My Reminiscenses

MY REMINISCENCES

LADY BLUNT
Wearing Order of Chefakat, "Order of Virtue," presented
to her by Sultan Abdul Hamid in 1886.

[*Frontispiece.*

MY REMINISCENCES

By FANNY, LADY BLUNT

Author of
"The People of Turkey"

With an introduction by
ADMIRAL SIR ROSSLYN WEMYSS, G.C.B.

WITH PORTRAITS

LONDON
JOHN MURRAY, ALBEMARLE STREET, W. 1
1918

DEDICATED TO

MY "EXTRAORDINARY NEPHEWS"

AND MY MANY FRIENDS IN THE
BRITISH NAVY

Malta, 1918

INTRODUCTION

By Admiral Sir ROSSLYN WEMYSS, G.C.B.

To many of the present generation the names
of Sir John and Lady Blunt probably convey but
little; but to those of us who are old enough
to remember events of the last thirty years, they
recall a very interesting period of history in which
they played a prominent part.

Not only as the gifted authoress of *The People
of Turkey*, but also as the wife of one of our
most successful Consuls - General in the Levant,
Lady Blunt's name ought to be enshrined in
the· grateful recollection of Englishmen.

Unfortunately, the English memory is short,
and the rewards for meritorious work in the
English Public Service are not, as a rule, adequate
to the services rendered. Moreover, the general
public is, more often than not, totally lacking
in appreciation or even in knowledge of those
by whose strenuous efforts and self-sacrificing
labours England's power, influence, and good name
abroad are upheld. How often after a life of
patriotic expatriation do these men retire, only
to find themselves strangers in their own land,

v

and to spend a lonely old age amidst a generation which ignores all their toils on its behalf.

Naval officers, who are generally better acquainted with the fringes of the Empire, more readily realise the magnitude and efficiency of the work done by England's civil servants abroad, and there are many of them who will remember with gratitude the warm welcome and charming hospitality of "Aunt Fanny"—hospitality which was accompanied by such kindly advice and instructive conversation as can only be given by a talented and clever woman. Those who have read *The People of Turkey* will peruse with pleasure these memoirs, and will realise how great were the services rendered by Lady Blunt and her husband to the country.

R. E. WEMYSS, *Admiral.*

ATHENÆUM CLUB.

PREFACE

I THINK it possible that my reminiscences, bound up as they are with the Near East and going back as they do to the early and middle parts of the last century, may prove of interest to my English friends at this present time when Turkey and Bulgaria, Greece and Albania are so much before the eyes of the world in the. great drama of War at present being tragically played in Europe. I will not try to foretell the future, but I think there is interest to be gathered from the incidents traced on the tablets of my memory, of the conditions of life as they were in my childhood. My father, Mr Donald Sandison, had come to Turkey in the beginning of last century and settled in Constantinople as the representative of the East India Company. His business flourished up to the time of the Janissary Rebellion, in the reign of Sultan Mahmoud. During this rebellion my father's house of business, like many others, was not only looted and burnt down but his business was so thoroughly disorganised that it could not be built up again in Constantinople.

My father married Miss Mary Zohrab, whose family had originally come from Persia. There

were two branches of this princely house who had
quitted Sistan in Persia during some revolutionary
upheaval.   One branch settled in Europe, the other,
my grandfather's branch, settled in Turkey.   My
grandmother on my mother's side was a daughter
of the Marquis de Serpos who belonged to an old
Venetian family, who had also settled in Turkey,
and of this marriage there were six children, three
boys and three girls, of whom my mother was the
youngest girl.   The boys were all educated in
England.   Two of them, my uncles Edward and
Paul, became distinguished men in the Turkish
and Egyptian Services.   The youngest son, John,
equally clever and of great personal attraction, was
a keen sportsman and settled down on a fine estate
in Asia Minor on the skirts of Mount Olympus of
mythological fame, where he spent his life hunting
wild boar, bears, and other creatures which were
then to be found in those wild regions, over-
shadowed by the snow-capped summit of that
wonderful mountain.   One of my aunts married
an Englishman, the other, a very gifted girl, died
of plague in Constantinople when about eighteen
years of age.

I give these few details with regard to my
forebears as I want my friends to know something
of my genealogical tree, for, owing to my cosmopolitan education and versatile knowledge of
languages, my origin I know has at times been
thought to be connected with a variety of
nationalities.   Admiral Harris, in his interesting

book of travels in the Near East, describes me as
a Roumanian when he gives a romantic account
of my marriage to Sir John Blunt, which amused
us very much. However flattering Admiral
Harris' description of me as a Roumanian girl
may be, I prefer to stand on the merits of my
English nationality, for like all Britishers who
are foreign or colonial born, I love the grand
old country which has produced the greatest nation
of the world, and claim it for my own.

It is now over forty years since I wrote my
book, *The People of Turkey*. Much has happened
in the mysterious regions of the Near East since
that time. The Near East is a land of prosperous
sunshine, interspersed with heavy storms of national
disaster, storms which follow one another as the
various Balkan States rise and fall. Each of these
storms has left its mark, without, however, attract-
ing any very definite European notice beyond that
of one or two Powers deeply interested in passing
events.

Many years have gone by since I left Turkey,
but I have never lost the keen interest with which
that country and its people inspired me. My
experiences in Turkey were so varied that the
desire to put them on record has brought about
this volume of reminiscences. The wish to make
my memoirs available for others was, I confess,
greatly stimulated by my long stay in Thessalonica,
the Salonika of modern days, and my good fortune
in seeing so much of our glorious Navy, a good

fortune which can rarely, if ever, have fallen to the lot of other women.

My most grateful thanks are due to Dr May Thorne, who, fortunately for me, is now in Malta attached to the Royal Army Medical Corps, and who has given much of her leisure time to prepare my *Reminiscences* for publication. I am most grateful for her sympathetic and able help, for, without her encouragement and devoted work, I feel sure these *Reminiscences* would never have seen the light. I should also like to thank Admiral Ballard, · Mr Ruck Keene, Dr Mizzi, Mr Alvarez, Mr Constantinidi, and many other friends, for their kind help in many ways.

In semi-savage countries like Turkey friendships develop and grow into delightful lasting intimacies. My husband and I had the privilege of many such friendships, which eventually culminated in my being adopted as "Aunt Fanny" by a number of young naval officers, who called themselves my "extraordinary nephews." Many of these "extraordinary nephews" are now distinguished men, as Admirals Sir Rosslyn Wemyss, Sir Stanley Colville, A. W. Waymouth, Mark Kerr, Allan Everett, Caley, Captains Sir Douglas Brownrigg, Cecil M. Staveley, and very many others, while the younger ones are fast mounting up the rungs of the ladder of promotion.

It only seems a few years ago since Jeanne and I measured some of these boys against the wall and registered their height in pencil marks. I mothered them, mended their jackets, took care of their boxes while they went off on expeditions, while Jeanne, who was always looked upon as the special guardian of the midshipmen, at times got her little friends out of all sorts of scrapes, took care of their money and their watches, and generally acted towards them as a good elder sister.

It gladdens my heart to see these young fellows come in now and again with an extra stripe or two on their sleeves, and I feel proud and full of gratitude as they bend down and embrace me, and say in voices of genuine affection, "Dear old Aunt Fanny."

CONTENTS

CHAPTER I

1840-1850

CHAPTER II

1851-1855

CHAPTER III

1856-1857

CHAPTER IV

1858

xiii

CHAPTER X

1876

CHAPTER XI

1876

CHAPTER XII

1877

CHAPTER XIII

1878

CHAPTER XIV

1882-1887

CHAPTER XV

1888

CHAPTER XVI

1889

CHAPTER XVII

1891-1895

CHAPTER XVIII

1895-1896

CHAPTER XIX

1897

LIST OF ILLUSTRATIONS

MY REMINISCENCES

CHAPTER I

1840-1850

I WAS born at Therapia, that beautiful suburb of Constantinople on the shores of the Bosphorus where the members of the Diplomatic Corps lived. Our house stood on the hill, and from the long terrace which ran down one side of it we had glorious views over the Black Sea, which was some two or three miles from us.

I was the youngest in a family of six children, five girls and one boy, and though I have no remembrance of Therapia in these very early days, yet I returned to it many times in after years and knew the house of my birth and the garden, and have often enjoyed the beautiful views from it. After my father's business in Constantinople had been destroyed by means of the upheaval caused by the Janissary Rebellion, he accepted, in the early days of Queen Victoria's reign, the post of British Consul at Brussa, one of the early capitals of Turkey, and the chief town of Bithynia when but little was known of Turkey, and still less of Brussa. Brussa at the time it belonged to the Greeks had been the centre of a flourishing and fertile district, but the laisser-faire policy of the Turks had let these fertile lands fall into disuse, so that when my father planned to go there with his wife and young family, he was strongly advised to go alone and see for himself what the place was like. My mother, however, was so insistent that she should not be left alone in Therapia that on a fine autumn day we were all taken to Stamboul to embark on board an old Greek trading vessel bound for Moudania, the nearest port to Brussa.

We must have been an interesting crowd, travelling as people in the East so often do, with all our servants and furniture, and the numerous "hangers-on" which a considerable household and the kind-heartedness of my generous mother gathered about it. There were my father and mother, my sisters and brother, my nurse, a tall, dark, somewhat awe-inspiring woman, a Greek who looked upon me as a doll to be dressed up and kept out of all play and mischief, and from whose arms I rarely escaped, except to be set down on a chair or stool till she was ready to take me up again. How well I remember the feel of her strong arms as she carried me about!

Besides the cook and the usual household servants, the horse-keeper and the cow-keeper, there was an old Armenian whose only duties as far as I remember were to turn the spit of the meat as it roasted before the great open fire, and to clean the boots; an old woman and her daughter whose duties were never in the least defined, and a sort of idiot whom my mother looked after because nobody else would.

The weather was fine and a fresh breeze swept
over the blue Sea of Marmora, and our journey
was accomplished more quickly than had been
anticipated. On our arrival at Mondania no one
expected us, and after considerable delay a farmer
was found, who, after calling upon Allah and
expressing astonishment at the number of persons
and things to be conveyed, said, "All the same I
will do my best to procure a couple of horses
and some mules for you. This is the vintage
harvest, and in the village I can get you some
grape-panniers which can be placed on the mules'
backs, in which your children, God bless them,
can be stowed away, and a man can be sent with
you to ride on the pack-saddle and pacify the
kicking beasts." My sisters, on hearing of this
novel mode of travelling, refused to be stowed
away in the sticky panniers like grapes being
taken to the press, but, *faute de mieux*, they had
to submit, and with many protestations got into
the baskets and followed my father and mother
who headed the caravan on horseback, and were
followed by children, several dogs, the precious
English cow, and an Angora cat. The servants,
hangers-on aforesaid, and carts with furniture
struggled along behind. It was now evening
and the whole procession was escorted by a dozen
or more tattered guards, armed to the teeth, as
a protection against a night attack by brigands.
The journey, well timed, neared its destination in
safety in the early morning, when the first sight
of beautiful Brussa was seen with the rays of
the golden sun just touching the points of the
minarets of the mosques and temples, with here

and there solemn cypress trees guarding the tombs
of the saints.   The whole earth, fresh and glistening with the heavy dew which is always present
during the summer months, now showed on a
wealth of flowers as the rapidly increasing light
let their brilliant colours be seen.   The whole
place was beautiful to the eyes of our party as
they approached the town.   But these impressions
rapidly gave place to feelings of disappointment,
when the narrow, ill-paved streets of the town
were entered, and stifling smells were encountered
from the heaps of decaying dirt and vegetation
which were on every side, the mangy dogs being
the only scavengers of the place.   They were
depressed, too, to see the poor appearance of the
unshaved Christians trying to hide themselves
within the shadows of the doors and narrow ways
as they went to their daily occupations.   These
poor appearances, we learnt later, were often
deceptive, for the Christians found it imperative
to give no sign of wealth or comfort, or they
would assuredly have at once been oppressed by
the Turks.   On many occasions I have seen the
interior of houses of an outward desolate poor
appearance, and been struck by the comfort found
in them.   A Christian in those days was a dog to
be harassed, starved, and thrashed on the slightest
provocation.   Little wonder that he did his best
to hide away any slight possessions he had
accumulated, so that he might in no way rouse
the envy and spite of his lords and masters.

On passing to the Turkish quarter of Brussa
our party found a great improvement.   The
houses were better built, the streets wider and

cleaner, the people better clad and of a more dignified appearance. My father was fortunate enough to have the offer of the best and finest house in one of the Turkish quarters. It had belonged to the last Dere Bey or feudal governor of that district of Brussa. The privileges of these Dere Beys or feudal lords originated · from the time of the conquest of Asia Minor by the Turks. As the Central Power began to weaken and become less affluent in consequence of this system, Sultan Mahmoud at the beginning of the nineteenth century suppressed the whole system and confiscated the property of these feudal land-lords, and caused some of the most troublesome ones to disappear. The Dere Bey of Brussa must have been one of the last to disappear, as his konak or mansion was in perfect order when handed over to us. Large, commodious, well situated, with the oriental finish of a fine garden, and a lovely Turkish bath built in marble. There was as well, a jail, or dungeon, which' my brother and I explored as we grew a little older. It was a place of gloom, airless, dark, half buried in the earth, with its strong walls facing each other barely more than a foot's space between, the walls furnished with heavy chains to be placed on the feet and hands of the innocent or criminal prisoners kept standing till death released them from their suffering.

My mother, with her refined taste and with the furniture she had brought, soon managed to transform this Turkish konak into a comfortable and pretty English country-house, without losing any of its oriental charm.

The town of Brussa, bereft of its past importance and style, still possessed some fine old
churches, mostly transformed into mosques, as
well as a number of others built centuries ago in
most exquisite Arabic style, an indestructible
Roman bath, and a few bridges. The old bazaar
was decayed and ruined.

There were a few coffee-houses and a big Han,
a business resort where all the mercantile offices
were placed. The town was almost divided into
two parts by a lovely ravine which separated the
Turkish from the Christian quarters. These latter,
occupied by Greeks and Armenians, made but a
poor show, for the reasons I have given. The
Turkish quarter appeared better than it was by
reason of the comparison with the poverty-stricken
appearance of the Christian quarter of this
neglected and abandoned capital of the Turkish
Empire.

Of European society there was none, not even
any foreign consulate. The Great Powers at that
time were represented, save the mark! by a
self-made consul, an Italian adventurer, Signor
Fortunato by name, who had married a native
woman and settled in Brussa where his knowledge
of foreign languages attracted the attention of the
authorities, so that on the rare occasions when a
European visitor made his appearance in the
country they referred him to Signor Fortunato.
Thus encouraged, Signor Fortunato represented
himself as a self-made consul for *all* the Great
Powers. It happened a short time after our
arrival that an old friend of my father's came to
Brussa to pay him a surprise visit. On inquiring

of some of the townsfolk where the British Consulate was, he was directed to Signor. Fortunato's
dingy-looking abode. He dismounted from his
horse, knocked at the door which was opened by a
slatternly, barefooted maid-servant, who said the
consul was not at home but the Signora would be
glad to see him if he would come in. The maid
led him through a sombre courtyard and stopped
in front of a huge tub in which a dishevelled, barefooted, fat woman was pressing grapes. "Ecco la
Signora," said the maid, pointing to the lady.
The astonished visitor, horrified at the taste of his
friend in the choice of his wife, asked her where
Mr Sandison, the consul, was to be found. "I
know of no consul but my husband, Signor
Fortunato," said the wine presser, "if you wish to
see him I will get out of the tub and send for
him." My father's friend thought it best to beat
a hasty retreat as he begged the lady not to
disturb herself, and remounting his horse soon
came across an Armenian who fortunately knew
where we lived. My father, delighted to see his
old friend, took him up at once to introduce him
to my mother, who had been one of the most
lovely ladies of Constantinople. Struck by the
contrast with that of his recent experience, he
could not help relating his meeting with Signora
Fortunato, which greatly amused my people.

Strange to say the same evening he happened
to fall into another adventure equally puzzling, if
less amusing. My mother had transformed a lovely
terrace covered with jasmine and honeysuckle into
a summer dining-room. The terrace had a deep
marble basin in the centre full of cold water which

gave a refreshing coolness. The dining-table covered
with the whitest of damask effectually screened
the marble basin beneath it. The evening breeze
sweeping gently over the scented creepers caused
the variegated lamps hanging overhead to sway to
and fro, and these attracted the attention of our
visitor, so that my mother forgot to warn him to
be careful not to stretch his feet beyond the
margin of the marble basin beneath. Whilst
enjoying the hot soup he gave a sudden start and
asked my mother whether a cold foot-bath formed
part of our oriental welcome to a guest. "No,"
said mother, with an apology smothered in laughter,
"it was a mere accident owing to my having
forgotten to warn you to be careful with your
feet." "Well," said he with a bow, " I can assure
you, Mrs Sandison, that I have found your
welcome as warm as this water is cold."

My childhood was spent almost entirely at
Brussa, and a very happy childhood it was. My
brother and I were great companions and had
many adventures in the country together. We
used to have lessons with the children of the
American missionary who lived near by, and the
daily interchange of ideas with a family brought
up under such different hereditary influences to
ours was an education in itself. Our holidays
were frequently spent at my Uncle John's house
on the lower slopes of Mount Olympus, where
close to the garden was a lovely little limpid
mountain stream, with the light glinting on the
water as it flowed over a bed of silvery sand and
multi-coloured pebbles, along the banks of which
willow trees grew, and where there was a little spot

which formed a perfect bower. Here as I grew a little older I used to sit and dream of the time when I should be able to roam into regions and countries revealed to me by books of travel which impressed themselves deeply on my developing mind. I believe there is no power stronger and healthier than Nature in her beautiful and harmonious moods for the development of love and sympathy in ripening youth. I still remember some of the impressions of those happy days, and rejoice to think how the memories of those sunny days recur to me often even now, and how they have outlived the memories, or rather, are stronger than the memories of the sorrows which came to us even then.

Hadgi Eivat was the name of the small Turkish village my Uncle John had chosen to live in, and where he wished to cultivate his farm in the English style. An utterly hopeless plan, alas! in a savage country full of ignorant peasants, who rendered useless and even dangerous the agricultural implements he had had sent to him from England. A thrashing-machine, being the largest of his implements, attracted a good deal of attention without, however, any of the farm hands and onlookers realising its power and weight. My uncle himself superintended the trial of this machine, but during a few minutes' absence one of the peasants lay flat on the ground in front of it and allowed it to go over him, with the result that he was at once crushed to death. On my uncle's return he saw with horror the mangled corpse, whilst the peasants gathered round merely said "that it was the devil at work," and none of

them would go near any of the machinery
again.

Soon after this event a case of savagery
occurred through uncontrolled jealousy, which
illustrates the small personal control which
ignorant barbarians possess.   A pretty, fresh-
looking young Turkish girl lived with her husband
in a single-roomed cottage by the roadside, which
necessitated her going out of the house to fetch
water from the well more often than her jealous
husband liked.   On one of these occasions, meeting
her on the road, he pulled her into the cottage,
threw her down and cut off her nose.   My uncle
passed by soon after, and hearing agonised cries
went in to the cottage and saw the horrible cruelty
which had been inflicted on the helpless girl.   He
asked her where the bit of her nose was to be
found, but all he could gather between her sobs
was, "pesherdi da yedi"—"he cooked it and ate
it, he cooked it and ate it."   My uncle doctored
the wound as best he could, but as it healed the
pretty little village maiden languished and faded
away and died a few months later.

I hardly think any children can have had so
free a time as we had during our holidays.   My
brother and I had many adventures as we roamed
about the countryside.   I well remember once
when he was just beginning to smoke and puffed
away at a pipe while we were walking through
some fields watching the cattle grazing, that we
noticed a solitary camel wandering along and
gradually coming nearer to us, and repeatedly
putting his head up and down and murmuring in
the disagreeable way camels can murmur.   Feeling

a little afraid of this evidently somewhat ill-
tempered brute we began to run away, but the
camel came after us considerably quicker than we
could get away from him and gained on us fast.
Searching hurriedly for some kind of shelter we
noticed a gipsy tent close by into which we hastily
ran.   No one was there, but the camel followed
fast on our heels, and though he could not get
into the tent he pushed his long neck in and made
the tent shake most alarmingly, whilst at the same
time he breathed harder and harder in his rage at
not getting at us.   Frightened to death we hid
ourselves under some heaps of horribly dirty rags
and rugs lying on the tent floor, hoping in this
way to escape the attentions of our pursuer.
Firmly convinced that this was a cannibal camel
bent on eating us we hid still more securely under
the filthy coverings, and my brother put the pipe
he had been smoking in his pocket.   Presently to
our great relief we heard a voice outside, and
someone drove the camel out of the way, and then
came into the tent.   We were so hidden that we
neither saw nor could be seen, but the language
we heard when the man saw his coverings topsy-
turvy was strong and forcible.

Our minds, excited by our recent adventure,
were ready to be afraid again and with thumping
hearts we both feared lest the gipsy, when he
found us, would kill us and put us into one of his
dirty sacks and carry us away.   Soon he saw an
arm and dragging us out accused us of trying to
steal his hidden money.   Standing us both in front
of him he made us turn out our pockets.   While
we were trying to tell him the reason of our coming

into his tent the pipe dropped from my brother's pocket, when the gipsy laughed and said, "Now I understand why the camel followed you, camels love the smell of tobacco and will always follow anyone who has a pipe. You must go home now and take me with you, when you must give a large backsheesh to the old gipsy for having made use of his tent."

Those who have lived in the East know with what rapidity ravines ordinarily dry, are filled by tempestuous torrents carrying down with them broken branches, stones, animals, and other debris. One stormy looking day, I, an irresponsible child craving for adventures, most unwisely wandered away for a ramble by myself when I was overtaken by a torrential storm. Hastening back as fast as I could, I found that the ravine I had to cross had become a deep and foaming river. I stood on the bank, a desolate little figure with the thunder crashing overhead and the lightning blinding my eyes, wondering however I should get home, when I heard a shout behind me and turned to see one of the farm hands running towards me. He caught me up in his arms and powerfully swung himself across the torrent, and managed to escape the boulders and uprooted trees which came crashing down. We reached home knee-deep in liquid mud, and I remember being given a hot bath and put to bed and fed on a good bowl of bread and milk, and got no harm. But this was a storm of unusual severity, and on waking next morning I looked out of the window and saw the whole countryside flooded, and we were prisoners in the house for

several days. Animals of all kinds strayed in or
near our farm, and one sight I shall never forget;
an ass was there holding a dead wolf by the neck
between his jaws. How the ass had ever been
able to attack the wolf remains a mystery, but
the villagers were in high glee at this extraordinary sight and roared with laughter as, with
considerable difficulty, the ass was induced to give
up his prey.

Another time my brother and I were playing
in the garden when a couple of ill-looking,
mysterious men came in by way of a gate which
opened into a deserted side street. .Frightened at
their presence we scampered into the house and
told my father who came out and ordered the men
off. About half an hour afterwards when we had
forgotten all about these men there was a great
uproar in the street, and on looking out we saw a
crowd of people, one of whom was holding a half-
strangled boy in his arms. I remember the horrid
blue look on the boy's face now. The man who
held the boy was the child's father, who said he had
seen two men trying to force what he had feared
was the dead body of his boy into a sack. But as
the men dropped their burden and ran away he
had rescued his boy and brought him at once to
the Consulate to seek redress and the expulsion of
these ne'er-do-wells. These mysterious people
turned out to be a set of primitive people who had
pitched their tents near the tombs of Sultan Orham
and of the saints and martyrs of his time, on the
lower slopes of Mount Olympus, because they
believed that great treasure was hidden in these
tombs. The treasure so they stated could only be

found by those who lighted forty candles made of
the fat from the bodies of forty children of the
district. These candles were to be lit when the
digging for the treasure commenced, in order to
gain the favour of the spirit guarding the treasure
so that it might not be turned into charcoal. I
had quite forgotten this incident, but it was recalled to my mind by the recent description of
the hideous method of the Germans to obtain
glycerine.[1]

Rich as Brussa was in natural products, the
town was unable to supply many of the ordinary
necessaries of life. Neither were there any schools
for the children, nor technical institutions for the
youths, nor a hospital. Such educational institutions as there were, were the strictly religious
colleges of the Medresses, which produced the
most intolerant order of students called Softas.
A court of justice (Mehkeme) was presided over
by a Kadi or Judge, who sat on a sheepskin and
gave judgment in accordance with the tenets of
the Koran. The Christian population had no part
in the administration of justice, and in cases
of litigation between Turks and Christians the
Christians invariably got the worst of it, as no
Christian evidence was accepted in the Mehkeme,
but on the contrary was suppressed or replaced by
the evidence of the Turkish false swearers.

The Turks provided no means for the care of
the sick ; they were stern fatalists, and were quite
content to rely on the prayers, charms, and relics

---

[1] The loss of treasure by being turned into charcoal, unless
some sacrifice is made to propitiate the Guardian Spirit, is a very
prevalent idea all over the East.

of their holy Sheiks, Mullahs, and Dervishes to
kill or cure all their physical and mental ills. It
was, I believe, subsequent to a report sent in by
my father to Lord Stratford de Redcliffe, then
ambassador at Constantinople, on the condition of
Brussa, that a Commission was sent by the Sublime
Porte, presumably to please His Excellency. The
Commission was composed of a group of Italian
architects who knew nothing of the country or of
the language, and who arrived in considerable
style, wearing black frock coats and top hats, a
costume which had never before been seen in
Brussa. The Commission made a tour of inspection of the Turkish quarter in search of an adequate
site for a hospital, and were much struck by the
appearance of the main street, which was wide and
clean and apparently deserted, and with plenty of
space between the fine-looking konaks or mansions
of the Turkish beys and hanoums. Well satisfied
with one particular part for the erection of a
hospital, they looked well all round, made notes
and took measurements, and proceeded to plan out
on the ground the area needed for the foundation
of a big building. Little did the Commission
suspect that they had chosen a place for the future
hospital in the centre of a veritable beehive of
enraged and alarmed Turkish hanoums, who
watched all the proceedings from behind the
jalousies of their windows, and were at a loss to
guess why a group of men dressed in so strange
and sombre a manner should by their unholy
presence desecrate the privacy of their quarter.
This unprecedented incident so keenly excited
these ladies, who were ignorant of the cause for

which the Commission had been appointed, and were
determined to show their strong condemnation of
proceedings they disapproved of, that they ordered
their eunuchs to unlock their gates and accompany
them to the konak of Fatima Kadin Effendi, the
doyenne and defender of female rights and privileges.
On being admitted to the presence of this grand
old lady, and after salaaming and kissing her hand
or the hem of her long train, they laid their
grievances before her. "Yes," replied the old
Kadin Effendi, after listening to all they had to
say, " I too have watched the doings of the infidels,
and though I have heard of the reason why they
are here I await the return home of the Bey to see
what he means to do in the matter. Should he
refuse to act out of respect for the Governor's
orders we must act for ourselves." "How can
we," said another old lady. "Of course," answered
the Kadin Effendi, "my son must demand satisfaction from the infidels for daring to defile the
privacy and sanctity of our quarters by their un-
called-for presence, and, at the same time, drive
them out of the country for unlawfully trying to
impose upon us, against the good will of Allah,
preventive measures to stop sickness or any trials
it may please him to inflict upon his chosen true-
beloved Moslems. We can take this step in defiance
of the new ideas of the Porte, and if need be, get
the approval of our Kadi (judge) at the Mehkeme
(court of justice), so prepare to follow my orders if
necessary, not later than to-morrow afternoon.
Get together a couple of hundred powerful women
and, at an hour to be fixed later, let them enter the
bazaar and go to the café where the infidels are in

the habit of taking their coffee." As the ladies obtained no satisfaction from the Bey the plan was carried out, and the following afternoon the door of the café, where the members of the Commission were peacefully sipping coffee and smoking cigarettes, was suddenly flung open and an infuriated group of veiled women, yellow slippers in hand, rushed in and pelted blows on the heads and faces of the amazed Italian architects. Outnumbered and taken at a great disadvantage the commissioners protected themselves by covering their heads with the stools they had recently been sitting on, and blinded such ladies as they could by putting their top hats completely over their heads. A regular pandemonium ensued and had reached its height when the door was once more flung open and Signor Fortunato, the self-appointed consul of all the Great Powers, appeared, accompanied by a body of police, who promptly turned out the veiled ladies and released the commissioners.

A few years subsequent to this battle of the yellow slippers some of the Great Powers followed the example of England in appointing consular agents at Brussa, chiefly with the object of opening the way for commercial interests with the interior of the country. This important step obliged the Turks to accept the inevitable and tolerate the presence of strangers in the land. It led to a few European families settling in the place, and a number of travellers visited Brussa and put a little more life into the neglected old capital. Among the visitors were a Russian Count and his wife, both very charming people, who were guests at the Russian Consulate; and as

c

my people were on intimate terms with the
Russian Consul and his wife they saw a good
deal of the Countess during the absence of her
husband on a visit to Roumania. One evening
when my three sisters were dining at the Russian
Consulate the conversation turned on clairvoyance.
The Countess asked my sister Nancy whether
she would like to get a glimpse of what the
future had in store for her. Full of the romantic
ideas of sweet seventeen Nancy willingly accepted
the invitation. She was seated in a chair placed
in the usual way between two tables, on each
of which was placed a mirror with candles, so
that reflections were formed which simulated
a long groove at the end of which there appeared
to be a dark patch or disc. The room was
darkened, and she was asked to sit down and
fix her eyes and concentrate her thoughts. Later
on she described to us that she noticed a faint
mist which gradually cleared away, and a picture
presented itself as taking place at the entrance
hall of our home, where although she felt she was
present yet as if the spirit and body were parted.
A great crowd of visitors appeared to stand
outside the door with sadness painted on every
face, and looking at a table raised in the centre
and covered with a black cloth on which a yellow
cross was seen beneath a mass of flowers. A
European with red hair and beard stood near
the table bending over it with his hand supporting
his head, and with tears streaming down through
his fingers. None of the family were to be seen
except my little brother Alfred, who appeared for
a moment and was then lost in the mist which

spread over the magic disc. The Countess was
the only one who could have understood this
strange vision, but she declared it meaningless and
wished my sister better success another time.
This vision was much discussed in the family, but
no one guessed what was in store for us. But
alas! only a few months later, what had been
considered a meaningless vision took the form of
reality. My poor sister Nancy was one of the
first victims of the epidemic of Asiatic cholera
that dropped on the town of Brussa, much as
many a bomb of the Huns has dropped on a
"fortified village" in England, spreading death
and destruction in every home it reached. In
one night four of our servants were taken ill, and
in the absence of medical care or any practical
knowledge of treatment, died. The family,
terrified by the calamity, were upstairs packing
up in order to leave for the country next day.
I was in my bed in the nursery when one of the
native maids came to tell me that Marechon, the
cook, was very ill. I, a little mite of five years
old, ignorant of sickness or death, sat on her bed
for a couple of hours and tried to help her. I
well remember rubbing her cramped knees with
an old stocking dipped in spirits. The poor
creature asked me to get her some broth; when
I had procured it and had her head resting against
my chest I put a spoonful of broth into her mouth
when her jaws snapped in a convulsion, and no
power of mine could get the spoon out from
between her teeth. In ignorance of her having
passed away I went upstairs to tell my sister Sophy,
who, horrified at hearing what I had been doing,

ordered me back to bed while she went to
Marechon. This was my first acquaintance with
grim death, but fuller knowledge soon followed.
No sooner did we move into the country than
the rest of the family, with the exception of my
mother, Alfred, and myself were struck down by
this terrible disease, and still no medical skill was
available.   Nancy was one of the next victims,
and died after a very short illness.   Matilda was
in a most precarious condition.   My father and
my two other sisters were all for a time in a
most critical state.   My brave, active mother was
distracted, for, where all needed her attention, it
was difficult to know whom to attend to first.   At
the time of greatest anxiety Providence came to
her aid, by the unexpected arrival of a clever
Viennese doctor who, in a few hours, marvellously
brought aid to this house full of dying patients, by
administering to each a strong dose of laudanum,
an unlimited number of little lumps of ice by the
mouth, and by friction to the abdomen.   I
consider these details worth giving as they might
be of service in an emergency.   The dreadful
results of the cholera visitation, so closely
connected with my sister's strange vision and her
sad end, obliges me to revert from one subject
to another.   My poor mother, while thankful
for the recovery of all but one of her patients,
was in great distress at the loss of her favourite
daughter, and was unable to cope with the
necessary arrangements for the funeral in Brussa.
Providence again came to her aid by the arrival
of an old friend who, on reaching Brussa and
learning of the family's misfortunes, rode straight

off to help her, and at once relieved her of all
anxiety with regard to the funeral. `This friend
had red hair and a red beard, and those friends who
attended the funeral bore witness to the fact that
it was in every way a repetition of the vision my
sister had had.

CHAPTER II

1851-1855

AFTER a series of somewhat monotonous years Brussa began to be more interesting, owing to the arrival of several groups of State prisoners from all parts of the Ottoman Empire. Some of these prisoners had been removed from their homes for the crime of protesting against the abuses of the Turkish Government, others, for daring to cast off the Moslem cloak with which, for a time, they had covered their Christian faith. There were also a number of political refugees as guests of the Sultan, chiefly Europeans. If I remember rightly, the first to arrive were some descendants of the family of Ali Pasha Tepeledin, that brigand adventurer who had come to the front in Albanian affairs at the close of the eighteenth century, and who by means of treachery and bribery had succeeded in obtaining the Pashalik (Governorship) of Janina from the Sultan. Ali Pasha Tepeledin had been beheaded in 1822 and his fortune, which was supposed to be enormous, is said to be buried deep in the sands of the river which flows by Janina. The children of Ali Pasha were reduced to penury and despair, and his son attempted suicide by swallowing a lot of arsenic. Regretting his action in time he is believed to have saved his life by half strangling himself in order to prevent the poison circulating in his system, and by swallowing the whites of eighty eggs!

Another State prisoner was Emîr Bekir, a Kopt and a great Syrian chieftain. He was accompanied by his staff, which included an Archbishop who was both friend and father confessor. This was a very interesting set of people who appeared to have suffered much and who were full of dignity and Christian resignation. The Emîr looked like an old saint with his snow-white hair and beard, and with a reverent aspect of true submission to all the decrees of Providence. His wife, a charming young woman full of life and intelligence, appeared to be the chief controller of the establishment, guided by the Archbishop, who was a man of the world, well versed in the intricacies of Eastern life. It was said that it was at the wish of his wife and of the Arch-bishop that the old Emîr had decided openly to declare his old faith. His courageous wife had managed to get hold of the keys of the gaol and in the silence of the night had given freedom to one or two hundred members of the Kopt religion who were imprisoned on account of their adherence to their faith. Doubtless our ambassador must have protected the rights of these people, for previous to their arrival all the sacred ornaments and draperies of their chapel were sent under the care of the Consulate, and all the time they spent in the country their lovely little church, nestling in a verdant bower of the garden, was left unmolested by the Turks. They all looked so happy in the peaceful security granted them, and enjoyed the blessing of freedom which enabled them to carry out their religious duties, a condition so very different to what occurred daily to many Christians in Turkey.

The famous Abd-el-Kader was a most fanatical Syrian chieftain who had fought against the French but was overcome and made a prisoner in the time of Napoleon III. Abd-el-Kader remained incarcerated in the Chateau d'Amboise for seven years, but was finally liberated by the Emperor and allowed to return to Turkey, where he was received as a guest of the Sultan and was given a fine konak (mansion) for himself and his family at Brussa next to our konak. This great Islamic Sheik of high religious repute among the followers of Islam was of delicate build, with regular features, curly red beard, and held himself with much oriental dignity, and was of a pleasing personality so that my mother had his name placed on her visiting list. His harem, however, was in marked contrast to himself. His chief wife looked a common woman, void of style or dignity. Abd-el-Kader's state apartment appeared to be the only decent place in the house. A Turkish sofa went all round the room. The walls were adorned by a single picture, a fine life-sized portrait of the Emperor Napoleon, which Abd-el-Kader pointed out to his guests with pride as a parting gift from His Majesty so long as there were any French officers in Brussa. No sooner, however, had the latter left the town than the face of the portrait was turned to the wall as evidently objectionable to his sight! Abd-el-Kader had a young nephew, Sidi Allal, who had adopted French manners, and though

handsomely dressed in the rich Syrian costume,
also wore elegant French top-boots, which gave
him a quaint appearance. He spoke some French
and wrote bad verses, but was a very good dancer,
an art he must have learnt in France where he
had accompanied his uncle. He appeared greatly
to enjoy this innocent pleasure at the small dances
at the Consulate, but on his last visit he appeared
in stockings only. As he was rather a friend of
mine I at once went up to him and asked him
whether he expected anyone to dance with a shoeless
partner. "Que voulez-vous, Mademoiselle?" said he,
almost with tears in his eyes, "my devout uncle
has forbidden me to indulge in simple practices of
this kind, and in order to save me from further
temptation has had all my boots and shoes locked
up." Poor Sidi Allal's punishment for his attempt
at emancipation did not end there. A few days
later he met my sisters going out for a ride and
joined the party. Unfortunately on returning home
they came face to face with Abd-el-Kader, who was
on his way to the Mosque, and though Abd-el-Kader
at once turned his face to the wall and stood there
till the riding party had passed, yet he detected his
nephew's presence in my sisters' company. The
unfortunate youth was at once sent to the local
gaol, where he had to stop for a week in filthy
surroundings and in the company of the worst
criminals. Incidents of this kind are common
in the Islamic world leading to unfavourable
comparisons between Christians and Moslems, the
former so amenable to the influences of humanity
and civilisation, the latter kept apart from both,
owing to the intolerance of their religious dogmas,

which will never permit of an *entente cordiale*
between the two races.

The following is another sketch of oriental life
with some variations. Some highly educated
Persian royalties, refugees in Turkey, had been
offered the hospitality of the old capital by the
Sultan. Prince Couli Mirza was said to have
been a pensioner of England, the other prince
whose name I forget was dependent on Russia's
bounty. The third personage, a fairy-looking
young princess, was the daughter of the Shah of
Persia and the wife of Prince Couli, her cousin,
with whom she had eloped. Besides her own
retinue there were forty Persian youths who were
supposed to be the sons of the princes. My
mother called on the Princess and was charmed
by her beauty and elegance and the distinction
of her manners, as well as deeply interested in
the account of the adventures of the whole
group of persons making up their establishment,
in their endeavour to avoid being caught by
the pursuing force which followed close on their
heels as far as the frontier. On returning the call
the Princess asked us all to luncheon for the
following day. Owing to the novelty of the
invitation I looked forward to it with great childish
delight. The Prince received us in the selamlik
(the men's apartments), and led us in state through
the mabhin or corridor leading to the ladies'
apartments, between a line of forty handsome
Persian youths, all salaaming as we passed. The
Princess, surrounded by a group of her ladies, all
young, pretty, and richly dressed in their lovely
court costumes, formed, in spite of the shabbiness

of their surroundings, a picture I shall never
forget. Some years later I managed to make
myself a copy of one of those lovely costumes and
wore it at a fancy dress ball at the Austrian
Embassy at Constantinople. Luncheon being
served, half a dozen girls bearing pretty silver
basins and jugs, and holding embroidered towels,
invited us to wash our hands before sitting down
on cushions on the floor round a big silver tray
which rested on a low stool. In the centre of the
tray as *pièce de résistance* was a silver bowl
containing rice, deliciously cooked, Persian fashion,
surrounded by several smaller plates containing
a variety of dainties. A long, beautifully embroidered scarf surrounded the tray and rested on
our laps instead of table napkins. A piece of
bread and a spoon in front of each person
completed the arrangements of the table. The
Princess placed my mother on her right side and
extended her long, white fingers towards the bowl
in the centre of the tray, took a handful of rice,
rolled it into a ball, and making a hole in the centre
with her thumb filled it up with a few trifles from
the side dishes and held it up to my mother's mouth
as her honoured guest. The rest of our party had
to help themselves in the same way as best they
could, but when it came to my turn to my dismay
I found it impossible to manipulate the rice ball
into its proper shape, or to convey it safely to
my mouth. The Princess, much amused at my
disappointed face, asked me to use the spoon which
had been provided for me. After that, no one
enjoyed the luncheon more than I did. There is
a considerable amount of resemblance between the

Turks and Persians in their customs and manners, doubtless owing to the sameness of their creed. Were it not for one or two tenets there might be considerable friendship and sympathy between them, but these tenets keep them much apart. I believe the Persians must be more amenable to the influence of modern civilisation than the Turks. Our friends did not make a long stay in Brussa, and doubtless England had something to do with their speedy return to their own country. A few persons who were of European renown in my young days, but are now all forgotten, as they are either dead or have given place to others in the various aspirations and objects which forced them to leave home and country, came to Brussa. Among the interesting persons who arrived, subsequent to the *sauve qui peut* which followed the defeat of the Hungarians under General Kossuth by the Austrians, were General Kossuth and his family, Count and Countess Batthyany, General and Madame de Denbinski, and several others. Short as their stay at Brussa was we saw a good deal of them, previous to their departure, under the pressure of Austria, further into the interior of Asia Minor. Madame Kossuth had a little girl of my own age and I was often asked to spend the day with her. She was not very entertaining, but I was deeply interested in watching the ways and manners of these great people in their home life, ways and manners which did not come up to the standard I expected of persons in such exalted rank and position. At meals, for instance, I noticed the General used his fingers in preference to knife and fork, but in spite of such failings in refinement he was a man of great personality and well worth listening to when he became animated and talked with his generals. Madame Kossuth, a homely looking person, hardly took part in the long discussions that daily followed meals. Count and Countess Batthyany, as well as some of the generals, struck me as being distinguished people with fine military appearance and courteous manners. They were all glad enough, to leave Kutaya after some months' stay and return to the civilised world again. Those times were not wanting in revolutionary agitations, which in some cases ended in partial successes as in Roumania and Greece. The latter, after terrible sacrifices and superhuman efforts which had started in 1821, ended by obtaining her liberty and independence. This great event enters within the boundaries of my reminiscences as, rather later, when still a little girl, I became a great favourite of the celebrated Grisioti Andarti, who was one of the chief Greek rebels on Turkish soil, where he had lost everything but his life. He subsequently took to the mountains with his followers, killing as many Turks as he could, and living on what he and his men could find as free looters. In one of these encounters one of his arms was severely injured and partially severed below the elbow. He managed to escape and reach one of his dens in safety when, cutting off the injured part he plunged the stump into boiling tar which cauterised the wound and saved his life. Grisioti was a big, handsome man with a Roman (prominent) chest, and an intelligent, expressive face which greatly added to the interest I took in him. I first saw him as

one of the Sultan's pardoned prisoners sent to
live at large in Brussa. An A.D.C. and one or
two followers were allowed to accompany him.
These latter often spoke of the tragic details
of the war, and all my admiration and sympathy
were roused on behalf of the heroes who had
fought and suffered for the independence of
Greece. The old Grisioti Andarti gave us a
picnic on the heights of Mount Olympus which
was to resemble as far as possible one of his old
haunts in the wilds of Thessaly or Macedonia. A
picturesque grotto embedded in creepers was fixed
on as the place of meeting. As our party
approached we were met by one of the chieftain's
palikaris (followers) who, saluting, offered to show
us the way. Presently we came face to face with
the grotto, when suddenly out sprang the chieftain
with a dozen followers, all armed to the teeth as if
ready for action. Looking round on all of us he said,
"Callos oriste," "You are welcome," and ordered
his men to take charge of our horses. Grisioti
then took me by the hand, and as we stood a little
in advance of the rest of the party said, "Little
girl, for this occasion I appoint you my chief.
You will find my gallant followers ready to obey
your orders, and in case any of our prisoners refuse
to hand over their purses you must decide whether
it will be their noses or their ears that will have to
be cut off." Horrified and alarmed at such a
suggestion I drew away my hand, saying, "I took
you for a good man and a great hero who had
promised us the enjoyment of eating a lamb
cooked cleft fashion, instead of which you want to
cut off the ears and noses of my people." "Well,

little girl," said he, with a hearty laugh, "those are
the laws of our 'order,' but since you disapprove
we will give them a free pardon and presently,
after everyone has been made comfortable, you
shall come with me and see how the lamb is to be
cooked cleft fashion for our dinner." As good as
his word, the old chieftain showed me what I have
never forgotten, any more than I have forgotten the
fun and delight of that picnic. Little did I dream
at the time that later in life I should have to
experience in reality what was then being acted in
comedy.

My father always did his best to help and
protect the various sets of refugees who came
to Brussa, and their frequent comings to the
Consulate did me much good service, for as a
child I got to know people of various nations very
well, and learnt all about their countries, their
sorrows as well as their patriotic hopes and
aspirations, and this knowledge enabled me to be
of much service to my husband in later years. I
well remember, for instance, that a set of Bosnian
gentlemen (Christians) were sent to Brussa as
prisoners at large. They were well-developed,
handsome people, and I came to the conclusion
then, and this opinion was confirmed when I came
across Bosnians years afterwards, that they were
the finest race in the Balkan States. They had an
air of independence and a personality that was
both charming and courteous. They were a
population absolutely separate from the Turks and
yet living amongst the Turks, and the Turks
appeared more tolerant of them than of many of
their Christian neighbours. The young Bosnian

women had much more liberty than most women
of the Near East, even going to the length of
choosing their husbands with whom they sometimes eloped. A custom of theirs at the birth of
a child was for all the inmates of the house to
leave it, with the exception of a very young girl
who, so soon as the baby was born, ran to tell
the waiting relations of the advent of the little
stranger. For her good news the girl acquired
certain privileges which brought her into close
contact with the family. I do not know if many
of these old customs still exist. Doubtless the
Austrian occupation of Bosnia altered to some
extent many of these quaint old customs of the
people, but I believe neither Turks nor Christians
felt happy under the control of a State which was
largely dominated and crippled in its action by the
silent but most powerful influence of the Jesuit
orders then resident in Austria. About the time
of which I am writing a fine school for girls was
opened by Miss Irby and Miss MacKenzie which,
I understood, did much good work.

The Roumanian political guests of the Sultan
consisted of a prince, one or two statesmen, some
distinguished artists, and one or two ladies. This
group of guests had been educated in France,
and were full of patriotic zeal and liberal ideas,
and longed for the opportunity to put into practice
in their own country much of the knowledge
which they had acquired in France. I well
remember an old Roumanian friend of those
bygone days who had fought for the same
cause the Roumanians are fighting for to-day,
who often used to repeat in a rich, sonorous

voice, "Dieu, Liberté, Patric." This group of
people were cordially received at the Consulate
by my parents, and my grown-up sisters had much
pleasure in the society of the younger members
of the party. I was rather an *enfant terrible* at
that time, and well remember how one day, when
running about the garden with my butterfly net,
I came across one of my sisters and one of the
young Roumanians looking at some object that
was interesting them both as their heads were
rather close together. I caught them in my net,
much to the indignation of my sister, who boxed
my ears for me, but her companion brought me a
big box of chocolates next day! After staying
in Brussa about a year the greater number of the
elder members of the party left, whilst a group of
the younger men remained to construct a very
fine road between Brussa and Moudania. Doubtless many of our friends eventually returned to
Roumania, where, under the able control of Prince
Charles, they would have plenty of opportunities
of helping their country.

During the Turco-Russian War of 1877 a
secret convention was entered into by Roumania
to tender help to Russia. Owing to the energy
of Prince Charles of Roumania and his small
army of about 35,000 men, the famous Graveio
redoubt, the strongest fort for the defence of Plevna,
was taken. The Russians were delighted at this
unlooked-for strength of the small Roumanian force,
and the Roumanians were pleased since it freed
them from the nominal protectorate of Turkey.
My husband followed this war on the side of the
Turks, and greatly admired the bravery, tact, and

D

savoir faire of Prince Charles's men. He felt that
if the Pashas of the Turkish Army, Osman Pasha
and Raouf Pasha, had been granted free hands in
this war, Turkey would have come out of it
much better than she did. Raouf Pasha was an
intimate friend of mine and was one of the witnesses at my marriage. I saw him last some time
after the war when I stopped a night at his konak.
One among many of the interesting details of
the Turco-Russian War he related to me was
when he and the Grand Duke were settling the
Articles of Peace between the two governments.
They were in accord up to a certain point, when
suddenly the Grand Duke turned to Raouf Pasha
and asked him to issue an order allowing six or
seven hundred of his soldiers to visit the Mosque
of St Sophia daily. Raouf, horrified at the
request, said that it would be impossible to give
such an order, since the worshippers at the Mosque
had services of prayer five times a day and the
presence of infidels would lead to a revolution in
Constantinople. The Grand Duke, having by
this request let the long wished-for Russian
ambition to see St Sophia once more a place of
Christian worship be known, pressed the matter
no further, but patting Raouf Pasha on the
shoulder smiled and said, "Et quand même, mon
cher, cela viendra, et je désire que nos braves
soldats apprennent le chemin de la Mosqué." Is this
wish of the Grand Duke nearer realisation to-day?

CHAPTER III

1856-1857

Two terrible catastrophies must next be recorded in my memoirs—the Crimean War and the great earthquake which visited Brussa and almost annihilated it.

The Crimean War was felt indirectly at Brussa, since it was a place of interest to the Turks and their allies as a recruiting and provisioning station. Commercial travellers, contractors, and speculators began to crowd in. It caused us no small pleasure to see some of our brave soldiers on leave from the Crimea, full of news of the war in which we were so deeply interested. Compared to the present abominable war the Crimean War appears to my memory to have been merely child's play. The Turks were much behind European nations in the art of war, and were unprepared in every way to meet the heavy demands of so great an enterprise. As for Turkish soldiers, ever ready to answer the call to arms, they too lacked much that was needful, and had no experienced officers as the following story shows. A Pasha in high command had a clever Polish officer, an engineer, to assist him. On one occasion the troops were in a place that was strategically bad and likely

to be unhealthy should wet weather prevail. The
Polish officer brought to his chief a map of the
district and pointed out a position that would be
better strategically and good should there be
much rain. The Pasha despised the map which
he was unable to understand, and said, "I must
consult the shepherd of the goats of this locality
as to what the weather will be." The shepherd
on being summoned to give his opinion asked for
a few minutes' grace in order that he might go
and see his herd, and returned saying: "I have
just inspected my herd of goats and find all their
tails up. Sure sign of fine weather." "There,"
exclaimed the Pasha, "the camp shall remain
where it is"; and it did remain there, with
disastrous results to the health of the troops.
According to stories current at the time, the
Russians were no better prepared, part of their
army being furnished with "show" arms made of
wood in place of genuine rifles and swords.

There were also errors on the part of the
English, owing chiefly to the want of proper
organisation, which led to the sacrifice of many
of our gallant soldiers. Large numbers of men
became victims of the great cholera. epidemic.
Unlike the present time there were not sufficient
means or knowledge either to relieve the suffering
or to stem the course of the disease. Many of the
officers and men who suffered from rheumatism,
due to the exposure they had experienced during
the bitter weather of the winter in the Crimea,
found their way to Brussa, where they were
greatly benefited by the quality and variety
of the mineral springs that are situated some

few miles from the town. These springs had
been made use of by the natives of Asia Minor
from time immemorial, and during the Roman
occupation magnificent baths had been built round
the sources of the different waters. These baths
were situated in the vicinity of a splendid mosque,
and were apparently of indestructible solidity since
they had withstood the ravages of time and miracu-
lously escaped both Ottoman destruction and the
earthquake. At Kucutlu there was a sulphur bath
which was curiously constructed, but the details
of which I regret I do not understand sufficiently
to make clear to my readers. I can only describe
it as I know it. There was a round marble swimming-bath some five or six feet deep, with foot-wide
steps ranged round from the brim to the bottom.
This large basin was of course full of water, and its
edge was on a level with the marble floor of the
bath-house, and at a good distance from the walls
of the building which supported a dome the size of
the round swimming-bath. It is possible to walk
beneath the bath, when one sees that the basin-like
portion is apparently held up by nothing, but it must
of course be suspended from the edges of the bath-
house floor. This under part is well worth a visit.
The natives have no knowledge about it, and as it
is rarely shown to visitors few people know of its
curious construction. The iron and alkaline baths,
equally strongly built in white marble but on a
smaller scale, are most efficacious in their healing
qualities. We used to spend a few weeks every
autumn at this lovely watering-place, which had
formerly been a favourite resort but which at the
time I knew it, was reduced to a poor Turkish

village. There were a few indifferent places one
could stay in, consisting of three to five mean
unfurnished rooms, but with a wide verandah
overlooking the rich country below, and with
glorious views of the hills above. These hills
were green and cool owing to the rich orchards
containing every variety of pear, peach, and plum
tree, as well as magnificent chestnut and walnut
trees. The verandah, the views, the baths, and
the fruit more than compensated for the poor
accommodation. The bathers could roam at will
in the orchards, and for a few pence to the
tattered guardians could eat or carry away as
much fruit as they liked. A perfect paradise
for a party of young people as we were then. It
is so long since I left Brussa that I do not
know what condition Kucutlu is in now, but
owing to the exodus of many wealthy Turkish
families from Constantinople who have settled
there within the last few years the place is
probably much improved. Strange to say none of
these baths were hurt by the terrific earthquake
which took place during the early part of the
Crimean War, and which shook the town to its
very foundations and destroyed most of the
buildings, and seriously damaged others such as
ours, which were built of wood. The earthquake
came with startling unexpectedness. We all,
except my father, were in the sitting-room upstairs.
I remember that, impecunious as usual, I was
trying to raise some money by a sale of nick-
nacks I had made. It was early in the afternoon
when we noticed a jet black cloud on the horizon,
and gradually the room became dark as I was

trying to pass off to my sister Matilda a faded
book-mark. In addition to the terrifying darkness
so alien to our usual brilliant sunshine, a stifling
odour of sulphur reached us from the outside. At
the moment when we were half suffocated and
ignorant of the cause of this extraordinary condition of things there came the first violent shock
which knocked us all down. This was followed
by a succession of equally strong shakings. By
the time we reached the door we found that the
windows of our exceptionally large hall, and in fact
the hundred windows of the whole konak (mansion)
were cracking in consequence of the bending of
the frames, and the glass was being scattered in
all directions. The whole house shook and we
feared its immediate collapse. We rushed to the
staircase and clinging tightly to the balustrade
we reached the ground-floor and ran into the
middle of the garden for temporary safety. The
shock continued, and in addition to the terror
caused by the blackness of the heavens the walls
of the garden fell, and clouds of dust were raised and
added to our discomfort. It was altogether a most
horrible, unforgettable calamity which destroyed
half the town. A silk factory built on a soft
stone rock came crashing down, and some three
hundred young Greek girls who worked in it were
either killed or severely injured. It was heart-
rending to hear the moans and cries of some of the
injured survivors caught beneath the debris, who
were unable to be rescued in time. Our troubles
were not ended with this terrific experience for
the shocks, some quite slight, others more severe,
continued for forty days and nights, an interminable

time so it seemed to us. We slept either in tents
or just at the entrance of the hall ; but if in this
latter place we often had to rise hurriedly from our
beds in the middle of the night and rush into the
garden. The effects of this disturbed life soon
began to tell upon some of us, and after the fortieth
night on which the great perpendicular shock was
experienced which did so much harm, we were
thankful that the Ambassador, Lord Stratford de
Redcliffe, sent to take us to Constantinople. I
need not say with what joy we left the ill-fated
town during a shock of lesser severity, but which
terrified our horses who neighed and stood with
their legs stretched well apart and rigid till the
shock was over. I thought my heart would break
with joy when next morning, on reaching the port of
Moudania, we first caught sight of a British man-
of-war. It was with great delight that we enjoyed
the welcome which the captain and officers gave
to us and to the few ladies, friends from Brussa,
who accompanied us. My father, unfortunately
for us, remained behind, faithful to his post.

Everything appeared to me like a fairy dream
after all the experiences of the last six weeks. I had
been greatly terrified during the last shock before
we left Brussa, as I had found myself a prisoner in
the dining-room owing to the door being jammed,
and although I threw myself out of a window
into the garden, the fear I had experienced for a
few moments when I thought I should have been
buried alive remained with me for some time.
However, such experiences in youth are not very
lasting ; the entire change of· scene and life on
board doubtless did much to quickly lessen the

memories of recent terrors.   After eating an
excellent dinner with which our good hosts regaled
us, we all went to our cabins so kindly offered to
us by the officers, who contented themselves with
a blanket and a pillow on the benches of the ward-
room.   In my youthful selfishness I gave little
thought to their discomfort, and getting into my
nightdress with my hair down my back I got into
my cosy little berth and soon fell fast asleep, but
alas! having had so many recent experiences of
disturbed nights owing to shocks and the need for
jumping up quickly when unexpectedly awakened,
I had a most ridiculous adventure.   Some sudden
movement of the ship must have disturbed me, and
in a half-awake condition I jumped out of the
berth, opened the door of the cabin and rushed
into the ward-room, where I stood in the centre
like a ghost in distress, gazed upon by half a dozen
young officers.   Wide awake now, and realising
my ridiculous position, I covered my face with my
hands and rushed back to my cabin horrified at
my silly action ; but, tired as I was, I tied my feet
together with my handkerchief before I got into
bed for fear of again being disturbed and rushing
out once more.   Next morning I was on deck
early and watched the rising sun dart its fiery rays
through the clouds flitting over the Golden Horn
and on the solitary Byzantine palace mirrored in
the calm waters of the Bosphorus.   This palace was
one of the very few that had escaped the ravages
of the Turkish conquest.   A few years later it was
burnt to the ground, an incendiary act on the part
of its inhabitants, the hanoums of the late
lamented Sultan Medjid.   In this palace or harem

lived several hundreds of old and young beauties, Kadin effendis, sultanas, odalisks, and slaves, who had been turned out of the Imperial Palace to be shut up within its solid walls. Justly resenting their monotonous lives they set fire to the building hoping to gain their liberty in the *sauve qui peut* that followed. But to go back to my own concerns. On hearing the breakfast bell I went below with rather a shamefaced look and took my seat at table, hoping my night's adventure might be attributed to somnambulism. However, no one made any remark about it. After breakfast we thanked the captain and officers for their kindness to us, and were then rowed ashore in one of the big boats and landed at the Tower of Galata, a filthy-looking place of business, crowded by Armenian porters who, as they saw us land, rushed in a body, fighting amongst themselves as to who could first get hold of our luggage. We mounted the two or three hundred steps of the dirty, ill-paved ascent to Pera, the European quarter, and reached the Grande Rue de Pera, a dirty neglected thoroughfare where numerous street dogs, the only scavengers of the place, were at work. We went to Messiri's Hotel, the only hotel that was then in existence I think. We stayed there but a short time, as the beautiful view of the opposite shore of the Bosphorus decided us to take up our quarters at Kadi Kieu, an old Turkish village, the right extremity of which was fast becoming a European resort. We chose for our home an old Turkish konak (mansion) on the Scutari side of the village, where the British Army was quartered. It was a pretty house with a fine verandah overlooking the main road which skirted the seashore. We soon made a number of pleasant acquaintances among English people, and for the first time I began to realise the soundness, charm, and delicacy of English society.

That short time during the Crimean War was one of the happiest periods of my young days, every hour of which I enjoyed. In spite of my being still considered a child, I learnt much that served me later on. I was allowed to go to balls owing to the scarcity of English girls, and well remember the first one I went to. I had many partners, and inadvertently engaged myself to several at once for one of the dances late on in the programme. When the dance began my numerous partners all came to claim it, and I was in much perplexity to know what to do. My sister, who saw I was in some difficulty, came across the room to me, and apologised for anything I might have done amiss as this was my first ball. I hastily made a knot low down in one of the corners of my pocket handkerchief, and crumpling the whole thing in my hand except for the four free corners, said, " Whoever chooses the corner with the knot shall be my partner." These balls were given by the various Embassies in honour of the English and other foreigners, and were a great success, owing to the number of officers, the variety of uniforms, and the efforts made by the Levantine ladies to excel each other in their efforts to please. I heard a French ambassador say that the best company at Constantinople was the Greek, but unfortunately the men did not come up to the mark. Of course no Turkish ladies appeared at these entertainments, and practically no Turks, except a few who held high official positions. Constantinople in those days was little known in England or the rest of Europe, yet it did not lack in interest and amusement to most of the visitors. Among the latter was H.R.H. the Duke of Cambridge, who after a short stay went to Circassia on an anti-slavery mission with my brother-in-law, Mr Longworth, and my brother Alfred. The latter, though quite a young boy, was very useful owing to his knowledge of languages. His Royal Highness wished to place before the people the desirability of putting an end to slavery, and, since it was the women who were said to be those who played the chief part in maintaining this odious custom, it was deemed wise to try and obtain their favour by giving them presents that would appeal to their taste for finery. The bazaar of Stamboul was ransacked for stuffs suitable to the taste of these ladies, and numerous boxes of rahat lokoum (Turkish delight) were added to the attractive stores. The mission naturally caused a good deal of sensation, and the invitation of His Royal Highness to the women to attend a meeting, was accepted by them after a certain amount of deliberation.

Mr Longworth and my brother, under the Duke's instructions, made a good display of the fineries by spreading out the multi-coloured stuffs which had been bought, and endeavoured to make them more attractive in the eyes of the audience by distributing amongst them the boxes

of rahat lokoum, in the hope that these presents
would more readily induce the women to give
the needed anti-slavery votes. The Duke began
his address by making a graceful appeal to the
ladies for their assistance, to help his country
and its great Queen in the efforts they were
making to put down slavery, that cruel and
inhuman custom so ruinous to the happiness of
the children, and so painful to their parents.
When the Duke's feeling speech came to an end,
the elderly matrons with one voice asked the
interpreter what the great English lord had said,
and on being informed they started up like a set
of demented furies, crying out, " How dares this
great lord come to our country with the object of
preventing our children from getting, through
the assistance of the slave dealer and the market
of Stamboul, the possibility, if their kismet
(fate) wills it, of becoming raised to the rank
of sultana. We will have none of these measures
in our country any more than we will have his
tempting gifts." Suiting their action to their
word they pelted the astonished Duke and his
party with the scarves and the rest of the fineries,
while the boxes of rahat lokoum rolled on the
floor. The mission having thus signally failed,
the members beat a hasty retreat. But it was
far from being fruitless, for from that time the
persistent pressure of England caused the gradual
disappearance of slavery in Turkey. Wherever
there was a British Consulate and a slave desired
his or her liberty, they had only to enter the
gates of the Consulate, for the Consul had it in
his power to get their release from the authorities.

In Salonika, for instance, my husband obtained
the liberty of about a hundred slaves, chiefly
blacks; to be rewarded for his good action by
being named Baba (father) by this wretched
community. It is doubtful, however, whether
this humane measure of giving them their liberty
is really likely to benefit them. So long as the
Turks are allowed to continue their fanatical
massacres of their Christian subjects, prisoners
will be taken, and to be a prisoner is worse than
to be a slave. An owner cares for and protects,
at any rate to some extent, a slave for whom he
has paid. He treats with cruelty the Christian
prisoner he despises and who has cost him
nothing.

Although during the Crimean War the Turks
were expected to be fanatically disposed towards
the Europeans, and though the enemy almost
reached the gates of the capital, yet nothing of an
alarming nature happened beyond a few incidents
of a personal nature. In one of these cases my
brother and my sister Matilda having failed to
receive in time an order from the Embassy to
abstain from assisting at a great Turkish cere-
monial close to the Imperial Palace, ventured in
that direction expecting to find us with a big party
as had been prearranged. As Alfred and Matilda
neared the palace the crowd became dense and they
sat down on two chairs at the side of the street,
without realising that they had fallen into the
midst of a crowd of Softas who were a most
fanatical order, and who closely surrounded them
and violently threatened to murder them then and
there. A fierce-looking nigger with dagger in

hand called out, "Shall I strike ?   Shall I strike ?" when, providentially, a Turkish officer came to their rescue and led them to the nearest haven of safety. This happened to be the kitchen of the Imperial Palace where they were confided to the care of the chef, who gave them hospitality in his private apartment, and a choice lunch from His Imperial Majesty's table !   When the crowd had begun to disperse a bodyguard of half a dozen kitchen boys, in red aprons and with bare arms, led the two chance adventurers into a safer part of the town.   As a rule, however, though we, with other friends, often roamed over the bazaars we rarely had any reason to complain of acts of rudeness on the part of the populace.   Often dear old Captain Borliss, the guardian of all the pretty young wives of the naval officers, took parties about the streets, and though he often felt anxious for the members of his parties, yet fortunately nothing untoward ever happened.   Our soldiers walked freely about and attracted a good deal of attention.   The Scottish Regiments were named "donsous" or "the breechless" by the Turkish ladies, whilst the Albanians proudly said that the kilt was a copy of their own "foustanelas."   The Crimean War was begun and ended on an honourable basis, free from disgrace or remorse on either side of the belligerents.   Fortunately for the brave generation that fought its battles, "German culture" was still in the nursery rearing and developing the monsters she has produced, bent on the destruction of the nations she has failed to conquer or beguile. How deeply must Turkey and her associates in misfortune bewail their connection in this

murderous war, out of which they well know
they have nothing to gain either in material profit
or in the esteem and sympathy of the rest of the
world.   Turkey is doomed and she deserves to be
left "chiplac" (naked), as prophesied by the late
Sultan Abdul Aziz who hearing, whilst in his bath,
of the birth of his son and heir said, "The country
under his reign will be reduced to the nakedness
I find myself in when hearing of the news of his
birth.   All will go."

But what about fair old Greece and her brave
sons brought to death's door by her erring king,
who has been an enemy to his own country while
earning the smiles and favours of the Kaiser.   It
is to be hoped that with the help of Providence
and the patriotic efforts of M. Venizelos, justly
named the "Saviour" of his country, that all will
be well.   To go back to the Crimean War.   At
its termination all the foreign forces began to take
their departure from Constantinople leaving behind
a dull monotony difficult to put up with even for
those accustomed to live in Eastern countries
where, socially speaking, the Government counts
for nothing, and where the brighter and better half
of the population is kept under lock and key.   We
were much pressed by our departing friends to leave
for England too, and my mother decided not to lose
the opportunity of travelling with friends, particularly as she wished to go to England then in order
to be present at the wedding of my sister Matilda
with Mr George Ricketts, a bright young officer
of the 5th Dragoon Guards.   At the same time
mother thought my brother and I might take up
our neglected studies better in England than else-

where. We both spent the two years we had in London more profitably than in book work, by seeing all we could of the marvels of that huge metropolis, for it is not possible to spend some time in the dear old country, breathe its pure healthy air, study its system, its organisation and greatness without learning a good deal that serves in later life. On our return to Brussa after our delightful two years in England our party was reduced to three, *i.e.*, my mother, my brother, and myself. I shall never forget the storm we experienced in the Atlantic. For three days and nights there were no fires in the engine-rooms. My cabin had a foot of water in it and yet I never got seasick or nervous, nor did I cease begging our kind captain to let me go on deck to watch the grand effects of the terrific storm. He consented at last, and at my request roped me to the great mast where I thought I should be perfectly secure. However, when the sudden impact of a huge wave carried off one of the long benches, the captain enveloped in his oilskins crouched by my side and asked me if I had not had enough. Before I could answer a terrific gust of wind struck the mast and broke it and the upper part fell crashing on to the deck. Fortunately neither of us was hurt, but I thought it was time for me to go below. As the weather calmed down the passengers began to show themselves at breakfast and on deck looking very green and seedy. Among the passengers were an English lady and her young and pretty daughter who soon became great friends with three Englishmen, well dressed and good looking. Somehow, my brother and I did not care to make their

E

acquaintance, nor did we join with them in a photographic group in which the English lady and her daughter took part. Later on, the latter, when dining at the Embassy at Constantinople came across, much to their discomfort, their late friends who served them at table with grace and *savoir faire!*

My brother and I were full of regret at having to leave England and return to Brussa, in spite of my dear mother's cheering encouragement that "tout vient à temps à qui sait attendre." Unfortunately young people are not always endowed with patience, and we felt ours would quickly vanish if we were destined to rusticate in Brussa without even the chance of making a stay in Constantinople. My father was very glad to have us back and so was our favourite Uncle John, known all over the country as "Chelebi John" (Gentleman John). Fortunately the country had not lost its old charm for us, especially for my brother, who became a great sportsman and settled down on my uncle's farm, where he had plenty to occupy his time and to interest him. It was a grand place for big game before a huge fire, which lasted for forty days, broke out and partially destroyed the forests. The fire started on the eastern side and gradually worked its destructive way in the direction of Brussa. It was a glorious sight to watch those grand old trees blazing away. As the fire approached the town the Armenian community came to the Consulate in a body to beg for help, as their quarter would have been the first to be burnt had the fire spread so far. My father naturally applied to the Pasha, who, twisting and turning his hands in real distress, said, " What can I do, Consolos Bey, what can arrest such a scourge if it please Allah to inflict it upon the country." My father persuaded the Pasha that the fire was not Allah's work but the charcoal burners' neglect, and that it could easily be stopped from reaching the town if he would get half the men of the place out to cut down the trees and leave a large bare space between the blazing forest and the Armenian quarter. The advice was taken in time, and Brussa was saved from a second calamity which, in its way, would have been as great as the earthquake.

Soon after this event my brother disappeared and for a week we heard nothing of him, when a letter came from him from Constantinople asking that some of his clothes might be sent to him, and adding that as he had had enough of Brussa he had in a moment of desperation got on his horse just as he was, with a hand-bag, and two fine potatoes from the farm, and had gone to Constantinople. Here he had presented himself to Sir Henry Bulwer, our Ambassador, and a very old friend of my mother, and had offered him his two fine potatoes. His Excellency, on hearing whose son the boy was, and much amused by the originality of the youngster, looked him up and down and, struck by his personality, asked him to be his guest, and sent him down to work in the chancery. This was the beginning of my dear brother's distinguished career and of his valuable services to the Government, first as dragoman and then as oriental secretary.

CHAPTER IV

1858

My brother's departure was a sad loss to me as he had been my best friend and chief companion from childhood, which accounted for my distaste for dolls and games more adapted to girlish enjoyment. I loved Nature and all her wonderful works that strike the youthful attention and elevate the mind to regions incomprehensible in their entirety, but sweet to dwell upon. But time passed on and my solitude ceased to trouble' me, and I felt happy to see my dear mother so pleased at the unexpected result of my brother's venturous enterprise. I had a most pleasant break to the monotony of my life by the arrival of a party of Constantinople friends, which included the interesting Monsieur le Baron de Lesseps, one of the brilliant celebrities of his time, whose charming personality won every heart. It is well known how his wonderful energy and engineering skill produced the Suez Canal in spite of extraordinary difficulties. The Brussa season was at its height and an expedition to the summit of Mount Olympus was planned, to my great delight. We rode up the lower slopes through densely wooded forests. Presently the ascent became steeper, and, if I remember rightly, it took

us some seven hours to reach the snow-clad summit,
the last part of the journey being accomplished on
foot. The lovely scenery and the bracing effects
of the cool breeze appeared to have an exhilarating
effect on all the party, with the result that we
started on a race to see who could reach the top
first. In my foolish, childish conceit I took the
lead, ignorant of the fact that we were walking on
an immense bridge of snow, beneath which a
silently flowing river found its way to the margin
of the plateau to fall 1000 feet in a cascade
below. As I neared the goal of my ambition to
my intense horror I felt myself gliding down to
eternity. Fortunately when I had slipped but a
few feet Monsieur le Baron de Lesseps came to
my rescue, and with great presence of mind and
agility saved my life, with no worse results to me
than a good ducking and the loss of my hat.[1]

A few days after our visitors had left I received
a letter from my sister Sophy asking me to join
her at Constantinople and to accompany her to
her new home in Bitholia (Monastir), the old
capital of Macedonia, where my brother-in-law,
Mr Longworth, had been appointed Consul. This
trip was to end the first period of my youth with
all its joys, its sorrows, its illusions, and its
delusions; all had to be left behind on my entering

---

[1] Some years ago a good deal of public attention was drawn
to the mysterious disappearance of an English traveller who
had gone up Mount Olympus and was never seen again, nor
was his body found in spite of careful search. In that
solitary region was a band of Albanian shepherds, cut-throats,
within whose mandra (fold) no one thought of looking, and
where, according to Keridly Mustapha Naily Pasha, after the
murder of the traveller the body had probably been buried.

this new phase of life. I had a vague idea that
my sister intended to keep me with her. Fresh
from England, I confess I did not relish her plan,
but the die having been cast, I put the best face on
it that I could and we started on our journey *via*
Salonika. We went on board an antiquated cast-
off paddle-wheel steamer belonging to some Greek
company. The voyage was neither comfortable
nor pleasant, but worse was to come. On the
third day we reached Salonika, where we landed
in a small boat on the sandy beach as there was
no harbour or landing-stage. Dozens of shoddy
looking Jewish boatmen surrounded our steamer,
fighting, swearing, and screaming amongst themselves for the first customers. I thought we
should never see the end of the fray, until there
arrived a clean, good boat occupied by a handsome,
bright-looking, young Englishman who scattered
the boatmen right and left and came on board,
cordially shook hands with my sister, and was
formally introduced to me as Mr John Blunt,
Vice-Consul at Uskub in Albania. This very
energetic young man soon got us ashore with our
baggage, and, in the absence of any hotel, drove
us to the house of Mr Calvert, the then British
Consul at Salonika.

Next morning we started for Vodena, half-way
to Bitholia. After a stormy night at this lovely
place, as guests of the Greek Archbishop, we made
a fresh start on posthorses for our final destination.
In spite of the absence of proper roads, of broken
bridges, and of overflowing torrents, we reached
Bitholia in two instead of three days. Dead tired
as I felt, I cheered up as we got on to a good bit

of road shaded by two lines of trees, a mile from
the town. This bit of road ended in an ill-paved
main street which, however, was wide, and both
sides were occupied by the best buildings Bitholia
could boast of. It looked nice, and I was glad
to see the Consulate appeared to be one of the
best amongst the houses. My brother-in-law was
absent on a mission and Mr Blunt stayed at the
Consulate as his representative.

On the day after our arrival half the town
called on my sister. Except for one or two
consuls and a small number of officers belonging
to the Turkish Army, which at that time had its
headquarters at Bitholia, there did not appear to
be anybody likely to be of great interest to us.
The rest of the visitors consisted of a mixture
of Turkish beys, Albanians, Greeks, Wallachs,
Bulgarians, and a few others who, stiff and
upright, sat on the edge of their chairs. The
ladies who came were mostly wealthy Wallachians
and looked like dressed-up boards. I had no idea,
till I saw them, that any human beings could be
so straight and thin as these ladies were from head
to foot. When we were relieved of the presence
of the somewhat trying company I could not help
expressing my disgust at Bitholia's social resources.
My sister laughed, saying, "Never mind, later on
you will find plenty to interest you in this part of
the world."

No doubt the country itself looked pretty and
interesting, in spite of the fact that nothing
remained in the way of buildings to attest to its
past wealth and grandeur, as everything had been
rased to the ground by the destructive Turkish

conquest, in accordance with the dictum of the
Turkish creed, "first the souls and then their
belongings." Several incidents shortly occurred
which were of interest to us. The first was the
sudden appearance of a very fine-looking Serbian
girl, armed to the teeth, who had walked all the
way from Serbia to seek the chastisement of a
young Turk attached to the medical department
of the army as a dispenser, who had promised to
marry her in her own country during the Turkish
occupation, and had afterwards deserted her. The
base deceiver was no longer at Bitholia, but my
kind, charitable sister at once offered the girl
hospitality till she could go back to her own
country. About the same time another girl, this
time from Kurdistan, arrived, dressed in man's
clothes. This one had found her way to the
Crimea in search of her lost lover. On finding
that her lover had been killed she entered the
army in order to vindicate his death, and, in spite
of being a woman, fought with such bravery and
success that within a short time, none doubting
the sex indicated by her clothes, she rose to the
rank of "Ramazan chaouch," *i.e.,* a sergeant made
during the period of Ramazan, a religious festival.
As a "Ramazan chaouch" she followed her regiment
to Bitholia, when it became known to the authorities
that she was a woman. His Majesty the Sultan
ordered that a pension should be given her for her
services, and this was at once awarded, but owing
to the greed of the official hands through which it
had to pass it never reached her. She therefore
came to the Consulate to plead for assistance to
help her to obtain her pension. During one of

her daily visits she came face to face with the
Serbian heroine and unwisely began with much
vigour to discuss the war. This led to a hand-to-
hand fight, the Serbian catching up a kitchen
knife, the "chaouch" a pair of tongs. I had the
greatest difficulty in separating these women, who,
forgetting their personal grievances, tried to kill
each other *pour l'honneur de la patrie.*

At this time the Turkish Army was, I believe,
at its worst—impoverished in substance, and
short even of the few necessaries the brave
Turkish soldier needs. Except for a few of the
superior officers, the army gave one the impression
of a tatterdemalion body of disorganised men.
Among the generals of this army were several
naturalised Poles and Austrians, and such well-
known Turks as Osman Ghazi and a few others
who were disposed to make changes in the
organisation of the army, and who had the services
of a French officer attached to the staff of the
commander-in-chief as àdvisor. Of the German
element, as far as I can remember, there was no
one of note. Polish officers were the most
numerous owing to a fine regiment which had
been formed under the command of General
Tchaykovsky; but this regiment only lasted a few
years because of the jealousies and intrigues of the
anti-Christian party. The army, however, such
as it was, gave some life to the otherwise dead
alive old country which was neglected, and its
fine natural sources undeveloped. My brother-
in-law, struck with the wealth and fertility of the
country, bought a big estate for a couple of
thousand pounds; but when he tried to cultivate

his property the neighbouring Albanians, armed, marched down in a body and threatened to shoot everybody on the place. The authorities being powerless to stop the Albanian depredations returned the amount paid by Mr Longworth, and took the estate over as Government property. Such was the condition of Bitholia (Monastir) over half a century ago. One evening, some time after our arrival there, when my brother-in-law's return was hourly expected, we heard a great clatter of posthorses at the gate, followed by a violent ringing of the bell. Mr Blunt, who happened to be below, called out in his impulsive way at the top of his voice, "Mrs Longworth, Mrs Longworth, Longworth has arrived." My dear sister, who adored her husband, rushed downstairs and fell into the arms of the traveller as he came into the hall before the lights were brought. The traveller so tenderly welcomed, instead of responding, was doing his best to free himself from my sister's embrace. When the light was brought she found to her dismay that the newcomer, not unlike her-husband in general appearance, was a total stranger. In order to punish what she considered an ugly joke on the part of Mr Blunt, she boxed his ears, and apologised to the stranger who introduced himself as Mr Dan Garden, M.P., on a trip through Macedonia. In the absence of any hotel my sister naturally offered Mr Garden the hospitality of the Consulate, which led to a fresh adventure in the evening owing to the stupidity of the maid-servant. This servant was a Slav, a silly, grinning creature, who was ordered to get Mr Blunt's room

ready for Mr Garden, and put a mattress and
pillow in the drawing-room for Mr Blunt. She
grinned assent and left the room, to rush back
ten minutes later shouldering the mattress and
accessories which she threw down in anger,
saying, "He wanted to murder me with his
revolver." On inquiring who wanted to murder
her, she said, "That solemn looking visitor who,
as I tried to lay the mattress on the floor, sat up
in his bed, saying, "Istemem, Istemem" ("I
don't want, I don't want.") We naturally thought
that Mr Garden, who had quickly fallen asleep
after his long journey, had been annoyed to be
disturbed by another person's bed being brought
into his room, just the thing we had endeavoured
to avoid. When I greeted Mr Garden next
morning he was looking a little more solemn than
on the previous evening, and was busy bandaging
his felt hat on to his knee, saying that this was
the best cure for rheumatism. Similar incidents
of wearing strange costumes in the Near East
are of the commonest occurrence, especially among
English people, who have often well earned the
sobriquet of "mad Englishmen" by turning up
in clothes so extraordinary that crowds of children
follow them in the streets. I recollect seeing a
traveller from India, who was, I think, the maddest
of mad Englishmen, with rows of beads round
his neck, and a hat on his head surrounded by a
range of little windows which opened and shut
when he pressed a spring!.

After a few weeks in Bitholia I had heard and
seen so many strange things that I began to
think my sister had been right in telling me

that I should become more interested in the
country later on. There were lovely rides all
round the country, which Mr Blunt and I greatly
enjoyed, as well as the company of each other.
As we became better acquainted our friendship,
as such friendships often do, ended by our
becoming engaged, and our marriage speedily
followed, in spite of the difficulties caused by the
absence of my brother-in-law, and the possibility
of arranging for a marriage ceremony in the non-
existence of a Protestant Church or missionary. I
had much to do when once I had made up my mind
to cast my lot in the wildest regions of Albania.
There were the arrangements for the marriage,
my clothes to make, my house linen to get, and a
thousand and one other things to arrange, of
which the most difficult was to arrange for the
marriage ceremony. On the return of my brother-
in-law a family council was held on ways and
means.

My sister proposed the Roman Catholic
service, which I refused, chiefly because it meant
changing my faith on account of *hors de l'église
point de salut.* Mr Blunt proposed the Turkish
nikiah or marriage, which he thought would be
quite binding, as it was a national institution. I
refused this suggestion with indignation, owing to
all the privileges of a Turkish marriage being on
the side of the husband. Divorce, for instance,
he can obtain solely by ordering his better half
" to cover her face," not to mention the still
greater right he possesses, that of having as many
wives as he chooses. Mr Blunt, who was only
joking, as he wanted to raise my indignation,

apologised humbly for his pretended ignorance of these important points, and turned the whole thing into such a farce that we all joined heartily in the merriment which ensued. My brother-in-law, now awake to his responsibilities, offered his privileged services for the civil marriage, and suggested the Orthodox (Greek) form for the religious ceremony, which I accepted willingly, as, unlike the Roman Catholic Church, there is no obligation to change the form of faith which is very like our own, *i.e.*, no belief in the doctrine of transubstantiation. His Holiness the Archbishop of Pelagonia kindly acceded to our request that he would perform the religious service, and the wedding was fixed for 25th November 1858. We all became very busy preparing for the event. My kind sister concentrated her energies on the confectionery, and prepared a beautiful wedding cake as well as many delicacies for the ball which was to follow the wedding. Mr Blunt and my brother-in-law helped us by approving or disapproving the arrangements. As for me, I had to become dressmaker and seamstress, and cut out and prepare my wedding dress which, as luck would have it, turned out a great success. I had, at the same time, to prepare two gala costumes for two little blackies (slaves) who, during the absence of Mr Longworth had taken refuge in the Consulate, thereby causing Mr Blunt a good deal of trouble to get the order from the Pasha to liberate them, in accordance with the English convention on the anti-slavery question. They looked nice little girls between thirteen and fourteen years of age, the one a regular Central African type with hair like a Turk's head broom, the other an Abyssinian with soft curly hair and regular dark features. As they were homeless I decided to take them under my care and bring them up as maids. These children entered into all the preparations with great joy, and stood and watched the marriage ceremony and the ball in the evening with wide open eyes and gaping mouths. No doubt overcome by sleep they disappeared, to be discovered later on by my husband fast asleep under the bed, with their little black legs protruding from beneath the vallance. It was luck, I thought, that in their savage ways they had preferred the floor rather than the bed to sleep on. The last day of my girlish freedom was not very cheerful, as my thoughts would go back to the past and the many plans and dreams I had made as regards the future, with its bright vista of life in a civilised country like England, with all her wonderful works of art and civilisation within the reach of rich and poor to enjoy in perfect peace and security under a well-ordered government. I could not help comparing this with what I had bound myself to in the future. In spite of the assurance I had of having secured a very happy home-life, I felt very low and depressed. My fiancé noticed my unhappy looks and asked me what was the matter. I told him all I felt and thought. For a few minutes he looked very sorry and concerned, but soon brightened up and said: "My dear child, do you imagine that I am the sort of man to be held down in a wild country like Albania? Every

career must have its beginning, and I am not at
all sorry to begin mine in Albania; but you can
rest assured it will be for only a short time, and
will end so soon as I have mastered and informed
the Government of all that is worth knowing.
So cheer up, and like me, think better of the
future, which I promise to make as happy and
cheerful. as I can." This comforting assurance
chased away all my sombre thoughts, and, recover-
ing my good spirits, I began to think of the morrow
and its complicated ceremonies in a brighter light.
There was still much to be done, for in Bitholia
we could get no outside help, nor could we obtain
many things usually thought to be indispensable,
but *à la guerre comme à la guerre*, and we had
to do without them. The ceremony was to take
place at the Consulate. An altar had to be
arranged in the centre of the drawing-room, and
two huge wreaths of orange blossom with white
ribbon bows and long ends had to be made (these
latter had to play an important part in the
marriage ceremony), as well as many smaller
details connected with the religious service.
There were two things which I flatly refused to
do, one was to be paraded all round the town in
my bridal costume, the other to be kissed by all
the company when wishing me happiness. I
accepted the good wishes but avoided the kisses
by carefully keeping my bridal veil down.

Next day soon after a few select visitors had
come, His Grace the Archbishop of Pelagonia
in his splendid gold-bespangled vestments, accompanied by his deacon and half a dozen priests
in the pleated robes and with their imposing

kalmosks (copes) over their long curly hair, walked slowly and quietly into the room and took up their appointed places. There were also a combare or best man and two witnesses, Raouf Pasha and Hassan Pasha who were Mohammedans. The service which was short but imposing began by my brother-in-law performing the civil portion of the service in English, followed by His Holiness the Archbishop reading the marriage service in Greek, and by placing or rather crowning both my husband's and my head with the orange blossom wreaths. These were exchanged three times on our heads. He first held them over our heads and then exchanged them to the other, each time repeating, " In the name of the Father, Son, and Holy Ghost." At the same time he exchanged our wedding rings in the same manner. Good wishes in the form of grain and bonbons were showered on us after the blessing. I should think but few weddings have been of so composite a character as ours. My brother-in-law was a Roman Catholic, His Holiness was the head of the Orthodox (Greek) Church, we were members of the Church of England, and our two witnesses were Mohammedans.

The ball in the evening was a great success, and I thoroughly enjoyed it as my husband and some of the officers proved to be excellent dancers. The journey to our home at Uskub had to be undertaken on posthorses, and as this was the rainy season it was not very pleasant. The bad roads were sometimes knee-deep in mud, and when crossing streams the horses were often up to their girths in the water, and yet in spite of all, since we were both good riders, the journey was done in two days instead of three. Uskub, as we entered it, impressed me as being a bright and cheerful town. The Consulate was situated outside the town on the fine Vardar river and appeared from the outside to be a large house, but within it proved only to be half finished and was tenanted by large numbers of doves and blackbirds whose cooing and singing broke the monotony of the solitude. The first faces we saw next morning were those of our two little blackies who had just arrived with the baggage. Much to my amusement visitors soon followed, headed by the Governor. There were also the Archbishop of Uskub, some Albanian brigand boys, the Hodjabachi or headmen of the Christian communities, which were composed of Serbs, Greeks, and Bulgars, who all appeared anxious and pleased to make my acquaintance as the first English woman that they had ever seen in their country. The establishment of a British Consulate must have been a great event and deeply interesting to the inhabitants. Next morning we made our first appearance in the main street of the town, arm in arm, and soon after callers came to make inquiries as to the Consolos Bey's state of health on the supposition that he must be very ill since he only went out walking supported on his hanoum's arm ! The Christian ladies next came in groups to call upon me. Some looked nice and pretty in their rich native costumes, often, however, made ridiculous by their attempts to improve these by a mixture of English and French fashions, such for instance as crinolines under their wide trousers

F

or bloomers, elastic-sided boots, and the hideous black silk or satin men's neckties of the day, which fastened with a spring. I could not help smiling when I thought of the effect this motley company would have made in a drawing-room at home. Yet these ladies looked dignified as well as satisfied with themselves. After sitting down each lady produced a bag mysteriously hidden in her garments, and brought out a lot of genuine jewellery with which they began to ornament their heads and persons. I asked them how it was they did not put on their jewellery before coming to pay their call on me. "No fear of our doing so," said they, "if we ventured into the streets with our treasures exposed, the Albanian beys would take them all, and we should never see them again." Although familiar as I was with Turkish, Greek, and a little Bulgarian, the conversation was neither flowing nor interesting owing to there being nothing in common between a free, civilised person and those ignorant, long-suffering creatures. As I was full of work and care in my efforts to set in order my small establishment, neither I nor my husband had time to give to the Uskub social circle. My husband, like the dear he was, set to work carpentering, papering the few habitable rooms, and working at the sewing machine. In a couple of weeks we settled down and organised our daily mode of life with the help of the two little blackies, a native boy my husband had saved from slavery, and a good, intelligent native woman who had freed herself from slavery by running away from the konak of a rich Dere Bey whom the Porte had seen fit quietly to clear out of the way. This woman who had kept out of sight for a time offered her services to me as cook. We had also engaged a groom who I found was stealing our provisions, and when he had the audacity to tell me that a fine goose which was in the larder ready for cooking had flown away he had to leave us suddenly. Fortunately grooms were not difficult to replace. We also had a fine young Albanian guard, Hussein Aga by name. After we had trained our staff somewhat the establishment began to look something like a home. Strange to say, all this work had absorbed our thoughts to such an extent that we lost all record of time so that we celebrated our Christmas a fortnight too soon. As we sat down to our first Christmas dinner together my husband produced a bottle of champagne, a trophy of the Crimean War, to celebrate the happy event. My plum-pudding, with which I had taken so much trouble, came in at the same time. Pleased with the product of my handiwork my husband cut into it, when to my amazement I noticed the spoon would go no further than a few inches. "Try another side," said I, with tears of disappointment in my eyes; "but what can be wrong when I myself measured the ingredients, mixed them together, and tied the pudding up." My amused better half made another dash into the inner part, when to my horror and humiliation what should come out but a whole egg in its shell. The incident was so preposterous that I at once sent for the cook for an explanation. "Madam," said she in a fury, "it was by your orders that I put in the eggs in their shells." I then remembered having asked her to boil a couple of eggs in the pot in which the plum-pudding was boiling for a salad I was making, and she, mistaking what I had said, had thrust the eggs into the pudding. Fortunately the pudding was none the worse. The post came in at that moment after some considerable delay, and on opening a letter from my sister Sophy I found a pressing invitation for us to go and spend Christmas at Bitholia. It was only then, on comparing dates and counting up days, that we realised we were celebrating Christmas a fortnight before 25th December. We came to the conclusion that there must be something wrong either in the air of the place or with our own selves to make us lose record of even time itself.

CHAPTER V

1859-1860

THE monotonous life at Uskub began to tell on both of us. My husband, who never knew what idleness was, occupied himself mastering all that was worth knowing about Northern Albania and its inhabitants. I believe he had only two cases during the two years we were at Uskub in which his Consular assistance was claimed. The first was the murder of an Ionian (British) subject. This man was murdered close to the town by a local Bey, who, on the day following the murder, coolly walked into the town and was arrested at the instigation of my husband by a body of police whilst in the shop of an Albanian costumier, when he was on the point of paying £50 for a rich costume he had just chosen. The day following his arrest all his womenkind came in a body to me begging me to get their Bey liberated, as they thought that, Turkish fashion, they might bribe me to persuade my husband to get the Bey freed. The Bey was not hanged, as Sultan Abdul Medjid was averse from capital punishment, but was imprisoned for a time. The women evidently thought nothing of the crime the Bey had committed.

The second case was that of another Ionian

(British) subject who rushed into the Consulate in an agitated condition, asking the Consul's assistance as his wife was about to have a baby. This funny incident Mr Blunt turned to his own use years later in Boston, when a very inquisitive lady newspaper reporter walked into his office to interview him respecting the duties of a consul in Turkey. Recollecting this incident he solemnly related it to the lady, who, evidently scandalised, put her notebook into her bag and hastily left the office.

Besides the absence of British subjects in Uskub there was no commercial connection, nor indeed any kind of connection with England. The Consular work consisted in reports on the neglected and impoverished state of the country, and on the habits and resources of its people, who greatly depended for their existence on produce stolen from the unfortunate Christians who lived in the towns and villages. The cattle, corn, and indeed everything the Albanians could lay their hands on, they carried off from the Christians after inflicting the most cruel and terrible outrages.

Looking over Sir John's Uskub correspondence nearly every paper I take up is labelled "Albanian atrocities"; and yet strange to say as a tribal people the Albanian Ghegs possess certain strict unwritten laws for the regulation of their home life with regard to the virtues of honour, honesty, and morality, which are far more rigidly enforced with them than among many more highly civilised and law-abiding peoples.

From time immemorial the Albanians have committed every outrage, every cruelty and injury on those who were not protected by their code of honour. As I lived among these people for two years, 1858-1860, and saw and heard much with my own eyes and ears, I feel convinced that for ages to come no power will break off the old well-established Albanian habits of utter disregard for life and property outside their own people. I consequently cannot help feeling deeply for the misfortune of those Christian towns and villages, barely free from their slavery under Turkish control, who are to fall beneath the yoke of the projected enlarged Albania. This will be worse than Turkish slavery, especially for the unfortunate Greeks of Epirus. This part of Greece, little known in England, counts for one of the finest and most patriotic parts of the old country, which for centuries has been at the head of the liberating national movement, and is known to have spent much of its wealth in embellishing Athens, and in subscribing funds to be utilised in the happy event of liberation. Should this project of an enlarged Albania come to be realised the blow will be terrible to the Greeks of Epirus, and the pacific healing difficult to accomplish. At the time we lived at Uskub it was an unknown part of the world, and remained so till the railway was built about a score of years ago, which brought it more into evidence. The railway, I believe, has not brought any great change or improvement to the country itself.

When the novelty of life in savage Albania had subsided we began to have a great longing to get away. I looked after my menage and took long rides into the country, fearless, thanks to

our perfect security from Albanian attacks, due
to the great name England had acquired all over
Albania, on the return of the Albanian forces
from the Crimean War. These forces had been
officered by Englishmen, and England's name
stood for justice, honesty, and greatness. The
kind care the Albanians had received at the hands
of the English made them known and spoken of
in every hamlet. As a matter of fact during the
two years I spent in that wild region, none of
the Albanian attributes of savagery ever came
nearer to me than by report. The Turkish
Governor himself was far from enjoying the
security that we did, for, while we could go
anywhere we pleased, he could not move out
of his house without an escort, and even in his
konak he was not safe, as a pistol shot at His
Excellency was of almost daily occurrence.

Among the few interesting natives I came
across in Uskub was a venerable old Sheik,
reported to have much success with the dreaded
effects of the evil eye, as well as for his gift of
predicting the future.

As his services were offered free of charge to
man and beast, Hussein Aga, our Albanian guard,
asked him to come and see my favourite horse
"Swift," which was sick. "Swift" was a fine
racehorse from the Crimea, which had been given
to my husband. I went to the stable to watch
the old Sheik's treatment, and found it consisted
of spitting and blowing into the mouth of the
horse, and pulling its ears. Wonderful to relate,
the poor beast soon shook off the effects of its
sickness, brightened up and neighed, and looked

at me for a bit of sugar. I thanked the old
Sheik and asked him in my most fluent Turkish
to come and have a cup of coffee. He willingly
accepted. When my husband left the room, the
old man with his deep-set eyes asked my leave
to predict what the future had in store for us.
I accepted. Who could have refused such an
offer, living in such a place as Uskub? "Your
husband, the Bey, is a man possessed of very fine
qualities, and of great bravery and courage. He
will have a long, wandering life, doing a great
deal of good, but he would do better still for
himself if he would follow your advice."

The Sheik was not wrong in his prediction. I
for one rarely, if ever, came across a man like
Mr Blunt who put aside his own interests in order
to serve his country.

"Khanum" (madame), said he, "Uskub is much
too small a place for you, and the sooner you
leave it and get to a place where you can exercise
your brain power the better. Your life will be a
long one with cares and joys, and will not end as
happily as you deserve." In all probability I
should have forgotten all about this prophecy but
for its parting words, which alas, have been
largely realised!

A wealthy Armenian of Constantinople,
Mardiros Effendi by name, came to Uskub on
business. He was clever and amusing and my
husband and I enjoyed his company, notwith-
standing that he was a bit of a coward, like most
Armenians were, under the Turkish administration.
Mardiros had a somewhat embarrassing adventure
while at Uskub. He took rooms facing the

konak of the aged but liberal Kadi (judge) of
Uskub, and as he was well dressed, of agreeable
presence, and living in good style, he soon attracted
the attention of the old Kadi, who was greatly
pleased to have Mardiros as his neighbour and
often went to see him. After a time Mardiros felt
a certain amount of curiosity with regard to an
opening in a jalousie of one of the windows in the
Kadi's house opposite to his rooms. The opening
was slightly enlarged and allowed two pretty
fingers, one ornamented by a beautiful ring,
representing the emblem of love among Turkish
ladies, to appear. The opening went on enlarging
till he could see two lovely eyes looking at him.
Impressed as he was, Mardiros resisted the
temptation of responding to the advances of the
lovely girl, one of the wives of the Kadi, no doubt
bored to death in her closely confined life.

One evening she asked of her husband, the
Kadi, leave to go to a wedding in the neighbourhood. Instead, however, of preparing for a
wedding she dressed up in the Kadi's robes, and
with a shawl over the turban went across to make
the acquaintance of her neighbour. She knocked
at the door, the servant opened it and led her
upstairs, announcing to his master,—

"Effendi, the Kadi has come."

Once well within the room she cast off her
disguise and, amazed by her beauty and her
courage, Mardiros stood speechless gazing at her,
and thinking it would be death for both of them if
her childish adventure were discovered. But she,
more amused than frightened, laughed and said,
"Effendi, where is your courage, your manliness?

Is this the way you receive the friendly visit of a neighbour? Take example from me˜ and look pleasant. The Kadi Effendi being out, I thought to replace his company with advantage."

Our friend, ashamed of the poor figure he was cutting, began to look more alive, when there was another knock at the door and the servant rushed in saying,—

"Effendi, Effendi, the Kadi has come."

Whilst her host once more became helpless she looked about, and seeing a recess covered by a curtain hid behind it just as the real Kadi walked in. Finding Mardiros in a speechless condition, the Kadi said he was sorry to have disturbed him, but as his wife had gone to a wedding he thought he would come and spend a pleasant hour with him. Poor Mardiros, now more dead than alive, as he thought of Madame Kadi within a few steps of her husband, felt, so he told us, that his last hour had come. Fortunately the considerate Kadi soon took his departure, but only just in time, as the next moment Madame rushed out saying she was suffocating and Kadi or no Kadi she must come out. There ended his adventure, which points out that even a Turkish girl kept under lock and key will gain her liberty at times. Next day Mardiros moved to the opposite end of the town.

Out of genuine sympathy or curiosity I called at the harem in question and was struck by the charm of the veiled beauty, who had a look of melancholy in her young eyes that roused my pity and sympathy.

As my husband had predicted our stay at

Uskub was of no long duration, for before two years were quite gone he was instructed to go on a mission of inspection over Macedonia and report on the result of a Turkish Reform Expedition made under the pressure of England. The Turkish Government sent Kibrisly Mehemet Pasha to carry out the suggested reforms.

Since I could take no part in this expedition, and as I did not care' to remain at Uskub alone, my husband kindly suggested that I should go to Constantinople for a change. I accepted the proposal with *empressement*, so we soon started on our separate ways. I took my inseparable "blackies" with me, and accompanied by our brave, intelligent, and faithful guard, Hussein Aga, I undertook the long land journey to Gallipoli, and then took steamer for Constantinople. I had rather despised Constantinople on my arrival from England some three years previously, but now the place looked to me like a terrestial paradise ; even the "blackies" seemed to appreciate the change. My brother met me and we drove straight to Therapia, where he had taken a small, pretty house for me belonging to my dear old nurse, just opposite to the house in which I was born.

Soon old and new friends began to call upon me, and I felt the dreadful Uskub depression clearing from my brain. Sir Henry Bulwer was still Ambassador in Turkey, and both he and Lady Bulwer were extremely kind to me. Sir Henry Bulwer and Lord Lumley took great interest in my statements about Albania and the little profit there could be in keeping on the Vice-Consulate at Uskub in so hopeless a country.

At the same time I pleaded my own cause so earnestly that both the Ambassador and Lord Lumley promised to do their best for a transfer for my husband. The time proved opportune, owing to a certain amount of political agitation at Constantinople. England was pressing hard on the Porte for the promised reforms in European Turkey. On the other hand, the Bulgarians had begun to wake up concerning their national rights and religious grievances against the Greek Patriarchate. In their anxiety to obtain support from wherever they could, they tried to interest France, and went so far as to make conditional promises that the Bulgarian nation should become Roman Catholic. The bait took at the Vatican. A fine Jesuit College was built at Salonika for the education of Uniates. An ignorant, worthless Bulgar priest was found willing to change his religion, and he was sent to Rome to be consecrated as the Bishop of the Uniates. On my husband's return from his mission in Macedonia, he was sent to Philippopolis to investigate these matters. He found the place upset by a Greco-Bulgarian polemic, *re* the ascendancy the Greeks had assumed over the Bulgarian churches to the exclusion of their own priests and of the Bulgarian language. The difficulties which had brought great dissension between the Greeks and Bulgarians were originated by the Greek Patriarch at Constantinople, the head of the Orthodox (Greek) Church in the Near East, as well as in Greece and in Russia. In course of time most of the states professing adherence to the Orthodox (Greek) Church

detached themselves from the Patriarch. Bulgaria
being still under Turkish dominion led to intoler-
able abuses, such, for instance, as the confiscation
by the Patriarch of churches built by Bulgarians,
and his prohibition of the Bulgarian service being
read in any other church. The fight continued
for years and came to be a national question, and
staunch patriots like Mr Stoyanowich, Mr Vulko-
wich, Dr Tchomakoff, and others worked with
the most astonishing zeal and activity in their
efforts to wake up the Bulgarians out of their
ignorant trance. My husband and I were much
interested to watch the Bulgarians use every
means they could to obtain the support of any
foreign power willing to help them. My husband
mastered the whole question, but limited his action
to keeping his Government informed of what
was going on. There was a good deal of the
Machiavellian policy in their methods with foreign
powers after the fiasco with France and the
Vatican. Hoping for better success with the
English Government, the Bulgarians made a
proposal through Mr Blunt similar to that which
they had made to France, namely, that they would
accept the English national religion in return for
English assistance. Mr Blunt listened with attention to their request, then turned to the deputation
and said, "Gentlemen, I thank you for your
important offer, but I regret to say that were I
to see you all on your bended knees taking your
oaths for carrying out this measure, I would not
believe you."

After looking at each other the deputation rose
in a body and asked my husband to shake hands

with them, saying, "You are perfectly right, sir, but necessity at times impels us to do strange things."

These were among the first steps the Bulgarians took to gain their independence in religious matters which years after they obtained by separating entirely from the Patriarch by the creation of the Exarchate at Constantinople. My husband supported the rights of the Bulgarians to hold their own services in their own churches and in their own language.

Mr Blunt's attitude in this matter raised the hatred of the Greeks, who tried to revenge themselves by filling their newspapers with abusive stories about him. My husband, naturally sensitive with regard to these reports, wrote to me to ask His Excellency whether he should reply to them. Sir Henry smiled, saying,—

"Have you seen one or two reports about me in the *Levant Herald?* I have just been informed that the author of these unflattering reports is the same man who has come to me to beg permission to reply to them. Unflattering reports in Levantine newspapers have no importance attached to them."

While my husband was endeavouring to clear up the rights and wrongs of the Bulgars and Greeks I was thoroughly enjoying myself, and received much kindness from everyone as a young grass widow. The French Ambassador kindly put the key of his lovely garden at my disposal, which facilitated my daily visits to my dear brother at the Embassy, by shortening the distance, as otherwise I should have had to go a long way round by the road. I also had the privilege of using M. l'Ambassadeur's fine horses, and greatly enjoyed riding all round the lovely hills bordering the Bosphorus. The presence of the Diplomatic Corps, which happened to be there at the time, gave much life and animation to the summer season.

I had the pleasure of meeting Mrs Suchodolska, the daughter of General Tchaikovsky, a clever, accomplished woman, who had been brought up in Paris by the Princess Czartorjska, and who became my greatest friend.

Mrs Suchodolska was but little known in Constantinople, and the French Ambassador meeting her at my house, asked me "Dans quel bosquet avez-vous ramassé ce bel eglantier." She was, however, better known in Austria than in Turkey, and received an offer from the Austrian Government to go on a mission for three years to Russia, with the object of collecting all possible information with regard to the constitution and working of the Russian Army. The salary for this arduous task was left for Mrs Suchodolska to fix. She was told that going from Turkey she would be less suspected of trying to gain information than if she went from Austria. Mrs Suchodolska talked the matter over with me, and we came to the conclusion that she should refuse it, since the post would be a risky one, owing to the espionage prevalent in Russia, and might lead to her banishment to Siberia. I merely mention this incident to show how, even in those early days, the Powers were heading against each other and building castles in the air

on their future possible conquests. England,
France, Italy, and Austria were much to the
front in those days, and even Russia, in spite of
the fact that she had always been looked upon as
a deadly enemy to Turkey. Germany was not
thought much of. The first I heard of her using
her influence was an act of confiscation of the
lovely piece of ground on which the German
Embassy was built. The property had belonged
to an old Patrician Greek family, but was taken
from them no doubt with the connivance of the
Porte. The unfortunate owners tried hard to
obtain something for this valuable property, but
without success so far as I know. England was
far ahead of any of the other European Powers
in her influence in Turkey, as the Turks from
all time had a liking for the English, so far as
their creed and sympathies would allow them to
have a liking for any Christian nation. Abdul
Medjid's sympathy and liking for England
naturally had its effects on the nation. Fond of
reforms Medjid made several good laws, but
unfortunately he had neither the knowledge nor
the courage to see them carried through. His
ministers were good and wise men, several of
whom were staunch partisans of England, earnest
patriots whose faults and errors, however gross
they may have been, were not of the treasonable
character of the present Young Turkey party who
would ruin their country by selling it to Germany.
I remember my brother telling me how pleased
Abdul Medjid and his entourage were to hear of
the projected visit of H.R.H. Edward, Prince of
Wales. This visit was the great event of the

G

day. The Grand Rue de Pera was repaved for
the occasion, the streets cleaned, and a variety of
oriental embellishments made, which added much
to the natural beauty of the place. On the
arrival of His Royal Highness the streets were
lined with dense crowds of people of various races
and costumes, which formed a picturesque
ensemble not to be met with out of the Near
East. The Embassy court was filled with British
subjects anxious to welcome the beloved popular
Prince, the future King of England.

Lady Bulwer kindly asked me to stay at the
Embassy during the visit of the Prince. I much
enjoyed meeting the pleasant people the presence
of His Royal Highness brought together at
the Embassy. I liked to watch the dignified
sympathy with which Sir Henry and Lady
Bulwer kept up a pleasant cordiality in that
cosmopolitan gathering of Turkish grandees,
foreign ambassadors, and other distinguished
people.

The Prince himself, young, handsome, and
full of life, gave the keynote to his host and
hostess by his kind and thoughtful courtesy, and
even insignificant I engaged part of his attention.
A big dinner was to be given to the Turkish
authorities in honour of the visit of His Royal
Highness, and on talking over the arrangements,
the Prince asked who was to be placed next to
him at table. Sir Henry, in accordance with
etiquette, suggested the Grand Vizier and Ali
Pasha, Minister of Foreign Affairs. The Prince
laughed, saying, "What can I have to say to
those two fat old Turks; better put Mrs Blunt

next to me, with whom I could have a pleasant talk."

Poor Sir Henry, nonplussed, thought for a moment and saved the situation by saying that I could be placed next to the thinnest of the Pashas, so that a conversation could be carried on in front of him.

The charm of the Prince of Wales' manner and conversation made a deep impression at Constantinople, and the whole population tried its best to get a glimpse of the future great King of England, Edward the Peacemaker.

CHAPTER VI

1861-1862

THE Sultan and his people appeared gratified by the visit of H.R.H. the Prince of Wales to their capital. The members of the Diplomatic Corps must have felt pleased to have the opportunity of exercising their pens on so unusual an event by stating to their respective governments their views and opinions on the apparent *rapprochement* between England and Turkey. Be this as it may, the excitement of the visit over, the cosmopolitan society settled down to its usual current of life. Owing to its many privileges Constantinople was looked upon as a pleasant and interesting official post by European diplomatists.

My husband's interesting reports on Philippopolis, which was fast assuming importance as the headquarters of the Bulgarian national movement, helped our desire for a change, and resulted in the transfer of the Uskub agency to Philippopolis. In spite of the long tedium of the journey I decided to go to Smyrna in order to become acquainted with my husband's family. I took one of the Messageries Imperiales steamers, I believe the first fine liner that appeared in Turkish waters. The sea journey was very pleasant, and Smyrna appeared to me to be the gem of the Near East. I wonder how much of her will be left after this terrible war! The Consulate was a fine, spacious building, well suited to my father-in-law's large family of five daughters and two sons. On my arrival, and during the time I spent at Smyrna, a fine British man-of-war was in port. The sight of the Flag filled my heart with joy by rousing the deep love and admiration I always felt for our naval service. During my short stay at Smyrna I was most kindly looked after by the captain and officers, who furnished me with a good hamper of provisions for my journey to Philippopolis.

I took steamer to Cavalla, where our Consular agent, Mr Whitaker, and his charming young wife put me up while I waited for the arrival of Hussein Aga, our faithful Albanian guard.

The country being infested by Albanian brigands at that time necessitated my asking my host for an escort; but he could recommend none worth taking, and said the best plan would be for Hussein Aga to engage two or three of his compatriots as escort. Fortunately for me the three men Hussein wished to engage had a fight between themselves, and Hussein told them we should have no need of their services. This led to a quarrel with Hussein, which ended by the ruffians vowing to attack us next morning on the road. The outlook was not very cheerful, but we started off and after an hour's ride reached in safety the dangerous pass at the head of the valley. I began to feel more easy in my mind when we were nearly through the pass. The descent was stiff but we hastened on, when, on turning a sharp corner, we sighted three shepherd boys walking three fine horses up and down the road. On seeing us they put their fingers to their lips as a signal for silence, whilst with their left hands they pointed to a small tumulus or mound where the three brigands were waiting for us. Fortunately for us the men must have been drinking heavily, for now at the critical moment they were fast asleep. The shepherds signalled to us to gallop on, and by taking their advice I had my first safe escape from brigands. The rest of the journey was safely accomplished *via* Adrianople. Philippopolis seen from a distance is most effective. The upper part of the town rests on three small hills overlooking a fertile plain encircled by a graceful range of hills, with villages dotted here and there, and by well-conditioned monasteries. I believe this part was chiefly inhabited by the Paulician Sectaries, and higher up the mountains by the Pomaks. The Pomaks were a fine set of mountaineers who remained faithful to their creed (Mohammedan), yet who lived in perfect harmony with their Christian neighbours. My husband came out part of the way to meet me, looking very well and very happy to welcome me to our new home, and I was so rejoiced to see him that I felt impelled to cry aloud to the wide country to tell it of my joy. Mr Blunt was staying as a guest at the house of Mr Stoyanovitch, the chief member of the Bulgarian community. Both Mr and Mrs Stoyanovitch were extremely nice people, he, a much travelled Europeanised man,

she, a sweet kind woman who spoke Greek
perfectly, and they both gave me a hearty
welcome. We stayed with them for three
months till a house to our liking could be got.
The change from desolate Uskub was very great,
and I was very happy and enjoyed the small
circle of acquaintances we made. Besides the
native element, chiefly composed of Bulgarians
and Greeks, there were two delightful American
missionary families whose company 1 greatly
appreciated, and whose earnest, simple lives I
much admired. They had not been long in the
country and did not know much about it, but
the people of Philppopolis, more advanced than ·
those of many other districts, had received them
kindly and soon began to value their presence
as advantageous to the country. Bulgaria owes
a great debt of gratitude to the American Robert
College at Constantinople, which helped to develop
the intelligence of the students and roused sentiments of patriotism among the Bulgarian youths,
who subsequently served as beacons of light to
the rest of the nation awakening from its trance
of long years of apathy. Besides Robert College,
schools for boys and girls were opened by the
American missionaries in some of the principal
towns of Bulgaria, where a liberal education, free
from religious pressure, was given. The good
work these institutes did was little known outside
their own spheres of activity, nor was it sufficiently
appreciated by the unintellectual sluggard masses
of the people. It will take a long time for the
Bulgarian nation to shake off the innate barbarism
of its nature, and it has led rather than followed

the Huns in their inhuman treatment of the
Serbians. The cruelty and intolerance of
Bulgarians are all the more regrettable since they
possess certain good qualities, but they have nót
the capacity to use them to advantage. Unfortunately, like the rest of the races in the Near East,
the sense of honour and rectitude are the least
developed of their virtues.

Subsequent to my husband's transfer to
Philippopolis some of the other Great Powers
nominated Consular agents. Educated European
influence had always a good effect in these semi-
barbarous countries which make up the Balkan
States, in spite of political outrages and national
rivalries. Mr Blunt's influence became very great
among the Turkish and Christian elements, owing
to his principle never to swerve from English rectitude. He was both loved and feared, and did a
great deal of good wherever he went, and I do not
remember his failing in any case he undertook to
set right. On the whole we were happy and
comfortable in Philippopolis. Owing to a considerable amount of commercial enterprise with
Vienna we could get anything we wanted. Living
not being expensive we were able to keep two fine
horses and to go about the country around us. On
one occasion I profited by my husband's absence
to go for a couple of weeks to Aslan, a renowned
watering-place about a day's journey from Philippopolis. In its time of prosperity under the
Romans it must have been a most lovely resort.
Now alas! its numerous mineral baths are roofless
and neglected, yet the gushing fountains of healing
waters ceaselessly pour into the deep swimming-

baths. These baths reminded me of abandoned orphans in a wilderness, there were none to care for them but a few Turkish peasants from the neighbouring village. I started for this place accompanied by Mr Stoyanovitch, my two blackies, and the faithful Hussein Aga. The road was mountainous and deserted, the country though much neglected was well favoured by nature. Half way on our journey we came to a guard-house half smothered beneath aromatic bushes. Mr Stoyanovitch suggested that we should call a halt and give our horses a rest. No sooner were we dismounted than an armed Albanian appeared, soon followed by six other armed men. They surrounded us, stared at me with their bloodshot eyes, salaamed, and asked Mr Stoyanovitch for some tobacco, which he hastily offered to the chief, who, we noticed, was minus one of his fingers. When Mr Stoyanovitch noticed the defect he became quite white and said to me in French, " For God's sake, get on to your horse as quick as you can." I did so, trying to look as cool and unconcerned as I could, when the bravo minus a finger came towards me and took me by the arm. I thought for a moment he meant to murder me, or worse still to take me as a prisoner, but with a smile on his cruel face he helped me on to my horse. I began to breathe again when that horrid hand was withdrawn. On a signal to his men they fell back, he salaamed again, thanked Mr Stoyanovitch for the tobacco, and signed to us that by his leave we might move on. We walked our horses in silence for a few yards to show confidence or bravery, and then galloped as fast as we could.

After a mile or so we drew rein, and Mr Stoyanovitch coming near to me asked me if I knew the
man who had helped me. "That ruffian," said he,
"is the most cruel and reckless brigand in the
neighbourhood. I thought he was still in prison
for the murder of one of our Beys in Philippopolis.
.The Bey's wife, in order to try and save her
husband, bit the brigand's finger so badly that it
had to be cut off. He must have bribed the
authorities and got out of prison and joined his
old band of brigands, or may have formed the new
one we have just met. How those ruffians have
allowed us to get off scot-free is more than I
can say ; perhaps it was your youth and bravery
that impressed the chief."

"Or rather," said I, "the Albanian superstition
regarding the ill - luck that attacks on women
bring."

Albanian brigandage was much to the fore in
those days, and crimes were committed in all parts
of the country with reckless courage and with
disdain of Turkish authority. The following
tragedy happened subsequent to my husband's
transfer to Adrianople.

Seven or eight brigands attacked a caravan of
seventy persons bound for Philippopolis some few
hours' journey from their destination. Mr and
Mrs Merion, two of our American Missionary
friends, were among the party. Since the object
of the brigands was wholesale robbery regardless
of loss of life, pistols and yatagans came at once
into use. Half a dozen people who tried a hopeless defence of the party were killed, Mr Merion
being amongst the number. In the confusion

that followed, the brigands disappeared with their booty, the survivors of the caravan hurried away as fast as they could, leaving behind Mrs Merion who waited beside the body of her dead husband in a desolate place under a burning sun, waiting for help from Philippopolis.   In the present terrible epoch, when lives are lost under most tragic conditions this case may fail to inspire the sympathy it deserves for the brave American wife.   When help came from Philippopolis she got into the carriage with her husband's remains, and a few hours after reaching home died after giving birth to a little girl.   In the absence of any American agency in those parts Mr Blunt received a telegram from the American Legation asking him to attend to the matter and to bring the assassins to justice. It was fortunate that at that time Kibrisly Mehemet Pasha, ex-Grand Vizier, had been sent to Adrianople as Governor-General.   Kibrisly was one of the sterling officials in Turkey, well known for his capacity in action and the fulfilment of his duties.   As soon as Mr Blunt received the telegram he went to the Governor-General and with him took the steps necessary to secure the arrest and punishment of the brigands.   Hearing that the latter were hiding in Philippopolis my husband immediately ordered posthorses to take him there.   He declined to take me with him that day, but the next day I received a telegram from him saying that if I still wished to come he authorised me to ask for an escort from the Governor.   This looked to me likely to be an exciting adventure, so I sent a note to the secretary of the Governor, a nice man and a

friend of ours, to come and see me. He came
at once, but on hearing the message I wanted
him to convey to the Governor, namely, that I
wanted an escort, he was amazed and said it was
impossible for the Governor to let me have one as
every trusty man of the police had been sent to
hunt for the brigands, so I must give up all idea
of my enterprise. Seeing I could get no assistance from that quarter and determined to go
if I possibly could, I said half in earnest, half
in play, "Kiamil Effendi, since you say His
Excellency has no reliable escort to give me I
will try to secure one among the Albanian cut-
throats, who, once engaged in my service, are
sure to prove faithful." I noticed that he did not
think I was in earnest, but as soon as he had left
I called Hussein Aga and asked him if he could
get three of his compatriots as an escort. I added,
"I do not wish to know who they are, or where
they come from. Provided you guarantee my
safety under their care, I will take all the responsibility of their engagement." Hussein's face ex-
panded with joy and he said, "Very well, Effendim,"
and withdrew. Next morning three villainous-
looking Albanians swaggered into the Consulate
for orders. One look sufficed to show that though
only in the prime of life, each had been through
some severe fights. Next day I started under
Hussein's and their care. Close to the half-way
station I noticed the mutilated body of a traveller
in a ditch who had probably lost his life in consequence of the valuable horse he was riding, and
which his assassins had carried off. I stopped the
night at the Governor's house, where I had an

excellent Turkish dinner, dressed Turkish fashion, which I had to eat with my fingers. Next morning, bearing in mind the horrid sight in the ditch, I asked for one or two policemen to join my escort.

"Turkish policemen," said my Albanians, "are like a set of frightened flies who disappear at the first sign of danger." "No, madam," added the spokesman, "trust to us, we undertake to leave you safe and sound at your destination before the sun sets." Thus assured, I continued my journey and reached the outskirts of Philippopolis before sunset; here my escort drew up at the roadside and salaamed. I asked them why they would go no further, but they said it was best they should leave me there.

Next morning Mr Blunt received a telegram saying the brigands he was seeking had left Philippopolis and were hiding at Adrianople. Shortly afterwards I heard from my husband that the escort which had taken me to Philippopolis was part of the band which had murdered Mr Merion and the others; consequently since Hussein Aga had engaged the escort he must return at once to Adrianople. I confess I felt quite nervous on Hussein's account, but on reflection I felt his part in the matter was only in obedience to my orders, which were in conformity with the notice I had given to Kiamil Effendi of the measures I meant to take, since the Governor could not give me the assistance I needed. I offered to attend at the court, but I heard nothing further of the matter. Owing to the energetic action of both the Governor and Mr Blunt, the whole band was caught and the murderers punished according to their deserts. As regards my escort, the part they had taken in the business was merely to help the assassins to get out of the country, and for their trouble they got a few years' penal servitude. This illustrates the state of insecurity existing in the country, owing to Turkish neglect and maladministration. Kibrisly Mehemet Pasha's prompt and determined action in the Merion case, at the instigation of my husband, cleared the country roads of brigands for some years, and confined Albanian ravages to the surrounding Christian towns and villages. My husband twice received special thanks from the President of the United States of America for his great services to the American missionaries in Albania.

CHAPTER VII

1862-1864

In a wandering life like ours there was always a certain amount of regret in parting from kind friends we were not likely to meet again, and in leaving behind such *lares* and *penates* as could not be carried away. Such feelings of regret were present with me when my husband and I dismantled our comfortable little home at Philippopolis. I much regretted leaving Bulgaria before I had had the opportunity of completing my collection of lovely old Chinese porcelain. Much of this porcelain had been brought from China *via* India a century and a half previously, for the benefit of the wealthy Dere Beys, whose descendants, reduced to abject poverty, were ready to part with these treasures for a mere trifle. I still have a few pieces left, but one of the finest I possessed I had the honour of presenting to H.R.H. the Duke of Edinburgh when he visited Salonika.

Philippopolis was rich in Roman antiquities. The wife of the Austrian Consul, a fat old lady who was an expert in antiquities, found many treasures. She drove about the country in a rickety country cart laden with valuable finds, looking more antiquated in her shabby old dress and coal-scuttle bonnet than many of the things she succeeded in finding. This lady and her husband lived in miserable surroundings, unsuited to the position of an Austrian Consular agent who, if I remember rightly, was the sole foreign representative at the time of my husband's transfer to Adrianople.

Our packing accomplished, we had to decide on the means of transit for our luggage and furniture. My husband suggested that it could go on a raft down the river Tunja, while I thought that something of the nature of a Noah's ark would be better. To this my husband agreed. Thereupon the ark was ordered, and when ready sailed under the care of our Armenian factotum, flying a glorious British flag, which I had made as a protection against Albanian looting parties. The ark started a week before our departure and arrived safe and sound ten days after we had reached Adrianople. But there was no dove to warn us of its safe arrival! The first box I unpacked was a big oblong one in which I had placed my linen with a few muslin wrappers on the top. I had covered these over with a white sack which I had not known contained a little rice. To my amazement, when I opened the box I found, instead of the wrappers I was looking for, a lovely emerald growth of young rice plants, so sweet and fresh looking that I plunged my face into it and enjoyed its fragrant perfume. The rice, evidently favoured by the soft, damp temperature had burst forth, and its rootlets had found their way through the loose texture of the muslin wrappers.

At the time of my husband's nomination to Adrianople (1862) the place still retained a semblance of its glory as the first capital of Turkey-in-Europe. The celebrated Mosque of Sultan Selim is there. The main part of this imposing building is crowned by an enormous cupola, which almost rivals that of St Sophia at Constantinople, and has four fine minarets, one at each corner, each with three galleries. Some idea of its size and grandeur may be formed from the number of its windows; the thousandth window, by the way, had been left incomplete by the Greek architect, who had been warned that its completion would cost him his life as, had it been finished, it would have brought ill-luck. This beautiful Mosque stands in one of the elevated parts of the Turkish quarter of the town. There was also the Teké, a sacred building of one or two orders of dervishes. It was in these sacred surroundings that one of the important local officials had built a very fine konak, out of the dishonest profits of his administration. The Governor, on discovering the frauds, confiscated the konak and ordered it to be sold by public auction, so that its price might to some extent recoup the State for the monies this man had taken. But this official was a cunning fox, who, in connivance with his friends, arranged that the price of the konak should be kept low and the house be bought by one of them, in order that it might be transferred to him later on. Our friend, the secretary to the Governor, Kiamil

Effendi, on learning of this plot, came to ask us whether we would like him to secure the konak in question for the Consulate. He highly praised it as a bargain and a rare find. We thanked him, and I asked his leave to visit the konak before the purchase was decided on. "That, Effendim," said he, "cannot be done for many reasons, but trust to my taste and you will have no cause for regret." I bowed my tacit consent whilst I considered how I could get to see it. On the principle that "Where there is a will there is a way," I concluded that there was no use in my having studied Turkish manners and customs if I could not transform myself into a perfect Turkish hanoum. I thereupon painted my cheeks, blackened my eyebrows till they met over my nose, cut my nails short and stained them with red ink. I got a well-fitting Turkish lady's costume with veil, cloak, and yellow slippers complete, and thus dressed I defied recognition as an Englishwoman, and with Hussein Aga's wife and an old woman I walked the length of the main street, in considerable trepidation lest I should let drop one of the yellow slippers from off my feet, an act which is a crime in a Turkish lady since it denotes ill-breeding. On reaching the konak without any misadventure the old woman knocked at the door and begged for admission, as the hanoum from the country, pointing to me, desired to visit so fine a konak, the like of which she had never seen. "Buyurun, buyurun" (Welcome, welcome), called out the lady at the top of the stairs. I stepped out of the yellow slippers and went upstairs with all the dignity I possessed, kissed the hand of the elderly looking lady of the house, salaamed to the younger ones, and looking round the spacious hall we had reached, I puffed out my lips in the most approved Turkish style three times, and said, "Mash Allah, Mash Allah, what a nice fine konak you possess, may Allah give you long life to enjoy it." "Ish Allah, Ish Allah, let us hope so, let us hope so," answered the good lady with a sad smile on her face; "would you like to see the rest of the house?" I gladly accepted her kind offer and went all over the premises, noticing everything with joy and delight, especially the beautiful Turkish bath built in marble. After partaking of a cup of coffee and cigarettes I bid these hanoums good-bye, got once more into the yellow slippers which this time I stumbled in, in my happy agitation over the success of my enterprise.. Next day Kiamil Effendi came to tell us that the konak was ours, and that I might go and see it when I liked. "That has already been done, my good friend," said I. He stared at me, and then complimented me on my English energy and *savoir faire*.

Both my husband and I were pleased with our new home, but our neighbours were not so pleased to find a Ghiaour (Infidel) family settled in their midst. Since, however, we both spoke excellent Turkish, and showed due respect to the customs and habits of our neighbours, we soon became good friends and remained such during the seven years we spent in Adrianople. There was a coarse wooden screen outside one of the drawing-room windows which I wished to have removed, as it blocked out not only air and light but a pretty view over the Imperial Park and Seraglio. This window had been blocked because it overlooked the courtyard of a Turkish house just beneath ours, and without it the ladies of the house could not have made use of their court, as someone from our window *might* have looked down and seen them. I bore the nuisance for a while in the hope of getting rid of it some way or another. Fortune favoured me, subsequent to a visit the Governor paid me. Knowing the right he had to object to the removal of the screen if I directly applied to him I said nothing about it, but as soon as he had left I told Hussein Aga to knock it down with the help of the groom during the night, and should the neighbours make a fuss about it, on the supposition that it was done by order of the Ghiaour Pasha, as Kibrisly Mehemet was called by the Turks, he was to diplomatise with the men and send the women up to me. Matters turned out just as I had expected. The men quickly calmed down, and so did the women when I took them into the drawing-room and showed them a big immovable sofa with a high back which I had had placed across the window, making access to the window impossible unless by climbing over the sofa. The women were so satisfied that no one could approach close enough to the window to overlook their private grounds that I heard nothing more of the matter.

In those days, living in Turkey had many advantages for those who understood the Turks and knew how to deal with them. In Adrianople the Turks were far more liberal and accommodating than those in Brussa. During all the years we spent there I do not remember any acts of violence or brutality either to the European or Christian residents.

Adrianople was a fairly large town, and extended from the region of the Mosque of Sultan Selim in a straight line to the walled part called the Frank quarter where the Europeans (Greeks, Armenians, French, etc.), lived, and then spread again right and left separating the Turkish from the Christian quarters. The country was fertile and well wooded, and well watered by the fine rivers, the Tunja and the Maritza. Altogether it was a pretty town, well placed and pleasant to live in outside the Frank quarter.

Sultan Selim, whose Mosque dominated the town, had been an enlightened and beneficent ruler. Among other things, he had inaugurated the merciful care of mad persons, for whom he built a fine institution, Timarhané or House of Health, well placed and airy, and had left a set of regulations for the care of such persons far in advance at that time of many countries ahead of Turkey in ordinary civilisation, such, for instance, as to the good feeding, the providing of music, and the outdoor exercise of the inmates.

Soon after we were settled in our lovely house we gave a house-warming to which everybody who was anybody was invited, *i.e.*, the Governor and staff, the members of the Consular Corps, the officers of the Cossack regiment stationed at Adrianople, many from the Frank quarter which included some Greek and Armenian families; but whilst the latter were dressed in their best, the *tout ensemble* looked antiquated and far from brilliant. A few of the men had white ties and gloves, and knew how to dance. Some of the elderly ladies were very much under the control of their father confessors and did not venture to wear evening dress, whilst the dowager chaperons felt so much out of their element that when some hot *consommé* was handed round shortly before the party broke up, some said, "Merci, mais nous avons pris la soupe chez nous." The young and pretty ones were more at their ease. When I asked the Governor, who had been a long time in England, what he thought of the company he smiled and said, "C'est bon pour remplir nos salons." We were, however, not quite devoid of social stars among the Consular Corps, the Cossack regiment chiefly composed of Polish refugees of high class, and a few others including some English people who had found their way to Adrianople. All these formed an agreeable circle of friends who managed to live happily by getting up plays, concerts, and picnics, hunting with the harriers in the summer, and in winter by organising skating parties. For myself, I never felt more delighted than when I heard from my old friend Mrs Suchodolska that she was coming to live with her father, General Tchaikovsky. We became inseparable friends, and many were the happy times we had together.

Of course, adventures of one kind and another happened from time to time to break the monotony of our lives. Young as I was, experience had already taught me not only to be cool and brave in any sudden emergency, but to try and find out

ways and means to lessen or avert any menacing
danger.   During one of Mr Blunt's absences from
home, when all the servants had gone to a " Festa "
at the other end of the town, my sister-in-law,
Lucy Blunt, an old Constantinople friend, and I
were the only people in the house.   About mid-
night we heard a violent knocking at the gate.
I rushed to the window and looked out thinking
my husband had returned, but instead I saw a
turbaned old Turk who called out, " Effendim,
Effendim, your house is on fire on the other side."
I rushed to the room opposite which overlooked a
yard where brooms were made, hundreds of which
were stacked against a wall close to our house.
The flames from the broom-yard nearly reached
the window I was looking from, and there was a
veritable firework display going on from the bits
of the brooms which were alight and were blown
upwards, and fortunately in a direction from the
house, by the strong wind which was fanning the
flames.   I went down to the old Turk and begged
him to keep guard, and only to let in about ten
of the neighbours known to him who would help
to get the fire under.   I then turned on the water
in the bath, and collected all the buckets I could
find and put them under the various taps to fill.
I got a long ladder and placed it against the
burning wall.   By this time the men had come.
I placed several of them on the wall, showed the
rest where the buckets and water were, and
directed them to fill the buckets and pass them
to the men on the wall.   Having got this all
going I went upstairs and found my sister-in-law
and our other guest quite dazed.   On learning

what was the matter Lucy became most excited, got a pillow and a pair of slippers, and implored me to leave the house. As for our guest, he quite collapsed; but this perhaps was not to be wondered at as he had experienced a serious fire in his own house when several members of his family and the English governess had all been burned to death. However, he went off for me to General Tchaikovsky Pasha who lived close by, and got him to send some of his Cossacks to help in pulling down the burning part and in extinguishing the fire. The efforts I had made and the help of the men succeeded in saving the house. Curiously enough, my husband could not sleep that night feeling that some calamity was menacing our home. Next morning to his surprise and relief he received a telegram from me telling him of the fire and of our safety. .

A few months later a very severe storm with much rain, which ceaselessly poured for several days, caused the rivers to overflow their banks and flooded the low-lying country, so that the houses and cottages in the lower part of the town were completely cut off from communication with the rest of the town. The anxious inhabitants watched for the boats which were employed in bringing bread and other necessaries to them. The sight of the flooded country was so unusual that Mrs Suchodolska and I decided to take a boat and see the Imperial Park which was transformed into an immense lake. It was curious to see the old trees giving shelter to myriads of birds chirruping, hopping about, and fighting for places of safety. The sight was so absorbing that we did not notice

that the current was taking us within the bed of
the river, and that the boat was getting beyond
the power of the boatman to control it. A sudden
call of alarm on his part made us join his call for
aid, when, fortunately, a rope was flung to us from
another boat which quickly pulled us out of danger
and brought us to the gates of the old Seraglio
where we landed. A fine flight of marble steps
had usually to·be negotiated when entering the
Seraglio from this side, but now all but the top-
most step was under water. We went into the
old reception hall which formerly had been a place
of much grandeur, where the Sultan's throne,
minus its jewelled ornaments, looked like a shade
of its former magnificent self, lamenting the glory
of times gone by. Opposite the throne stood the
curious Imperial cage, solidly railed all round, in
which the heirs to the throne used to be placed
when receptions were given to Foreign Ambassadors, who used to sit on the then luxuriously
covered benches which ran round the walls. The
chief beauty of this well-proportioned hall lay in
the exquisite old tiles of all kinds and designs,
which covered the walls and floor, in which the
colours, grave and gay, blended harmoniously.
The whole Seraglio had unfortunately been
neglected and allowed to fall into decay, and
during the last Turko-Russian War the ruins
were burned down. There was a graceful tower,
approached from one corner of the reception hall,
where the Guardian of the place, an old Janissary
with many scars on his shrivelled face, denoting his
old profession of cut-throat in the glorious days of
his youth, lived. According to his statements he

nightly conversed with the ghosts who frequently appeared to him and kept him company. He spoke of the ghosts and their doings with such authority that he almost made us believe that the tales we listened to were of real persons.

One of the last of the Dere Beys who had lived in Adrianople and had had jurisdiction over a vast area, evidently had a keener desire for sanitary reforms than his predecessors, since he viewed with disgust a great mound of decaying manure and refuse which had accumulated during some years in front of his palace. The Dere Bey expressed his dislike of this evil-smelling and fly-accumulating mass in the hearing of one of his attendants who noted his master's complaint. This attendant, a small, thin man, on his own initiative went all over the town and ordered men and boys to assemble with spades, baskets, and carts in front of the palace at a fixed hour that night when he set them to work to remove this immense heap. By the morning the mound had been completely cleared away, and the Dere Bey on leaving his rooms noticed with delight and surprise that the festering heap had disappeared. On inquiring who had accomplished this great feat, the small, lean, delicate-looking attendant salaamed and said, "Effendimiz, I did it to please my Lord and Master."

The Dere Bey gave vent to a burst of incredulous laughter and said, "You! You! In future your name shall be Dagh Deveran" (Remover of Mountains).

A reputation for sagacity and acts of justice soon became associated with Dagh Deveran's name.

People from all parts appealed to his unerring judgment to settle their quarrels till he rose to great distinction and finally occupied his master's position. Among those who came to seek his help in the settlement of a dispute were three Pomak giants from the mountains. When these men were ushered into a large room the only person present was a lean, shrivelled individual who, with crossed legs, sat gathered up in the corner of a sofa. The Pomaks looked all round and asked for Dagh Deveran, the Remover of Mountains.

"I am he," said the little man, drawing a mental comparison between his size and that of the applicants for his judgment.

"You," said the astonished Pomaks, "why you could not remove a bok (a bit of dung), and you enjoy the name of Remover of Mountains!"

"Yes," answered Dagh Deveran, "it was an act of mine that earned me the name, and I have since gained a reputation for levelling human disputes, and now I am ready to listen to yours."

My sister-in-law, Lucy Blunt, stayed with us for some time and was a great addition to our lively set as she was young, pretty, and clever. She was much admired by many people, especially by two extremely pleasant Russian Consuls. One of the Consuls had to leave Adrianople suddenly and was succeeded by the second, who came to Lucy one day and begged permission to tell her that his predecessor had bade him come and ask her on his behalf to marry him. "And now, Mademoiselle," he added, "since I have given you the message with which I was entrusted, I would ask you to marry me." Lucy, however, was half engaged to a charming old man, a Mr Taylor, Consul at Erzerum, whom she had never seen but whom she knew through her brother George, who was Mr Taylor's assistant; and whom she subsequently married. I do not know that I should have mentioned this family incident had it not been for the realisation of a curious prophecy about her. An old Russian soldier, subsequent to one of the wars between his country and Turkey, had deserted, and had lived for thirty years in a marshy, swampy little island in one of the rivers. Our Cossack friends having discovered this hermit got up a picnic in the vicinity of his abode, and in answer to their whistles he came out of his lair, much like the old Russian bear he looked. He was said to have the gift of clairvoyance. When Lucy heard this she at once extended her hand; the old man looked at it and said, "Vous, Mademoiselle, vous allez vous marier deux fois, vous batterez votre premier mari et vous serez battue par le second."

The prophecy came true. Good old Mr Taylor was like wax in her hands and did all she demanded of him, whilst her second husband, a Russian of high position, was a villain of the first order, and tormented the poor girl nearly to death up to the time he died.

CHAPTER VIII

1865-1871

In 1864 we had a temporary break-up of our home at Adrianople, as Mr Blunt was called to Belgrade, the capital of Serbia, to act as temporary Consul-General while Mr Longworth went on leave. This post was a great advance for my husband, and we gladly undertook the long and tedious journey on horseback over the Babouna Pass, through the Iron Gates of the Danube, by Kezanlik, the world-famed garden of roses and of love, where the Bulgarian youths meet their sweethearts in the spring, and passed the gruesome Tower of human skulls. This tower, which stood on territory recently and temporarily acquired by the Turks close to the Serbian border, served as a lesson and menace to the Serbs, and was for a long time a daily demonstration to the Serbs of the brutality of the Turks. I believe one of Serbia's first acts on her liberation was to pull down that awful tower, for when I passed the same spot some years later all trace of this horrible sight had disappeared. We started on 6th November and our party consisted of my husband and myself, a Russian Consul, who was my husband's colleague, my two little insepar-

able "blackies," who were now young women, our
faithful guard, Hussein Aga, and a boy who.had
been rescued from slavery. The continuous down-
pour of rain during this, the wet season of the
year, and the want of proper roads made it very
hard work for the posthorses, as they often had to
cross gushing torrents and muddy swamps. However, we reached Sophia, the capital of modern
Bulgaria, safely, and were hospitably received by
the Hodjabachi or headman of the town. Unlike
Philippopolis, Sophia at that time did not look like
a progressing populous town, nor did its inhabitants, a good number of whom honoured us with a
visit, seem bright or in any way disposed to be
influenced by modern ideas.

None of this company of the *élite* who came
to lay their grievances before Mr Blunt and the
Russian Consul appeared conversant with any
foreign language but Turkish, which did not
please the Russian Consul, as he would have
preferred to talk with them in private, but as it
was he had to make use of an interpreter. When
the Russian Consul heard me encourage these
people with hopes of emancipation from the
Turkish yoke he became annoyed and begged me
not to foster ideas of rebellion, saying that Russia
already did a great deal for Bulgaria and she
preferred to do things in her own way, from which
later on she reaped nothing but ingratitude and
treachery. At that time Bulgarians appeared to
have no knowledge of European civilisation or
usage for its productions. The only European
article I noticed was a baby's feeding-bottle, not in
use for the purpose for which it had been designed,

but filled with slevovitzha, a spirit made in Serbia from plums, and passed round to all the guests, who each took two or three sucks at the anything but milk-like contents. When our turn came we refused with thanks.

Extreme surprises often greet one in uncivilised countries. When I was about to retire to bed that night the lady of the house asked me whether I would prefer to have my milk and rosewater bath before going to bed or in the morning. Amazed at the offer of such a luxury I could not help asking her whether Bulgarian ladies were in the habit of indulging in- such baths. My hostess in her turn looked greatly surprised and said, "Oh, dear, no! We make better use of our milk by drinking it, by making cheese and yaghourt, one of the best of foods, which makes our men strong and healthy ; but some time ago two English ladies stayed with us and both took these baths, so we concluded it must be an English custom ; besides, madame," added she, "we are not used to baths and seldom indulge in one, except when we go to the mineral baths now, alas, ruined, which are found all over our country."

At Kezanlik, that pretty, clean, interesting Bulgarian town, noted all over the world for its attar of roses, a comic adventure befel us. Our Russian friend proposed that our entry into this town should be in state, in order that our import- ance might be impressed on the inhabitants. Calling up the postilion he ordered him to utter his shrillest whistle-call in order to announce the arrival of distinguished travellers. In a few moments all the windows and doors in the main street were crowded by the inhabitants, anxious to find out who the arrivals could be, a subject of great interest to them owing to the near approach of the great fair that took place each year in the neighbourhood. The fair used to last a week when a vast amount of merchandise exchanged hands, and the variety of people and costumes met there was a sight not to be forgotten. One of the attractions this year was to be a company of tight-rope dancers. Seeing the arrival into the town of strangers in this imposing manner, a loud voice called out gaily,—

"Here comes the company of tight-rope dancers, here comes the famous company, including two black girls in hats." The news spread all down the street with electric-like rapidity, with additional, if not flattering remarks on our personal appearance.

My husband and I were greatly amused; not so the Russian Consul, who was furious at our being mistaken for a group of entertainers, and tried to lash with his whip the surprised and indignant villagers. The postilion, seeing the unpleasant turn the joke was taking, urged his horses to a gallop and saved the situation.

I was not sorry when we sighted the grand Babouna mountain, towering over a small village nestled at its foot, where I hoped we should get a good night's rest. On arriving at the village the owner of a nice-looking house came out and kindly offered us hospitality, which we gratefully accepted. I went upstairs, where a room comfortably carpeted and with a bright fire burning in the grate was put at my service by an exceedingly pretty young girl, who went by the name of Nivesta (bride), who helped me to take off my wraps and made me comfortable by the fire, when the door opened and Hussein Aga came in in a mysterious manner to tell me that the Bey had given orders that in an hour's time we must all be in readiness to start again. The postilion refused to attempt the narrow pass by night, owing to a recent snowstorm, and Mr Blunt and the Russian Consul coming in, we discussed the matter and decided not to start before the morning. After a good dinner, when Mr Blunt and the others were settled by the fire smoking and talking, I slipped out of the room and went to find the pretty Nivesta, who was not only pretty but bright and intelligent. She wanted to know all about our habits and customs, particularly as regards dress. As we were both much the same size I proposed an exchange of costume to see the effect. Delighted with the suggestion she brought out some of her best clothes and soon transformed me into a Bulgarian Nivesta, while dressed in my tea-gown she became a pretty English girl with her hair hanging down her back. While we were enjoying the fun we heard clapping of hands from the opposite room, and the Russian Consul calling for a basin and jug to wash his hands. I took up the needed things, and with all the modest seriousness I could assume walked up to our Russian friend, while the Nivesta stood near by. The Consul, whilst washing his hands cast a casual look at me, then put his monocle in his eye and began to examine me more attentively, calling out at the

I

same time to my husband to come up and see a
young Bulgarian girl with soft white hands, and
with features that could not belong to that race.
"What can she be, and from where can she have
come," said he. As my husband came up my
eyes met his, and we both burst out laughing and
revealed the mystery to our astonished friend,
who apologised for his mistake. It is quite a
remarkable thing what a difference an exchange
of clothes can make in a person. The Nivesta
in my clothes looked transformed into an English
girl, in spite of the fact that she had a slight
touch of the racial defects of wide nose, and eyes
set wide apart.

We started on our journey next morning, soon
to find some difficulty owing to the snow, which
got deeper as we approached the dangerous
parts of the Babouna Pass. Owing to the drifts
of snow, which sometimes reached the horses'
girths, we decided to get off our horses and to
walk or crawl across the narrow bridge of rocks,
precipitous on both sides, over which we had to
go. I fixed my riding habit under my arms,
put the sleeves of my jacket inside my gloves,
and lay flat on the snow and crawled quietly
across the dangerous pass. In spite of the
discomfort and the danger, I greatly enjoyed the
lovely views as I looked down both sides of
the pass, on the rich woods and fertile country
in its variegated autumn colouring, and on
the hills and dales, carpeted with soft emerald
growth slightly sprinkled with snow glistening
in the sun.

On entering Serbian territory I was struck by

the poor appearance of the small villages which were situated some distance from the frontier. On inquiring the cause of the bareness of the country and of the scarcity of cottages or villages, I was told that the vicinity of neighbours provoked discords and fights, and that that part of Serbia was too near to the Turks to make it wise for Serbs to live there.

I greatly rejoiced when we finally reached Belgrade and were warmly welcomed by my dear sister, Mrs Longworth, who was delighted to see us, as we were to see her, after long years of separation.

The Consulate at Belgrade was large and commodious, and I was delighted with the rooms assigned to us. A small Turkish force was still in occupation of the grand old Fort of Belgrade, whose sole duty appeared to consist in raising and lowering the Turkish flag on its four sides on "festas" as a testimony of Turkey's lingering power in Serbia. After I had been in Belgrade for some time the Pasha in command of the Fort, whose harem consisted of his wife and daughter, the latter a victim to ill-health, which neither prayers, amulets, nor the skill of the family doctor could alleviate, asked me whether I would accompany his wife and daughter to Vienna, so that they might have the benefit of the opinion of the medical specialists there. I accepted at once, glad to be able to be of use to these sweet helpless ladies too terrified to go by themselves. It amused me at the same time to become the chaperon of two nervous Turkish women, perhaps the very first of their nation who had ever visited

a European capital. I soon arranged a costume
that disguised their nationality more or less, as
well as a costume for myself that looked something
like theirs. The family doctor, a handsome
Slav, vain of his personality and importance,
accompanied us. It was Easter time when we
started, and all the people of the country-side
appeared to be in gala costume, and to have
nothing to do but stop and stare at us as we
crossed the Danube to take the steamer direct to
Vienna.

The news of the arrival of a party of Turkish
ladies had preceded us, and on board we found
a crowd of travellers anxious to get a glimpse
of so unusual a sight. The Turkish ladies,
frightened out of their wits, each took hold
of one of my arms, which made it still more
difficult for us to pass through the crowd, obliging
me to talk to the doctor in two or three familiar
languages, and at the same time to keep saying,
" Place, mesdames, place, messieurs." Arrived in
the cabin, the ladies at once closed the door and
turned the key, and stood with their backs to the
door for fear of its being opened. The doctor
enjoyed the fun, and went on deck full of
importance, and gave the impression to the
inquisitive travellers that we were a runaway
party from the Sultan's Seraglio at Constantinople.
Some among the crowd, by conjecture and
supposition, turned the supposed incident into a
regular romance, and honoured me as the runaway
sultana, owing to the assumed importance I had
exercised, and discussed my merits and qualities
as those of a real sultana. The doctor came

down and induced me to accompany him on deck,
where I graciously bowed to the salutes and
attentions bestowed on me. I found the farce so
amusing that I forgot for a while the responsibility
I had undertaken of chaperoning two frightened
women, absolutely ignorant of the ways of the
world outside their harem.

All the way to Vienna both sides of the
Danube presented some of the most delightful
scenes I have ever witnessed. Apparently all the
population in their picturesque native costumes
were enjoying themselves on the banks of the
river. On arriving at Vienna we went to
"Goldenes Lamm," the best and largest hotel in
Vienna at the time. Next day three Viennese
medical men came to see the Turkish invalid, with
the happy result that they were, after a little
while, able to restore her to good health.

It was interesting to see how the nervousness
of these ladies in surroundings strange to them
was gradually overcome. At first they insisted
upon having the door of their sitting-room locked,
and I had some trouble to persuade them that
there was no need, as no one, unless called up,
would venture in; but when I rang for a waiter,
and a handsome liveried man came in, they
changed their minds and frequently found some
excuse to make him come up. This is not
surprising as Turkish ladies hardly come in contact
with men outside the narrow circle of their own
families, consequently a handsome, well-dressed
man with deferential, quiet manners is a subject of
interest to them.

Opposite to the Consulate at Belgrade was

the palace of Prince Michael Obrenovitch. The Prince was, I believe, the most refined, liberal, and progressive ruler Serbia ever had. Prince Michael had spent a great part of his life in exile, and appeared to have studied all that was best in different capitals of Europe, with the object of making every effort to introduce such of the reforms as he could into his unsettled principality. Unfortunately the rivalries existing from generation to generation between the two ruling families, the Obrenovitch and Kara Georgevitch, not only greatly restricted his power but from the beginning of his reign menaced his life, with the result that he was in constant danger of assassination. Prince Michael's wife, Princess Julia Obrenovitch, *née* Countess Hunyadi of Kethely, was a most charming person who never obtained the popularity she deserved. There were endless intrigues and rivalries among the representatives of the Foreign Powers to gain the confidence of this much-tried princely couple. Unfortunately Michael Obrenovitch was much in advance of his time and too brave and too unwilling to cope with the treacherous dealings of his adversaries.

The Prince and Princess gave most attractive balls that charmed and in part softened the hatred and spite their enemies nourished in their vindictive hearts. The Serbian society, small as it was, was much divided, some people favouring at times one political agent of some great Power, sometimes another, which at times caused a good deal of coolness. I believe the representatives of England, who kept as much as possible out of intrigues, were the most respected. Yet in spite of this, one

of our political agents before Mr Longworth's
time was said to have given so much trouble to
his Government by constantly threatening to
lower his flag, that when his death was announced
at the Foreign Office a fervent prayer, "Thank
God for the removal of *that* public calamity," was
said.

My husband had some trouble, which it
fortunately was not necessary to report home, as it
was a purely personal affair. While dancing at
one of the balls given by the Prince and Princess,
he inadvertently stepped on the toes of an officer,
who hated the English. My husband apologised
at once and then went on dancing. Next morning
he received an impertinent letter calling him out
to a duel, and later on two friends of the officer
presented themselves for the answer. My husband
replied that the matter would be referred to the
authorities, and thereupon asked an audience of
the Prince and stated the case. The Prince
apologised for the rudeness of the officer, had
him put under arrest, and sent Mr Garachanine,
his Prime Minister, officially to Mr Blunt to
present his apologies. So ended this storm in a
teacup.

The Prince was a great lover of the free
constitutional government of England, and tried
in every way to introduce into Serbia some of
the laws and customs of our country, confidently
hoping for England's support in more propitious
times. The Princess, sharing her husband's views,
undertook a journey to England, where her charm
and her cleverness were employed to help Serbia
gain England's support with regard to the settle-

ment of her claims with Turkey. The famous pun made by Lord Palmerston, though well known, is worth repeating. The Princess was entering one of the Premier's receptions when her dress caught at the door. "Princesse," said the witty host, coming forward to release her, "la Porte est sur votre chemin pour vous empêcher d'avancer."

It was perhaps fortunate for Michael Obreno-vitch, in view of his sad and tragic end, that he had no children. Regardless of dangers, many of which he was warned of, Prince Michael often went about Belgrade without an escort. It was, if I remember rightly, on his return from Paris, where he had gone to visit the Exhibition, that a woman fired at him in church, but fortunately missed him.

On the morning of his assassination he received two anonymous letters warning him not to drive to Topchi Dere, the public park where he often went; but on principle he paid no attention to such letters. As a rule he drove a pair of splendid black horses which had been presented to him by Sultan Medjid as a peace-offering. These horses became his favourites, as besides their beauty they were so perfectly trained that a child could drive them. On that fatal day they seemed conscious of impend-ing danger, for when brought round at the usual hour of the Prince's drive, nothing would induce them to start. They backed, reared, kicked, till the Prince, tired of trying to get them to start, ordered another pair of horses to be brought. Hardly had the carriage entered the park than four men, well-known criminals, fired at the

Prince, and afterwards mutilated his body in order to make sure he was dead.

Prince Michael was truly lamented by his friends in Serbia and elsewhere.

My husband left Belgrade after Mr Longworth's return from leave, but, as I was not strong after a rather serious illness, and my husband's work necessitated his travelling in Macedonia where I could not follow him, I stayed on with my sister and brother-in-law. I watched with great interest the progress the country was making in all directions. Good roads were made, while schools and colleges sprang up in many places.

After a very pleasant prolonged stay in Serbia I began my return journey to Adrianople under the care of Hussein Aga, whom my husband had sent to take me and my black maids home. I had lived so economically while at Belgrade that I had saved enough money to buy a carriage and a pair of Hungarian horses (greys) at Baziash Fair, and since the roads had been greatly improved during Midhat Pasha's short but efficacious rule the journey home was made under very comfortable circumstances. The weather was lovely, the roads safe, and a hamper of good things generously furnished by my sister completed my wants. I greatly enjoyed the scenery from the Babouna Pass, across which I walked and chose a pretty nook amidst wild roses and honeysuckle "to spread my carpet of rest and smoke my pipe of peace." I fell into that train of perfect repose that solitude at times brings to the heart and mind when contemplating the marvellous works of Nature, when Marion, the blacker of the blackies, came to ask

me if I would have lunch. I nodded my head,
native fashion, and presently saw her approach
with a tray of good things, but missing a piece of
excellent Gorgonzola cheese the Italian Consul-
General had given me for the journey. I asked her
to bring it.

"Yes, mame," said she with a grin, and returned
holding a plate with the cheese on it, as far away
as her arm would stretch, whilst with averted head
she squeezed her stumpy nose with the fingers of
her other hand. Absurd as she appeared in the
midst of such lovely surroundings, I kept as serious
as I could and asked her what she meant by such
funny ways.

"Mame," answered she, "cheese grow quick,
making walk about plate, p'haps it wants to get
to the violets which smell so sweet."

"Take that thing away," I said with indignation, instead she placed it under my nose. So
soon as the blackie with the creeping cheese had
gone I left off romancing and returned to terrestrial
matters, and ate a good lunch.

My next station, if I remember rightly, was
Nish, where the Governor invited me to stay the
night in his harem in order to show me the improvements introduced into the town by Midhat
Pasha. The town looked clean. The Governor
was most pleased to take me over a model jail that
had recently been built. It was a large square
building opening on to a good-sized courtyard,
round which were cells adapted for the different
classes of prisoners, and included workshops for
different trades, where things of all kinds were
produced. Beyond the workshops stood the silent

cells in melancholy isolation away from the sound
of human voices or the sight of human beings.
A hole in the door, which opened from the
outside to admit the daily portion of bread and
water, was the only communication each prisoner
had with the outer world. The Governor ordered
three of these doors to be opened. It was a sad
sight, since the three prisoners we saw were fine-
looking young Albanians, pale and depressed, who
cast an indifferent look on us without uttering a
word. Evidently since hope was dead in their
hearts they disdained even to use the power of
speech. I felt more sorry than I can say for the
lot of those unfortunate beings, in spite of the
justice of their punishment, and it gave me an
impression of sadness that will last to the end of
my days.

As we came down the steps of this long
range of buildings, kept wonderfully clean and
tidy for a Turkish Institution, we came to a
strong iron door which led to the part where the
worst criminals were confined. The door was
swung open and I followed the Governor for a
few steps with Hussein Aga close by my side,
and one or two guards behind us. The place
appeared to me to be vast, bare, and dark. As
we stood I heard a terrific jangling of chains and
the rush of what seemed to me of an innumerable
crowd of wild-looking creatures, with heavy iron
chains attached from hand to foot on both sides.
The crowd hastened towards us and fixed their wild
sunken eyes upon us, clamouring to the Governor
for their freedom. I felt startled for a moment
and tried to back out when the Governor, with his

oriental calm and dignity said, "Korkma, korkma, Effendim! Do not be frightened, do not be frightened, Madame, these are helpless beings now."

Not caring to see any more, I made a sign to Hussein to get me out where I could breathe pure air again. That night, though most kindly received and hospitably entertained in the Governor's locked-up harem, I got but little sleep since the picture of those brutalised creatures was ever present to my mind, and I wondered if by chance they were favoured with freedom, what use they would make of it.

The rest of my journey was uneventful, and I was very glad to reach Adrianople and to find my dear husband in our pretty home, where everything had been kept in perfect order by my good old Bulgarian housekeeper. Our beloved horses "Swift" and "Jack" were alas! no more. For the first few days I felt rather out of my element at having to make a new start in the old life. Except for a few changes in the Consular Corps the social circle at Adrianople was much as we had left it, and appeared to me to be very monotonous; but less so to my husband who had gone heart and soul into Macedonian affairs, and, since he had no assistant in writing his report, I helped him as much as I could.

A change had occurred in our immediate peaceful neighbourhood, which was not favourable. A ruined house on our right had been made into a prison for female (Turkish) prisoners, while on our left a drunken Sheik had married a fine young wife, who, I believe, used to thrash him

daily. One morning as I was dressing I heard
a terrific cry of "Fire! fire!" from the Sheik's
house. Seizing two jugs full of water I rushed
down calling to the servants to follow me. I
reached the house by a small door which opened
into the garden and witnessed a battle royal
between the couple. The Sheik had been knocked
down on the floor, while his vigorous young wife
sat on his chest beating him with her strong
fists while he bellowed like a bull, "Yangen var!
Yangen var!" (Fire! fire!) Owing to the disturbance caused by this false alarm I punished
both by emptying my jugs on their heads, which
quickly put an end to the fray. The girl who
had been forced to marry this degraded creature
soon afterwards disappeared and nothing more was
heard of her.

During the silkworm season the whole population of Adrianople was absorbed in rearing silkworms. This was, when successful, a most
lucrative business, but was a great speculation,
owing to the prevalence of a disease that killed
the worms as they crawled about on the little
forest of mulberry bushes made for them by
breaking off branches of the trees and sticking
them into the ground so that the worms could
be watched and cared for. A silly fancy induced
me to make a trial in rearing worms, though
I had no notion of the food and care they
needed. The seed, as the minute grubs are called,
was given me by a friend in a tiny bundle of
twigs, which I put on one side; but on looking
at it the following day I found myriads of
microscopic maggots seeking nourishment. I

soon procured leaves from the mulberry tree in
the garden, chopped them up on a plate, and
shook the maggots over them. Next morning
every vestige of leaf had gone and the plate was
black with a mass of living moving life seeking
space and food. In my ignorance regarding both
necessities I went on defrauding my tree of its
leaves and spread them on all the tables I could
find in order to give space to these rapidly growing mites. The growth of these worms was so
rapid that I got into difficulties with regard to
space, even after I had secured an outhouse for
their special benefit. As week succeeded week
they went on eating, sleeping, and developing
into beautiful worms when I had a fortunate
inspiration, and applied to my drunken neighbour
for the key of a disused mosque under his care
at the bottom of the narrow passage between our
houses. "Mash Allah, Effendim," said he, "all
I possess is at your disposal, and you will find
your silkworms thrive and grow fat there while
elsewhere most of them drop and perish." I
thanked him and sent him a couple of bottles
of Mastica, and in return received the key. The
garden surrounding the mosque proved an ideal
resort for my worms, and there I watched my
treasures develop and swing their heads right
and left as they crawled up the branches of the
boughs I broke off for them, in search of the
precious leaves on which to weave their lovely
silk cocoons, ready for their change before entering the happy state of a love-stricken butterfly
in search of her mate, with whom she could live,
love, and die. My mosque-reared family was

the only one that prospered and outlived the epidemic that killed those I had in the other places. After defraying all expenses I had a balance of £50 in my pocket, but interesting as this enterprise had been I was never tempted to renew it.

CHAPTER IX

1872-1876

In 1872 my husband was appointed to be Her Majesty's Consul at Monastir (Bitholia of my earlier days). The appointment was a great blow to me as it meant a return to the wilds of Macedonia, to be cut off once more from the civilised world and left in that dull town which had been further impoverished by the withdrawal of the Turkish Army. The music, wild and soft, of the band of the Turkish Army had been not unpleasing to listen to during the time I spent at Monastir before my marriage, and when " God save the Queen " and other foreign national anthems were played, they often touched the hearts and brought tears to the eyes of those who, like ourselves, were away from home.

The very thought of this removal was enough to crush all hope of a pleasant life; still I tried my best to look contented for my husband's sake and for the sake of my baby boy, whose presence in our home was like a ray of sunshine. We sold most of our furniture owing to the difficulties of carriage along bad roads and across broken bridges, with which the way to Monastir abounded.

My husband preceded me and the boy, in order

to secure a decent abode and prepare it as best he could for us on our arrival. My child, who was now a year and a half old, necessitated my taking the journey *via* Salonika in a talika, a springless, uncomfortable vehicle which I often had to get out of and walk. I stayed only one day at Salonika, heartily wishing we could have stopped there for good. Nearing Vodena a terrific storm overtook us, barely allowing time to cross the flooded torrent tearing down from the heights above, while the talika was flooded as high as the seat, obliging me to hold the child up to my shoulders. The ascent up the hill was equally difficult and dangerous. I fortunately got out and walked to the top of the hill, the rain pouring down, and sat on a great boulder with my baby in my arms waiting for the talika, when to my horror I saw it rolling down the precipice with the horses and groom. Providentially it came to a stop against some projecting rocks; but it took over an hour to get it up, and during the whole time I sat on the boulder with my baby pressed against my heart, the picture of despair. The rain did not cease to pour down, the thunder crashed overhead, and sheets of forked lightning crossed one another in a magnificent display over the hills and the valley below. I never remember so terrific a storm or so beautiful and angry a mood of Nature. Had there been an artist to paint the whole tableau with me and the child as a group of despair in the centre of these wild surroundings, it would have made a striking picture. Fortunately the storm gradually subsided and we were able to get to a miserable hostelry

K

before it grew dark, where I spent the night in a
kind of barn open on all sides. Next day we
reached Monastir, where in the twilight I could
see the impoverished look the town had assumed
on the main street. Most of the once fine houses
were bereft of occupants and going to decay; the
shops were almost bare, goods being no longer
needed; while the natives looked more wretched
and miserable than before. My husband had
secured, as the Consulate, the best of the deserted
old konaks. Choosing the smallest of its rooms
we settled down, leaving the rest of the big edifice
to the rats and mice to gambol about in, in
freedom and security. Disheartened as both my
husband and I felt, Providence once more came to
our aid by the unexpected arrival of Colonel Synge,
a most charming man and delightful companion.
We at once got him to come and share our
unsettled home *à la guerre comme à la guerre.*
Sport was Colonel Synge's chief object in coming to
Monastir, and both he and my husband thoroughly
enjoyed this to their hearts' content. I naturally
took no part in their expeditions after big game,
but stayed at home in order to try and give a
semblance of comfort and respectability to the
Consulate, for which I had neither the energy
nor the means to do more than was absolutely
necessary. The task was difficult, but had to
be done, as no official in Turkey could possibly
acquire influence, or secure the confidence and
esteem of the authorities or the inhabitants unless
he put his Consulate on more or less a proper
footing. I believe this all-important question of
living in adequate style never attracted the serious

attention of the Foreign Office, whose chief object
seems always to have been to keep the salaries of
the junior officials in the Consular Corps at a
minimum, obliging them either to get into debt in
order to set their consulates on a proper footing,
or else to live like "Zingari" or gypsies, as the
natives are in the habit of calling them, and whom
in consequence they do not regard as the representatives of a Great Power.   I consider it is
better not to nominate Consular agents than to
expose them and their Government to unavoidable
humiliation.   The great influence my husband
enjoyed during his long term of service in Turkey,
and the good he did was in part due, not only to
his personality, but to his continuous efforts to
keep up the Consulate in proper style.

On our arrival at Monastir political ferment
had already begun, and many were the evils my
husband was able to modify by his influence and
the pressure he brought to bear on the tactless
Governor, who neither knew nor was competent to
deal with the just claims of the people, Christians
or Turks.

We had only been a few months in Monastir,
and I had not got to the end of hanging up
curtains, when as I was sitting on the top of a
ladder fixing some draperies, my husband rushed
into the room with an open despatch in his hand,
saying, "The Consulate of Monastir is suppressed
and I am appointed Consul at Salonika."   I nearly
dropped off the ladder with joy and ran to give
Colonel Synge the welcome news.   He was equally
glad to hear it, and reminded me that he had told
me more than once that I need not trouble to do

too much to the house as he was certain we should
be transferred to Salonika. We were all three
delighted, the Colonel particularly so, as he had
bought a nice property not far from Salonika as a
hunting-box to retire to when he was tired of the
formalities of civilised life.

Before leaving Monastir I visited many of my
old haunts in memory of the good time I had spent
there with my sister and her husband, Mr and Mrs
Longworth. There were also a few acquaintances
to call on, including the fat old Dervish Pasha, who
was not only the politest of polite Turks, but a clever
and amusing old hypocrite. One afternoon as I was
driving home, and just as the carriage passed the
door of the konak where Dervish Pasha lived, a
wild-looking " Perishan " (religious lunatic), with
hair and beard innocent of brush and comb, rushed
out of the gate, and with one bound jumped into
my carriage and sat at my side, staring at me with
his bloodshot eyes and murmuring words I could
not hear. Frightened and horrified to feel myself
at the mercy of this demented beast I tried to get
out, when he took hold of my arm and held it as if
in a vice, while Hussein did his best to throw the
man out of the carriage. Dervish Pasha witnessed
all that was going on under his window, and, to my
disgust, told me not to mind, as the Perishan was
a very holy man whose touch was sure to bring
me good luck. These pretended holy madmen,
highly venerated at that time by the Turks, were
a terrible nuisance to people in the streets on
account of their disorderly looks and deeds, and
yet none of them were ever proceeded against.
I have not seen the face of a Perishan for years,

but I. cannot forget this last sample without a
shiver of disgust. It would not be surprising if
the Kaiser in a freak of religious zeal may not wish
to join the Perishan order, thereby trying to revive
his departing influence on the unfortunate Turkish
nation he has brought to ruin.

Among Turkey's shattered dominion it is difficult to predict what the destiny of Macedonia will
be, with her mixture of nations, a regular *Salade
Macedoine*. Every one of the races will wish to get
a bit. It reminds me of the representative of a certain Power who came to me and asked me to write
an article on his countrymen living in Macedonia.
I asked him where these fellow countrymen were to
be found. "Mais voila! Madame, c'est qu'il faut
les créer là ou ils ne se trouvent pas, et pour cette
belle œuvre je vous promets de la part de· mon
Gouvernement, une décoration et une· somme
d'argent." I expressed my regret, saying that
. creations of the kind were so entirely out of my
power that I should have to forego the promised
decoration and payment.

I was again obliged to travel without my
husband as my child became very ill, and I
desired to start at once for Salonika to place
him under the care of a good doctor there. We
again had a miraculous escape that might have
cost us our lives. A bridge over a deep ravine
suddenly fell. On our previous journey the
condition of the bridge was so bad that my
men had to pull up several planks of the bridge
and put them together to make a safe road for
the talika. This time, though it was getting
dark, I noticed a big cloud which I took for

the smoke from a fire of bushes in the vicinity
of the bridge. The horses trotted close up to
the bridge when a man rushed out and stopped
them. At first I took him for a brigand, when
he pointed to the supposed smoke and said,
"Look, the bridge has just fallen." In another
minute, had it not been for this warning, our
horses might have fallen down the ravine. This
poor man richly deserved the present he got,
not only for averting from us a great calamity,
but for taking us some distance round where
the ravine was fordable. Such were the
adventures that travellers had to face in the
Turkish Empire in those days.

On arriving at Salonika I was hospitably
received by Mr and Mrs Crosbie, very kind
Scottish friends. Mr Crosbie, a missionary who
had come to Salonika to try and convert the
Jews, was a very well-known character and a
most kind host and friend to all the clergy
who came to Salonika. My son soon recovered
under the care of a good doctor and my good
fortune went further, for the second day of my
arrival I secured one of the best and prettiest
houses in the centre of the town, which had
been occupied by a dear old Russian Consul
who, on hearing that I wanted a nice house,
at once came and offered me his Consulate, saying
that it was best we should have it rather than
a solitary old man like himself.

As soon as my faithful blackies and the
luggage arrived I set up house for the tenth
time, always under difficulties but rewarded by
success. There is nothing like experience to

LADY BLUNT, 1876.

[To face page 184.

develop one's capacities under the pressure of
necessity. My husband, well pleased with our
new home, and leaving the cares of the house
to me, started making acquaintance with the
town, the people, the authorities, and his
numerous colleagues. He instituted a club, the
Cercle des Étrangers, of which he remained the
active President for over twenty years. (The
club was burnt down in the great fire of 1917.)

Salonika (Thessalonica, as the old Greeks called
it) at the time we went to it had nothing new
like so many other towns of Macedonia. The
old walls surrounding the town were crumbling,
and there were gaps in all directions, but the two
arched gateways, one at each end of the Strada
Via or principal main street had been marvellously
retained. To the discomfort of the inhabitants,
these gates were closed every night at sunset;
an absurd measure of security kept up by the
authorities for the trifling revenue it brought.
In the Frank quarter, where the Christians
lived, the houses were built of wood and were
neither elegant nor comfortable. The Jewish
quarter consisted of a number of abominable,
poverty-stricken, filthy hovels of which the sight
and smells were so repulsive that the only time
I went round it with one of the Sisters of Charity
of the Roman Catholic Convent, I determined
never again to set foot in it. I need hardly
say that the system of ghettos did not exist in
Turkey, consequently all the well-to-do Jewish
families could build and rent houses in any part
of the town they pleased. The Turkish quarter
as usual was airy and clean, but, barring the

Strada Via and one or two other streets, the
streets were narrow, ill-paved, and unlit. There
were only one or two carriages in the town belonging to private families, and a few Tahtervans
(a sort of palanquin) for the special benefit of
Turkish brides who were conveyed in them to
their new homes. The rest of us, when we
went out at night, had to walk with men ahead
of us carrying not only lanterns but our shoes,
which we had to change on arriving at the house
where the dinner or soirée was being given.
There was no municipality to look after the
needs of the town, so that no attention was paid
to cleanliness nor to the epidemic diseases which
frequently visited it. All refuse was cast outside
the gates, where it formed dirty, evil-smelling,
disreputable looking heaps. There was neither
pier nor landing-stage of any kind. Salonika
was very picturesquely situated on the shores
of the splendid bay of that name with the
Hortiach Mountain behind it, and the glorious
Mount Olympus mirrored in the blue waters of
the bay.

The town possessed a bazaar where lovely
articles of every description could be got for a
trifle. Shops were scattered all over the town,
and unlike Malta, every industry for supplying
the needs of the people was carried on by the
natives. Carpets, all kinds of wool and linen
tissues, and beautiful articles in wood, copper,
and silver, and other metals were made, some of
them quite works of art. Life in Salonika at
that time, if not luxurious, was easy going and
inexpensive. Turkeys cost 10d. to 1s. each,

partridges 10d. a brace, eggs 4d. a dozen, fish,
milk, fruit, and vegetables were all plentiful,
good, and cheap.   European articles of luxury
or even of necessity were not yet in use, except
in the houses of a few wealthy families who had
imported them by special order.

On the whole Salonika came next to Smyrna
with a promise of a fair future, at least such
were my impressions of the place.   When I
came to know it better, the things I could
never endure were the filthy state of the streets
and the untidy, ill-kept shops; but in the East
one has to endure many things one does not like.

It did not take my husband long to master
the situation, nor did he fail in his untiring
efforts to improve, as far as it lay in his power,
the spirit of unrest and discontent prevalent in
the place on our arrival.   His tour in Macedonia,
Thessaly, Albania, and the Epirus were beacons
of light that continued to render him good service
in his work, as every place he had visited enabled
him to learn much, and to secure the services
of trusty agents who continued to the last hour
of his office in Turkey to keep him perfectly
well informed on all that went on in those
unsettled countries, beginning to ask for changes
and improvements which were tardy to come.

CHAPTER X

1876

THREE events of great interest to us happened in 1876, the first two, namely, my husband's transfer to Monastir and then to Salonika were of private interest, the third, the massacre of the consuls at Salonika, was a tragedy in which many people were involved.

The ferment of discontent in Salonika was very great but was not too readily seen. It reminded me of a deep, fast-running river, calm on the surface till a point was reached where the waters were agitated, when bubbles of discontent and dissension arose, and of a sudden the aspect of calm disappeared.

My husband minimised the importance of the various rumours which abounded and, though new to Salonika, tried with his tactful *savoir faire* to put off the evil day of a massacre of the Christians by the Turks, when suddenly a matter, small in itself, gave rise to the murder of two innocent men, M. Moulin, the French Consul, and his brother-in-law, Mr Henry Abbott, the German Consul. A peasant girl of the Orthodox Church from a village in the interior had a Mohammedan lover, and in order to be able to marry him

decided to accept the Islamic faith, and came to
Salonika to take her vows in her new religion.
By chance this girl met her mother in the train
on her way to Salonika, when there was a battle
royal between them.   The mother lost all hope
of retaining her daughter in the Orthodox faith,
and telegraphed from one of the stations at which
the train stopped to her Greek friends in Salonika,
begging them to rescue her daughter on the
arrival of the train.   It happened that it was the
Feast of St George, a general holiday, and all the
Greek population, probably having nothing better
to do, collected round the railway station, and on
the arrival of the train got hold of the girl and
threw her into the carriage of Mr Lazaros, a
Greek gentleman who was the American Consul.
The coachman was ordered to take the girl to
the Metropolis (the Archbishop's palace) but took
her instead to the American Consulate.   As Mr
Lazaros was not at the Consulate the girl was
taken to a house in the Greek quarter.

That evening a meeting of Greeks was held,
when it was decided not to hand the girl over to
the Turkish authorities, as it was hoped in this
way to prevent her making her declaration as a
Moslem.

Now Mr Henry Abbott, the German Consul,
and his sister who had married M. Moulin, the
French Consul, though half Greek were British
subjects, and Mr Abbott and M. and Madame
Moulin all appear to have greatly favoured the
detention of the girl.

The Turks also held a meeting and determined
to get hold of the girl and so the fight began.

It might be added that it was because the girl
was thought to be under age, and therefore still
under the jurisdiction of her parents, that all the
trouble arose.   Later on, when the girl was seen
in Court, and at Mr Blunt's request and with the
support of the Kadi or Supreme Judge and the
Archbishop, she was asked to put off her veil,
she was seen to be a woman of two or three and
twenty, and of course perfectly free to follow
what faith she desired.   But "how great a matter
a little fire kindleth." This incident of the
peasant girl was the spark that set ablaze a
conflagration which had been smouldering for a
long time.

The day after the girl's arrival in Salonika,
when she was in the hands of the Greek community,
Mr Blunt, attaching no importance to the affair,
left the Consulate early in the afternoon without
stating where he was going.   In his absence matters
began to be serious.   On the reiterated refusal of
the Greeks to hand the girl over to the Moslems,
a body of fanatical Turks, armed with all kinds of
implements, poured down the main street and took
up their positions with their backs to the wall,
awaiting instructions, whilst the Muezzins on the
minarets called the faithful to protect Islamism.

I went on to the balcony overlooking the
Consulate gate and saw the French and German
Consuls, M. Moulin and his brother-in-law, Mr
Henry Abbott, with their kavasses (guards) go
up the street in the direction of the Government
House, which was just opposite the Mosque and
the telegraph office.   The Governor and the
Mejlis (Council) and a great number of the

populace were gathered together in the Mosque.
Whether M. Moulin and Mr Abbott went into
the Mosque or were forced into it remains a
mystery, but their presence there was revealed by
a few lines Mr Abbott wrote to his brother, Mr
Alfred Abbott, saying, "We are kept prisoners
here. You had better send the girl to the
authorities as this is our only chance." I cannot
say how long it was after the receipt of this note
that Mr Alfred Abbott came to find my husband,
who had not yet returned. About the same time
Hussein Aga came to inform me that the two
Consuls were held captives in the Mosque, and
that if the girl was not handed to the Turkish
authorities within two hours they would be
murdered. At the appointed time I heard pistol
shots, and there was a considerable movement
among the Turks in the street.

A Jewish gentleman, Mr Allatini, a man of
great influence whose office was in the Consulate
courtyard, ordered the Consulate gates to be
closed, whereupon in my husband's absence I
wrote and asked him to have them reopened, and
to allow people seeking protection under the
British Flag to come in. It was a risky thing to
do, but I felt that the town, and indeed all of us,
were passing through a great crisis which demanded
coolness and presence of mind. Hussein reported
to me that the Consuls had been murdered, and
that the excited Turks were leaving the Mosque
and going to the Greek quarter to begin the
massacre from the house of Mr Lazaros. I
thereupon decided to send my little boy to Mr
Allatini's house where I felt he would be safe,

while I remained at the Consulate to await events with my faithful guard, Hussein Aga.

Shortly afterwards my husband came in, surprised and horrified to hear what had taken place. He immediately sent a peremptory note to Mr Alfred Abbott, since he was a British subject, ordering him to hand over the girl to Hussein Aga and a small body of police at once. He was about to go out to the rescue of his colleagues, if perchance they were still alive, when I called to him from the balcony not to do so, or at least to put on his Consular cap in order that he might be recognised. But to no avail ; he just called out, " I shall be all right," and walked off in the direction of the Mosque. Although a comparatively newcomer some of the armed Turks recognised him and begged him not to venture into the Mosque, as they were sure he would be murdered like his colleagues. His reply to them had a good effect as a number of them offered to, and did, accompany him to the Mosque. He found the Pasha and all his Mejlis (Council) coming out of the Mosque terror-stricken and horrified at the recent tragedy. They in a body opposed Mr Blunt's entrance since the colleagues he wished to assist were past all help. The Pasha himself, shaking from head to foot, begged my husband to accompany him to his konak. My husband consented to do so on condition that he should be admitted to the privacy of the harem, where he thought he might find quiet and security to think over the measures to be taken for the safety of the town. Before going into the konak he went into the telegraph office and sent a message to Athens for one or two men-of-war to be sent at once, and wrote me a note saying he was safe.

On entering the harem he was met by a crowd of screaming women, terrified at the sight of a strange man. Some covered their faces, others tried to run away, but the Pasha coming in gathered them like a flock of frightened sheep and swept them into the inner rooms.

During this time Hussein Aga and the police had found the young woman and were taking her to the authorities when, providentially, they met the murderous Moslems on their way to the house of Mr Lazaros to commence the massacre of the Greeks. At first, disbelieving the personality of the girl, they fired at Hussein, when one of the band recognised her and got the crowd to acknowledge her, and took her to the Governor's konak, where my husband was laying before the Pasha and his Council the gravity of the consequences should they fail to take immediate steps to prevent further mischief when once the girl was in their hands. Coming to their senses they, like frightened schoolboys, begged for instructions.

In the interval, Madame Moulin and her brother, Mr Alfred Abbott, heard of the murder of M. Moulin and Mr Henry Abbott and were frantic with fear and sorrow ; the former, in an attack of hysteria, threatened to throw herself out of the window unless the body of her husband was brought home. I went to try and comfort Madame Moulin. On my way to the French Consulate I came face to face with a party of the murderers who were besmeared with blood.

I continued to walk on, apparently calm and cool, when one of the wild brutes about three feet from me cocked his pistol and pointed it at me. I stopped and gave him a look of defiance such as I suppose real danger and terror inspires. The man lowered his pistol and murmured some words which I failed to understand. I found it best to bring Madame Moulin to our Consulate. A few minutes later my husband came in, when Madame Moulin again lost all self-control and called out wildly for revenge, and insisted that the body of her husband should be brought to her. After an hour or so Madame Moulin wished to go back to her own house whither I accompanied her, and spent the night watching her with my ears alert for noises in the street in dread of an attack.

The next morning on leaving the French Consulate I slipped into Mr Allatini's house to see my dear boy before returning to the British Consulate. I noticed there was a good deal of agitation prevalent in the streets. The Turks looked savage and discontented, the Christians meek and frightened, whilst some of the foreign consuls who had ventured out were insulted by the populace. My husband, brave and fearless as usual, had not returned from the inspection he had made during the night in the dark, and quite alone, of the Turkish quarter. He walked down every street to make sure that the Governor's promise to have each street guarded by soldiers to prevent further trouble was fulfilled. On returning to the Consulate my husband saw a dense crowd near the gates, which suggested a fresh attempt at massacre. He pushed his way into the centre of the crowd only to find a donkey, heavily laden with wood, which had fallen down and lay stretched across the street barring the way. He scattered the crowd and walked into the Consulate where all the British subjects, in a very nervous condition, awaited his return for instructions as to the measures they might take to prevent further trouble. My husband took them all on to the balcony and pointed out to them the guns of H.M.S. *Swiftsure* pointing right on the Turkish quarter, and at the same time told them of the scare caused by the fall of a donkey, and so ridiculed their fright that they, though shamefaced, felt comforted and hastened home to assure their womenkind that all danger was over.

During the evening the body of M. Moulin was brought to the French Consulate by the French monks, and as Madame Moulin persisted in her desire to see her husband's remains I got the doctor of the French *Stationnaire*, which had arrived from Athens, to make the poor body presentable after its terrible mutilation in the Mosque. Poor Madame Moulin calmed down very much after seeing her husband's body and became resigned to the inevitable. I was much struck with Madame Moulin's sorrow, which so absorbed her that she never expressed one word of thanks to me or to a few others who had risked their lives to help her in her hour of need.

During all this critical time I hardly saw anything of my husband, who appeared to be everywhere except at home. I felt proud of the confidence he had placed in my *savoir faire*, and took courage and decided to face the agitated crowds in the streets and go and see my good friend, Mrs Henry Abbott, who lived at the other end of the town.   Mr Henry Abbott's mangled body had been taken to his home and there I found his widowed mother calm and resigned, like a Grecian mother of olden times, accepting the decrees of Nemesis.   Her daughter-in-law, Mrs Henry Abbott, one of my dearest friends, a highly accomplished and gifted young girl and a member of the Caratheodori family was sitting by her side in accordance with Greek custom.   Overpowered with her grief she fell into my arms like a wounded bird.   Filled with pity and sorrow for her I did my best to comfort her.   The body of her husband and that of M. Moulin were taken respectively to the Greek Metropolis and the Roman Catholic Church to receive the last sacred rights of the Requiem.

Both Mrs Abbott and Mrs Henry Abbott received large indemnities from the Turkish Government and soon left Salonika never to return there.   Mrs Henry Abbott made England her home, where she settled down with one of her sisters, and where, perhaps, I may meet her some day.

The presence of H.M.S. *Swiftsure* moored in front of the Turkish quarters, her guns in readiness to fire if needed, soon brought the quarrel to a close, while the Turkish authorities in order to make a show of activity made some arrests in their endeavour to calm down the irritation and anger of the Islamic population.

Most of the foreign embassies sent representatives to Salonika, while my husband, with the support of Sir Henry Elliot, stood his ground firmly and settled this complicated quarrel without the occupation of foreign Powers which some desired to impose on the town. The degradation of the Pasha and his imprisonment with a few others connected with the case, and the death penalty paid by some of the supposed or real murderers was all that appeared to be necessary. One of the murderers, a gigantic nigger, who a few months previously on our arrival had carried some of our heaviest luggage on his back, was one of those who were hanged. His wife stood by at the time and, putting her hands on her breast as a sign of contentment, said, " Och olsoun " (Serves you right).

So ended this tragic massacre of the Consuls. Several people, both Christians and Turks, testified to the fact that it was due to my husband's tact and energetic measures that Salonika was saved from a more general massacre.

CHAPTER XI

1876

Soon after the funeral of the consuls all the foreign ships, with the exception of H.M.S. *Swiftsure*, under the command of Captain Baird, left Salonika. The présence of the *Swiftsure* was most welcome to us after all we had gone through, and my husband took the opportunity of impressing upon the Turkish authorities the serious responsibility that rested on their shoulders with regard to the welcome and safety of the men of all ranks of our men-of-war whilst at Salonika. My husband was so successful in having the measures he imposed upon the Turkish authorities fully and faithfully carried out, that during his twenty-five years' residence in Macedonia nothing of an unpleasant character ever happened to an Englishman, though shooting parties into the interior and the free access of the liberty men to the town were of daily occurrence ; and this, in spite of the fact that the spirit of hatred between Moslems and Christians was never modified ; that the Balkan States—Albania, Macedonia, Thessaly, and Epirus —were all in a state of ferment ; that the agency of the Komitadjis or armed marauding bands, Bashi-Bazouks, the Andarti (Greek freebooters living on their casual earnings), and Greek brigands were all ready to fight all and sundry ; yet, thanks to my husband's influence, Englishmen of all ranks, except in two instances, were safe to come and go as they liked.   Among the Greek brigands was a man named Nico, well known for his savage cruelty. He would commit a murder or two in a town or village and carry off boys of tender age, and then barter the noses and ears of his victims for cash with the helpless parents ; or he would send the heads of the boys to the horrified relations in cases where the stated amount was not forthcoming.   It was in 1880 that our dear old friend Colonel Synge, while staying at his country house at Tricovista, had the misfortune to fall into the hands of this monster. In the dead of night Nico penetrated into Colonel Synge's room, dragged him out of bed, and carried him off to the inaccessible fastnesses of Mount Olympus.   This was a terrible blow to us both, but especially to my husband upon whom rested the responsibility of Colonel Synge's release.   On the second or third day an ultimatum addressed to my husband arrived from Nico claiming £12,000 as the price of Colonel Synge's head.   The Government took the case up and after weeks of parleying the amount was reduced to £8000.   Our poor friend during this time went through great suffering and privation, to say nothing of the feeling of horror of finding himself the victim of a band of assassins.   H.M.S. *Condor* was at once sent to Salonika from Constantinople, and greatly facilitated my husband's journeys across the bay to Catarina in his efforts to come to an understanding with the unscrupulous Nico who held poor Colonel

Synge's life entirely within his power.   It was a day
of great rejoicing to us when the *Condor* brought
Colonel Synge to the Consulate, though he, poor
man, was reduced to a skeleton and looked more
dead than alive.

Salonika was daily becoming more and more
important, rendering Mr Blunt's work over the
vast area under his jurisdiction more difficult of
control.   The timely appointment of Mr Alvarez
as Consulate Assistant was a great relief to my
husband, and at the same time it afforded both of
us great satisfaction to have a countryman of our
own in the midst of the foreign element with
which we were surrounded.   Mr Alvarez was
the first of the Consular assistants appointed
to the Salonika Consulate who served under my
husband before becoming a Vice-Consul, and he,
and those who followed him, have distinguished
themselves in the Consular Service.   Mr and Mrs
Alvarez, who are now settled in Malta, are the
oldest and dearest friends I have connected with
the Service, and are a source of great comfort to
me as the last link of the old happy days at
Salonika.   Those were indeed happy days, even
at their worst, when my husband on returning
from a journey in the interior fell ill, and for
weeks hovered between life and death.   Even at
this distance of time my mind often reverts with
deep gratitude towards Salonika and its inhabitants
for the interest and sympathy they showed in his
case.   All the clerical heads of the communities,
bishops, priests, hodjas had special services, and
asked leave to be allowed to come and pray at his
bedside or breathe over his head.   The monks of

Mount Athos sent a special deputation from all
the monasteries and gave prayers for his speedy
recovery. The Turkish Government Department
sent me two stones of great medicinal value which
had been in its possession from the time of the
Conquest. These stones were given into my hands
on loan as a precious remedy for his case, and I
was asked to give a receipt for them. The strange-
looking objects entrusted to my care were very
hard greenish stones of the size of a small walnut,
and were to be applied where the pain and danger
were most severe. When I applied one on the
head it caught and stuck there as if drawn by some
invisible electric force. The same thing happened
with the one I placed on his body. During the
night a change for the better began to show by
the abating of the delirium and by one of his
drawn-up legs stretching into a normal position.
Next morning I was overjoyed when three or four
doctors, who had come to perform a serious opera-
tion, said there was no need to operate since his
life appeared to be out of danger. This opinion
of the doctors gave me a certain amount of faith
in the efficacy of the stones, especially as I tried
them on my own person and on several others, and
found they would neither catch nor stick even
when damped, whilst· reapplied to my husband
they caught on and held like a limpet on a rock.
These wonderful stones are found at rare intervals
in the veins of a donkey's neck, perhaps only one
stone may be found in a million donkeys. Is it
possible that these stones may be the petrified
serum which benefits such cases of disease as Mr
Blunt was suffering from ?

As soon as my husband had recovered and was sufficiently strong to travel, we went to Constantinople to stay with my dear brother and his wife, Sir Alfred and Lady Sandison. My brother's kiosk was placed on the top of the hill at Therapia, facing the Bosphorus towards the entrance to the Black Sea. The sweet reviving air and the lovely surroundings soon restored us both to our normal condition of health, and enabled us better to enjoy the family gathering which included my adored old mother, my dear sister Matilda and her husband, Mr Ricketts, and my cousin, Sir Edward Zohrab, and his charming wife. It was a most delightful party, and after so many years of separation we all had most interesting adventures to relate of the places we had been to, and the people we had met. The Ricketts had wonderful things to tell of their life in the Caucasus, where Mr Ricketts had been Consul until the fashion of murdering consuls had reached that wild place disturbed by political agitation. Prince Karaja, who represented the interests of Turkey, and his wife were cruelly murdered whilst at dinner, and Mr Ricketts had . good reason to suspect that his turn was to come next, as a certain Great Power had notified its objection to Turkish and British agents in that quarter.

My cousin Sir Edward Zohrab's stories of his experiences in the Khedival Court from the time of the first Khedive of Egypt were exciting enough to form a fine romance. One of his experiences was when he played a great rôle in the rescue of the Khedival harem at the time of Arabi Pasha's rebellion. It will be remembered how Arabi suddenly surprised Alexandria with a force of some 10,000 men. The Khedive was practically isolated in his palace, and fearing an attack by the rebels, and being anxious for the safety of his harem he entrusted the latter to the care of my cousin who was attached to the Khedival house. Edward managed to convey the precious inmates of the harem from the Abdin Palace to a palace outside the town. He had to take many carriage loads of veiled ladies through crowded streets held by Arabi's adherents, while the arch-rebel, instead of directing affairs himself as one would have supposed he would have done, obeyed my cousin's orders and rode ahead of the procession of carriages, whilst Edward, revolver in hand, warned Arabi that at the first sign of disturbance on his or his adherents' part he could consider himself a dead man. The menace having succeeded to perfection, Edward placed the innumerable princesses, kadin effendis, and hanoums in safety, and then, without any credentials, boarded the *Condor* and begged that a body of sailors might be landed. Edward's appearance in no way harmonised with the importance of his mission, and when watching the faces of the officers he despaired of success, as they appeared to doubt the truthfulness of his story. However, his candid face and his evident anxiety to obtain help carried the day, and a party of bluejackets was landed. This small force and the clever management of the *Condor* by its gallant captain, Lord Charles

Beresford, saved Alexandria; and later on the same ship and same captain earned the praise of "Well done, *Condor*," at Fort Mex, thus immortalising the name of the ship and that of its captain which has become identified with the best interests of the Navy. I think this well-known incident is worth repeating, if only to show the utter incapacity of the oriental mind to organise any undertaking properly, and how the *savoir faire* of a few young Englishmen enabled the whole rebellion to be cut short.

Mr Ricketts, Edward Zohrab, and my brother, with his great knowledge of the Turks and his talent in telling a good story, formed a trio well worth listening to on the mysterious political, racial, and religious workings in the Near East. Everything, alas! in these countries is worked like wheels within wheels, crushing what is worth developing and developing what ought to be crushed.

I had to stop at the Dardanelles for two days on my return from Constantinople in order to wait for the steamer to take me to Salonika.

By good luck I came across Dr Schliemann, the great explorer of Troy, who kindly asked me and my two friends to visit his excavations. We gladly accepted so unexpected and valuable a treat. We first had a short journey by sea and then a delightful ride on horseback across fertile country which rose gently towards the famous old city. Dotted here and there were picturesque ruins interspersed with modern Turkish defensive works. We reached Dr Schliemann's home, perched high like an eagle's nest on a mount of

some considerable height, just as the glorious
rays of the setting sun lit up the prehistoric
remains of Troy. My enthusiasm grew in
proportion to the beauty of the scene, and our
gallant host welcomed us in poetic style and
honoured each of us with the title of one of
his favourite goddesses or queens. I was
supposed to impersonate Diana, the huntress,
while he represented Homer, and loaded me
with flattering eulogies from the *Iliad* which
he quoted with a strong German accent. My
feminine vanity was flattered to the height of
my desiring to well impersonate the great
goddess I represented, and as I was hungry
after my journey I longed for the nectar she
had drunk and the ambrosia which had nourished
her, when casting a glance around my gaze fixed
itself upon a bottle of beer and a fat German
sausage! My illusions of greatness were quickly
dispelled by so mundane a sight. "Dr Schliemann,"
said I, with a resentful look at the beer and the
sausage, "it is time I think we retired as we are
keeping you from your supper."

Next morning our host sent a smart handsome
Greek youth with us to be our guide. The
ordinary business of this young Greek was to
make friends with the wives and sweethearts of
the labourers engaged on the excavations, in order
to extract from them any of the precious finds
which the workmen might have carried home
in their pockets. I dare not enter into any
archæological or historical details of the remains
of the buried cities we were shown dating from
the Stone Age, but if I remember rightly we

were told that the cities, three in number, built
on this hill have each in the course of ages
passed away, submerged by water which left
behind sea-shells, sand, and débris so deep that
a second and then a third city was built, each
one showing steady improvement in the form
of houses, ornaments, and extent over the
previous ones. Proofs of the long intervals
between the three cities were supplied not only
by the houses and ornaments but by the sea-
shells and débris left by the receding floods. I
believe Dr Schliemann's most valued and precious
finds were made on the part believed to be the
Grecian Ilium. Numerous skeletons, human
and animal, were found, with a large amount of
pottery and a variety of other objects, which
enabled him to trace the manners and customs
of the various peoples who had at different
epochs inhabited this site. We left next day
after taking a tour round the different excavations that were being made, and carried away
a lasting remembrance of the wonderful work
which Dr and Mrs Schliemann were doing under
considerable discomforts and difficulties. Troy
is in such close proximity to the Dardanelles
that I doubt not that the careful and detailed
maps which Dr Schliemann took of the whole
district have proved of great service to the
Germans in this war — I believe the very
acropolis of this ancient city has been used as
a fort.

The last time I saw Dr Schliemann was in
London when we both dined at the house of the
late Mr John Murray. After dinner the lady

who had sat on his left hand while I had sat on his right, said to me, "How on earth did you get that German celebrity to talk when all the efforts I made to start a conversation with him failed?"

I smiled to myself as I thought of his personifying Homer and said to her, "You see I have had the great privilege of meeting him in the midst of his beloved work and was able to ask him how it had progressed."

CHAPTER XII

1877

MY VISIT TO STAMBOUL

WHILST at Constantinople I became much interested in the changes in connection with the treatment of the women of Turkey, which took place subsequent to the death of the much regretted Sultan Medjid. Sultan Medjid was succeeded by his brother, Sultan Aziz, a person of insipid personality, possessing none of the strong characteristics of his father nor any of the virtues of his brother. The only way in which he benefited his country was by the efforts he made to create a navy. These efforts did not have much practical result, however, owing to mismanagement and the corrupt administration of the naval department. His Majesty possessed no fighting tendencies, but reared a regiment of fighting cocks which he loved to watch, and childishly honoured the most valiant by hanging military decorations round their necks. In spite of his many failings Sultan Aziz did pretty well for the first ten or fifteen years of his reign, owing to a number of able Ministers like Ali Pasha, Fuad Pasha, Midhat Pasha, and one or two more, anxious for reforms and better administration.

Unfortunately his palace *entourage* consisted of a set of ignorant upstarts who prevailed on him to set aside the whole of his old and tried Ministers, and to replace them by a new set who traded in the purchase and sale of every post of importance within and without the capital. All the pashas and functionaries who bought these posts, for which they had paid heavily, and uncertain as to the length of time they were likely to hold them, drained in their turn the unfortunate people under their jurisdiction. The evils which followed this utter disorganisation were great, and ended in the dethronement of Sultan Aziz. During his imprisonment in Tcheraghan Palace overlooking the Bosphorus, and when standing at a window one morning he saw one of his men-of-war lying at anchor. On the deck was a sailor who took his belt from round his waist and bound it round his neck, and then walked three times round the deck. The Sultan rightly understood this to mean that the navy for which he had laboured was to be the means by which his death would be brought about, and that the three turns the sailor had taken round the deck signified that in three days he would be murdered. Some of the Sultan's ladies who had been allowed to accompany him in his imprisonment told me that on the third night they heard His Majesty cry for help, and that, when discovered dead the next morning, his death was found to be due to hæmorrhage from a severed artery in his arm. The rumour was spread abroad that he had committed suicide, a rumour which these ladies strongly denied, since they declared that not only

had they heard cries but that a belt belonging
to the Sultan, worth a fortune owing to the fine
gems with which it was ornamented, had
disappeared.

The next monarch to sit on the Imperial
throne was Sultan Aziz's nephew, Prince Murad,
a gentle, humane, liberal-minded prince, who for
years had lived in great seclusion, and who had
not been permitted to go out of his palace nor to
receive friends in it. This young prince, taken
by surprise, and horrified at the tragic fate of
his uncle, was dragged out of his quiet surroundings and put at the head of affairs. Quite
unsuited for responsibilities for which he had had
no training, and unable to cope with the intricacies
of the corrupt administration he was so suddenly
called upon to govern, this young prince fell into
a nervous condition, and after three months'
troublous reign was deposed in favour of his
brother, Prince Hamid, who, it is believed, worked
hard to bring before the people the undesirability
of Prince Murad's occupation of the throne and
his own pre-eminent suitability for the position
of Sultan. A friend of mine told me that during
Prince Murad's short occupation of the throne
he went for a drive one day followed by a big
escort. When passing down the street where my
friend lived the latter inadvertently opened a
window, unaware that Prince Murad was passing
that way; and this simple act put him in mortal
fear, as had the knowledge of it reached Prince
Hamid's ears it would undoubtedly have been
construed into an act of conspiracy, and he would
have paid for it with his life. I was present at

the coronation of the luckless Prince Murad at Stamboul, a most interesting sight. A large party of English residents, headed by the Ambassador and his staff were given most excellently placed seats from which to view the ceremony, while at the same time they enjoyed the friendly attentions of the newly crowned Sultan.

As soon as Prince Hamid had consolidated his power on the throne he dropped his hypocritical mask of modest humiliation, and took within his own grasp every branch of the Administration, rendering his Ministers, one and all, helpless machines who could only move and work subject to his personal control and orders. The Sultan's helpers in this immense and despicable undertaking consisted of a large body of spies who daily and hourly brought him information on all that happened, or that was supposed to be happening in his Empire. This system of controlling everything himself was enlarged and carried to such an extent that even so insignificant a person as a sub-lieutenant could not obtain a short leave of absence unless the leave was personally approved by the Sultan, nor could a governor in the interior take a step even in a small matter concerning local interests without the Imperial consent and approval. Besides the terrible system of spies, Sultan Hamid kept in his pay a body of Albanian cut-throats, under whose valiant activity men of all ranks and of all ages completely disappeared, and no family dared ask or try to find out what had become of its missing member or members. In spite of this terrorising system Sultan Hamid

M

managed to reign for thirty-three years, owing to his great cunning and ability in safeguarding his own life. His system was to help in turn the different peoples and countries in his Empire, and so soon as he found the favoured country was becoming too forward or too strong, to drop it and give his Imperial favour to its natural rival. In this way there was perpetual discord in the units of his Empire but safety for himself. The Foreign Office of Turkey was absolutely under his sole and personal control, and he managed by treachery and false promises to hoodwink by turns all the Great Powers. This condition of things disgusted the patriotic Turks, who found all their zealous efforts to improve matters utterly frustrated.

It was during the zenith of Sultan Hamid's power and the extraordinary use he was making of it that I determined to spend a week in the vast and mysterious city of Stamboul where the *élite* of Turkish society lived. The city was like a city of the dead. The streets were silent; there were no carriages or pedestrians; here and there a mangy dog turned over a little heap of refuse. Only the bazaars, squares, and business parts of Stamboul teemed with crowds of all races and nationalities rushing wildly about in pursuit of their business. The fine old konaks and palaces were silent; no one was seen at the windows which were apparently hermetically sealed, while the entrance gates were strongly guarded. Yet crime could, and did run a free course in these apparently silent houses, similar to the crimes committed in monasteries in times gone by; and none beyond

those within the walls of the buildings were any
the wiser of the acts of murder and cruelty that
were committed there.   The gates of the selamlics
or men's apartments in these silent palaces stood
always open ; but at the time I visited Stamboul I
was told that visitors were very rare as the Sultan
had given strict orders that there should be no free
intercourse between families or friends.   The only
people who were allowed freedom of entrance were
the Imperial spies.

My first visit in Stamboul was to the palace of
old Dervish Pasha.   This palace comprised two
vast separate portions, the haremlic for the women,
the selamlic for the men.   The apartments were
carpeted with priceless Turkish carpets and had
long low sofas running round three sides of the
walls, spread with rich stuffs and cushions, but the
whole rendered bizarre and truly oriental by the
introduction of a few odd chairs and tables of
common modern European work.

The family consisted of Dervish Pasha, his
wife, a sweet, middle-aged lady, his two sons and
his daughter-in-law, the wife of his younger son.
I was most kindly received by all, and after sunset
a most sumptuous dinner was served ; our fingers
were used in the place of knives and forks.   We
did not dress for dinner ; the great lady took her
place on the cushioned floor in a sort of white
cotton tea-gown and with stockingless feet.   None
of the party appeared to have any idea or any
knowledge of modern modes of living.   The sons
seemed to be utterly uneducated in spite of the
fact that the younger had married one of the
daughters of the Sultan, a clever little minx.

Since she was of the Royal house her husband,
according to Turkish etiquette, had to stand with
crossed arms awaiting her permission to sit down
or her invitation to converse with her.   After
dinner, which the Pasha out of compliment to
me had honoured with his presence, he returned to
the selamlic, when his wife, profiting by a few
moments of freedom, bitterly complained of the
hard life ladies were compelled to lead under the
rule of Sultan Hamid.

"He allows none of our friends to visit us, but
instead imposes four of his lady spies on us who
are in and out of the harem all day long.   I dare
not say a word, and though Allah knows how
devoted my husband and all of us are to His
Majesty's interests, yet I tremble for my dear sons
lest some mischief-making spy reports falsely with
regard to them."

The foxy old Dervish Pasha was so full of
compliment to me with regard to the English
nation, which I knew at heart he detested, that
my curiosity was aroused, and I tried to find out
his object in pretending to admire the English and
their methods.   Not to my surprise but to my
disgust, I found that he daily collected numerous
members of the Ulema (priestly) order about him,
and that with much care he was preparing them to
go to India on a mission to stir up the hatred of
the Mohammedan population against the British
rule.

My impressions on leaving the palace of
Dervish Pasha after a couple of nights under his
apparently hospitable roof were of the saddest.
I felt that since for his own personal interests

Dervish Pasha, greatly hated by the people, was aiding the Sultan in his various nefarious practices the outlook for the future of Turkey was grave, and that sooner or later a catastrophe must occur.

My next visit, to the harem of the Minister of Police, proved more interesting than that to the palace of Dervish Pasha as it brought me into closer relationship with the feminine element, an element most difficult for an outsider to know in that wonderful Empire of Turkey. The Turkish woman lacks neither intelligence, feeling, nor dignity, but hampered as she is by insurmountable religious prejudices, by lack of freedom and knowledge of the world, she has no chance of moral development. My friend, Fatimé Hanoum Effendi, a gifted, intelligent lady, was delighted to see me after the lapse of a number of years, and at once broached the subject of feminine grievances, saying that everything had gone from bad to worse under Hamid's cruel, despotic rule. " We now," said she, " have lost even the little liberty we formerly enjoyed. We are shut up like my canaries in their cage to pine indoors and to peep through our barred windows as they do through the bars of their cage, while we long for liberty, life, and knowledge such as the rest of the world enjoys. Surrounded as we are by police spies and prevented from meeting our friends, unable to talk on any subject, even the question of dress is placed under strict control, what can we do ? A few of us who have the courage to defy these ridiculous orders have to pay dearly for it by having our cloaks cut to shreds in the streets, obliging us to return home hurriedly and making us objects of disgrace to all who see us. Under such circumstances as these, and there are others far more serious, how can our nation hope to progress? What we need is free intercourse with our friends and relations, both men and women, when the supposed soulless woman could prove her worth by sharing in the responsibilities of life, thus lightening its burden."

"I am glad," added Fatimé Hanoum, "that you chose the season of Ramazan for your visit as you will notice with interest how this holy month, when we fast during the day and feast during the night, is spent by us in Stamboul, when most of the closed doors of the konaks are open in hospitality to rich and poor, and alas! to Hamid's spies also, who hover about like bees round a hive. In spite of the strictness enjoined at ordinary times, at this season we are allowed to drive down the main streets, teeming with crowds of men loitering about in search of some chance fortune, as we leave the Mosque of St Sophia after service, when indignities and rudenesses are offered to us in a way that I am sure would shock you. By the bye, this evening ladies are allowed to take part in the service at the Mosque seated behind the lattice work of the part reserved for them. Though out of sight of the congregation of men we can both see the solemn ceremony and take part in the service. If you care to come with me dressed like a Turkish woman, and you do not mind the risk of some unpleasant adventure, do come, as you are sure to be interested."

I willingly accepted, confident that no one would be likely to pierce through my disguise, and

fortunately for me there was no question of having
to put on the abominable yellow slippers. My
instructions before we left were as follows :—

When we leave the carriage at the door of the
Mosque you must on no account get separated
from two strong women guides who will be one on
each side of you, even if pushed and pinched and
hustled generally by young Turkish sparks. On
no account look up or answer anybody who might
address you, and once safely in the Mosque sit
by your hostess' side and perform the external
ceremony of worship exactly as she does.

The enclosure set aside for the women
worshippers was so crowded with ladies, old and
young, that it needed great efforts on the part of
the two guides, veritable old hags, to push their
way towards the front and get us good seats so
that we might watch the ceremony and follow the
service. The sight appeared to me so imposingly
solemn and impressive that, forgetting all my
friend's instructions, I stared at the grand sight
before me, when she whispered, " In Allah's name
attend and do exactly as I and all the other
women do. Should you be suspected of being a
Ghiaour (infidel) the old hags here will tear you to
pieces ; as it is they are already staring at you and
whispering among themselves."

I needed no further warning ; but while taking
all care I was still able to watch with the greatest
interest the *ensemble* of that lovely Mosque, lit
up by thousands of lamps swaying gently in
harmony with the devout attitudes of the
worshippers, who looked so entirely absorbed
in their prayers to Allah and Mahomet his

prophet, that I felt sorry their solemn address was not to Allah alone, free from the superstitious influence of a false prophet by whose decrees no belief in or justice to women was permitted; and no mercy possible to anyone outside the pale of the Moslem world. As we left the Mosque we found a still bigger crowd watching for the exit of the women worshippers towards whom I found the conduct of the young Turks impudent and disorderly. They pushed themselves close to the various carriage doors, addressing rude remarks to the occupants whom they tried to pinch. One or two of these impudent young men who tried to get near me had to give up the attempt, as I was well protected on each side by the repulsive but useful guides who did not spare these young men in language or in blows, much to the amusement of the onlookers. As we went along the main street thronged with promenaders our carriage was followed in spite of an escort of police. All kinds of things were thrown into the carriage, *billets-doux*, fruit, flowers, bonbons, and lighted cigarettes. My friend Fatimé, greatly to my surprise, instead of feeling shocked or scandalised, appeared to enjoy the fun saying, "This is our Carnival, and the freedom it affords us is so great and so rare that we willingly pass over what to you must appear to be both improper and unseemly."

Although I found the ladies I met at her house intelligent and liberal-minded, yet they lacked the refinement of an educated European woman, doubtless owing to the want of a sound education and a lack of worldly knowledge. I

paid one or two other visits in Stamboul and
noticed much discontent among the younger
generation wherever I went, a discontent that
seemed to me to be on the whole of a whole-
some nature, but I saw no hope of their ideals
being attained. I felt that possibly in time
some improvement in the conditions of life for
the women of Turkey might come, but I felt
convinced it would not be during the reign of
Sultan Hamid.

My last visit was to our dear old friend
Raouf Pasha, one of the witnesses to my
marriage at Monastir. I found him very much
down on his luck, expressing, like so many of
the other old friends I had met, his regret at
being unable to go and see my husband for
fear of giving offence to the Sultan, who strictly
opposed any friendly intercourse of his Ministers
with persons outside his ôwn *entourage*. Raouf
told me that, as it was, he was far from enjoying
the Sultan's favour, and would have been placed
on the list of the disgraced but for the great
need the Sultan had of him in his diplomatic
relations with European Powers, and went on
to say, " When my opposition to some of his
proposed acts becomes determined he tries me
with bribes which I politely refuse."

As my companion Mademoiselle Jeanne came
at this moment, the Pasha insisted on keeping
us to dinner. I was glad to stay for the sake
of our old friendship and the charm of his
personality, which he still retained in spite of
the many restrictions imposed upon him by
Sultan Hamid. Raouf Pasha dined with us,

and after dinner his wife dressed in her rich court costume of embroidered satin and delicate veil honoured us by bringing us our coffee herself. The coffee was served in dainty little gold cups studded with diamonds, and fulfilled the triple desiderata of Turkish coffee, namely, that it should be as "Sweet as love, as strong as death, as hot as hate."

Our evening spent with His Excellency and his harem was most pleasant, and he kindly sent us back to our hotel in Pera in one of his carriages. When seated in the carriage I noticed two ugly faces flattening their noses against the glass door trying to get a good look at us. The persons to whom the faces belonged followed the carriage, while at every turn of the road other undesirable looking people joined them, so that quite a number of them were present at the door of the hotel when we alighted. These people ranged themselves in a circle round the hotel door in order to get a good look at us as we entered. I asked the porter who these people were and what their object was. He only laughed and said, "Madam, you need not trouble about these people. They are only the Sultan's police spies anxious to find out who His Excellency Raouf Pasha's guests were and where they were going."

Next morning Raouf Pasha received a pressing message from the Sultan requesting his presence at the palace.

"Who were your guests last night," said his Majesty in a suspicious way.

"My guests," replied Raouf Pasha, "were

Mrs Blunt and her companion, old friends who I was very glad to see."

"Mash Allah, Mash Allah (Thanks be to God, Thanks be to God). The Blunts are good friends of Turkey. I am pleased you received the hanoum. Give her my compliments next time you meet her, and tell her I am sorry not to have seen her at the selamlic for a long time."

This gracious message was an act of courtesy on the part of His Majesty which I do not pretend to have deserved after all I had thought and said about his mischievous mania for sacrificing the lives of so many innocent people in his endeavour to secure the safety of his own.

CHAPTER XIII

1878

MY husband was temporarily transferred to Adrianople during the Turco-Russian War (1877), and for several reasons I felt that I might well spend the time of his enforced absence from Salonika in a visit to England. In those troublous times no British official or his family could avoid being mixed up with the general current of events.

The Consulate was left in the temporary charge of Mr Suter, Vice-Consul at Volo. Mr Suter was a dear old gentleman but so nervous that on hearing that he must proceed in his official capacity on board a man-of-war that had just come into the bay he sent a message to say that it was too great a responsibility, and that I must telegraph to Mr Blunt for someone else to be sent in his place. Feeling at a loss as to what I ought to do I drove at once to his hotel where, to my dismay, I found him in bed almost suffocated by the fumes of a charcoal brazier, which would have killed him but for my timely arrival. When I got him round from his partial suffocation he was shaking all over in a condition of nervous

172

fright, and declared he would not face a man-of-war and that I must do my best to send someone else. Fortunately on my return to the Consulate I found the captain who had come in to see what was amiss. I explained the situation and begged him to express my regrets to the commander-in-chief, who not only kindly overlooked the lack of formalities but was the first to call at the Consulate. In the meantime I did my best with the Turkish authorities and attended to a number of other details such as my husband would have done. I felt greatly comforted on receiving a telegram from my husband saying that Mr S. would soon be relieved. At the end of a week Mr B. who was to relieve Mr S. arrived with his wife and daughter, a trio unsuited, so it seemed to me, for the position they were to occupy. Mr B., I learnt later, had earned the honour of representing the English Government by aiding some Member of Parliament who had been stranded in the part of Asia Minor where Mr B. lived. This gentleman in return for the hospitality shown him had obtained for Mr B. the post of Consul. Be this as it may, the impression Mr B. made on the naval officers was unfavourable, and when some of them were talking about him, ignorant of the presence of the two ladies, he was described as an imbecile who had no right to be at Salonika, when Miss B. got up in a huff, very natural under the circumstances, and said, "My papa is not an imbecile."

It annoyed me very much that Mr B. insisted on taking me under his official care, since the Governor and Dervish Pasha, who was Com-

mander-in-chief at that time of the Forces in
Macedonia, were most attentive, inquiring daily
after me and often coming to see if I needed any
help. Dervish Pasha, the old hypocrite, used to
make himself so much at home at the Consulate
that when he came in the afternoon he would order
one of the maids to spread his carpet of prayer and
would go through his Namaz, very likely praying
Allah and his prophet to forgive the crime of his
doing so in the presence of a Ghiaour.

If he did, he would have been like one of the
Sheiks-ul-Islam at Constantinople who, on receiving a visit from Mr Alison, the First Secretary at
the Embassy, who was a fine Arabic scholar, called
for his prayer carpet and devoutly petitioned Allah
and Mahomet to forgive him addressing a dog of
an infidel. When this devout Moslem had finished,
Mr Alison asked permission to use the sacred
carpet for the same holy purpose, and kneeling
down he repeated a form of prayer in excellent
Arabic, and ended with a special appeal to the
Almighty to forgive him holding speech with a
dog of a Mohammedan. The Sheik-ul-Islam
learnt his lesson while Mr Alison enjoyed the
joke.

At that time Albanians began to crowd into
the streets of Salonika boasting that a big Albanian
force was marching on the town, which news very
naturally alarmed the Christian element. I did
not credit the rumour, but, as our faithful Hussein
Aga was with my husband in Adrianople, I thought
it wise to ask Dervish Pasha to send a trustworthy
policeman who could be in the house since our
position was rather isolated. About dusk a wild-

looking, powerful Turk came in, salaamed, and
said that Dervish Pasha had sent him to guard the
house. I did not like the look of the man and
liked much less his boastful manner. I therefore
ordered him to remain outside the house and guard
the door. As we were about to retire for the
night one of the maids, Kusha, opened the door
and walked in the direction of the garden gate,
where she came across the policeman very drunk
and excited. Drawing his sword he rushed on
Kusha calling her a dog of a Ghiaour whose head
would have to go. Kusha rushed into the house,
locked and barred the door, and came upstairs
breathless, followed by the two blackies who
were trembling with fear. The beast of a man
hammered at the door, calling out that he must
come in. I knew the native character and the
best way to impose upon it, so I opened a window
and ordered him, with an apparent bravery, to
leave the house at once and not to show his face
again if he hoped to keep his head on his shoulders.
On my repeating the order with still greater force
he turned away and stumbled in the direction of
the gate and cleared out. We watched him till
he had gone some way down the street when the
maids ran out and locked the gate. We locked
and barred all the doors and shutters, but in spite
of this we had but little sleep, watching for a
possible return of our drunken policeman and
packing in readiness for our voyage to Marseilles
on the morrow. My party consisted of myself,
my boy and his governess (Miss Garnett), and
his nurse Milly the blackie who had had charge
of him since his birth.

My decision to go to England and to stay
there until my husband could return from
Adrianople, proved a success. No sooner had I
set foot on the soil of the dear old homeland than
I felt that restful peace and relief which is so
greatly appreciated by those whose lot it is to
live in wild unsettled countries, where wars and
massacres come unexpectedly, and where it is
difficult to escape from their brutal effects. It
was fortunate that in those now somewhat remote
times discords leading to wars affected only a
comparatively small number of people, whilst in
this so-called civilised twentieth century, alas!
the evil has taken so general a line, that hardly
any part of the world appears to be free from its
baneful blight. So far, Malta can be described
as one of the few happy exceptions. Even on the
question of food, thanks to. the untiring efforts of
His Excellency, Lord Methuen, we have been
better off than elsewhere. Prices have, of course,
gone up, and eggs and a few other luxuries are
not to be found every day in the market, but
these things are mere trifles.

My stay in England lasted nearly a year and
gave me ample time to finish my book, *The People
of Turkey*. There was a threatened delay in
publishing it, owing to someone inaccurately
describing it to my husband as a book dead
against Turkey and in favour of Russia. Naturally
at that moment (1878) it would not have been
desirable to publish a book with such a tendency,
consequently both my husband and Sir Henry
Layard asked me to hold it back, as it might be
objectionable to the Government. The thought

of delay in publishing was a great blow to me, but I was fortunate enough to be able to avert it by mentioning the incident to Lady Salisbury, who asked me the name of my publisher. On hearing that Mr John Murray was bringing the book out, she said, " Oh ! that must be all right, as Murray would never publish a book opposed to the views of the Government, but, to make sure on this point, I will ask Mr Murray to send me the proof sheets which I will look over, and will consult with Lord Salisbury as to the publication of the work."

This most kind offer of Lady Salisbury soon settled the matter, and the opposition of my husband and Sir Henry Layard vanished when I wrote and told them of Lady Salisbury's kind action. The book, which is out of print now, was based on genuine facts free from all political questions with regard to Turkey and her people, while these memoirs, equally based on facts, but written in a freer manner, may, I hope, prove equally interesting to those who desire to know something of life in the Near East.

During my stay in London I had the privilege of a long talk with Mr Gladstone, whom I met at dinner at the house of the Marchioness of Bath. Mr Gladstone showed great interest in our conversation, especially regarding the unsettled state of Bulgaria, and wanted to know whether the Bulgarians would rest content with what they had got. I said, "Certainly not, as a country divided into two would not rest contented till it had got back all it could." The conversation then turned on Turkey and England's influence

over her. Although at the time I was a great
admirer of Mr Gladstone, I could not help
expressing the prevalent opinion in Turkey of
the great harm his anti-Turkish policy had
effected, and illustrated what I said by two or
three examples, showing the great and powerful
influence England had enjoyed in former times,
and the very low position she now occupied in
the opinion of Turkey. I do not think that Mr
Gladstone much liked to dwell on this subject,
but nevertheless both he and Mrs Gladstone were
very kind to me, and said a lot of flattering things
about my husband, in spite of the fact that my
husband's political views were not in harmony
with those of Mr Gladstone. I feel sure that Mr
Gladstone was too great a statesman to ignore
the merit of those who were opposed to him in
political opinion.

I arrived in England in the height of the
season when Hyde Park teemed with crowds of
well-dressed people promenading in the spring
sunshine, while Nature's soft green carpet and
floral array made a pleasant background, and was
repeated in the miniature gardens on the terraces
and balconies of pretty houses and stately mansions.
The fine shops too were full of the luxuries of the
season. Cares and worries seemed left far behind.
The whole *ensemble* of a London season make a
most striking impression on visitors from abroad,
who witness on a fine day a picture not to be
seen elsewhere. I have heard many foreigners
express this feeling, whilst others regret not being
able to visit England owing to their ignorance
of the language. Lady-Burdett-Coutts, to whom

Sir Henry Layard had kindly given me a letter of introduction, sent me a card of invitation for all her receptions for the season. I much admired the sweet dignity of the hostess, and the beauty of the lovely gems which ornamented her evening gown at the first of her receptions I went to. After the exchange of a few kind courtesies, I found myself in a densely crowded room, but to my disappointment I did not see a single person I knew. Feeling rather out of it I sat down beside a solitary lady on the chance of getting into conversation with her. Unfortunately the lady was a strict disciplinarian on the question of etiquette, such as the French at that time, less acquainted with the English than they are to-day, represented as a people who would not make an effort to save a drowning person unless they had been previously introduced, and limited her replies to a distant "Ye-es" and so pointed a "No" to the two trifling remarks I made, that I thought it best to go elsewhere in the hope of better success. At the opposite end of the room I noticed a group of young people in lively conversation. I worked my way in their direction and accosted a young man gesticulating to a very pretty girl, and said in a sympathetic way, "What a pity such a pretty girl should be dumb," when he replied to me by pointing to his own mouth and ears, and made me understand that he too was deaf and dumb! I had a third unhappy experience in my efforts to make friends, and then beat a retreat and quietly walked to the supper-room, when, after enjoying some delicious dainties, I got into my carriage and drove home. I was

more fortunate at a few other receptions I went
to, meeting old and making new friends. But
the reception which stands out *par excellence* in
my memory was that given by the Foreign Office
to Lord Beaconsfield after he had been invested
with the Order of the Garter. It was a grand
and beautiful sight. All the Royal Family were
there, with the exception of Her Majesty Queen
Victoria. The foreign representatives were in
full state uniform, vieing in colour with the ladies'
lovely dresses. I was delighted to have had the
opportunity of taking part in so interesting a
reception, and though only the wife of an official
in troubled Macedonia, I left the Foreign Office
probably the happiest of its guests, for on meeting
Lord Salisbury he stopped me and asked me when
I was going back to Salonika. "That depends
on your Lordship," said I. "Why, I am not
keeping you here." "No, but considering that
for nearly two years my husband has been with
the disorganised Turkish Army under the very
guns of the Russians, following this dreadful
Russo-Turkish War, I am not going to leave
London unless I have something good to tell
him." This was an inspired little speech on my
part which must have amused Lord Salisbury, as
he began to praise my husband and added that
no one in the Service had done such valuable
work as he had. I bowed, thanked him, and
added that I feared that would not be enough.
He laughed and said, "Well, in a day or two
you will hear something good." "In that case,"
I replied, "I will begin to pack up." On the
third day I received a note from Sir Philip Currie,

the Under-Secretary of State, telling me that my
husband had been appointed Consul-General at
Salonika, and that my request that my expenses
to England and back should be paid had been
considered just, and that I should receive a
cheque for the amount from the Treasury.
Needless to say the news of these two important
matters was a pleasant surprise to me, whilst my
husband was much gratified to learn that his
efforts to serve the Government to the best of
his ability had been recognised.

Another pleasant surprise soon followed. On
a warm bright day about the middle of May,
Milly, the blackie, came to tell me that a gentleman
had asked to see me but had given no name. I
told her to show the visitor up, wondering who it
could be. A fine handsome man, past middle age,
dressed in a long sheepskin coat that went down
to his knees, walked in. I could not hide my
surprise, and wondered whether my visitor was
quite right in his mind to come out in so wintry a
coat on a hot day in the middle of the London
season. He warmly shook hands with me, saying,
" I am Lord Lucan—you must be surprised to see
me in this sheepskin coat, but I put it on in
memory of your good husband who had secured it
as a precious possession during the Crimean War.
When I asked him to get a similar coat for me he
insisted on giving me his own, and it proved of
such great service to me that I put it on to-day in
order that you might see it, as I want you to tell
him how much I appreciated the gift." I thought
it most kind of Lord Lucan, who I had never met
before, to come and see me and talk so nicely

about my husband, who had begun his career in the Service by being attached to Lord Lucan's staff as First Interpreter to the British Forces in the Crimea. In consequence of my husband's useful services and the part he took in the Battle of Balaclava, he was awarded the Crimean Medal and clasps and the decoration of the Turkish Medjidié, which he valued with the friendship and confidence of his chief (Lord Lucan) to whom he became deeply attached.

Though alone in London and not knowing many people yet the little I saw of society greatly charmed me and made me feel prouder than ever of the superiority of the English nation.

My return to Salonika preceded my husband's return as he had to remain at Adrianople during the Russian occupation, when he earned further approval in his difficult task of trying to settle the local questions in which the Russians, Roumanians, Turks, and Christians were concerned.

Shortly before my return a new Russian Consul had been appointed to Salonika who had been with the Russian Army on the Shipka Pass. On learning that Mr Blunt, whose return to Salonika was daily expected, was Consul-General at Salonika he was heard to say, " Blunt, Blunt, surely he cannot be the same man I was ordered to ——! " and he made a click with his mouth, and passing his hand round his neck he made his friends understand that he been empowered to cut Mr Blunt's throat if he could. He called on me and I found him to be such a nice-looking, refined man that in spite of his having been ordered to try and compass my husband's death I asked him to come to lawn tennis on the following day, an invitation he gladly accepted. Unfortunately the fates willed it otherwise. The poor fellow, whilst washing his hands before coming to the Consulate, dropped down and was found in a dying condition by his faithful kavass. The kavass, horrified, rushed for the doctor and came to me for assistance. I went at once, and I shall never forget the impression of that room of death where the young fellow lay stretched on the floor. A bright ray of sunlight played on his face, and an old doctor bent over him trying to feel his pulse, while a solemn group of ten fat, well-fed Russian monks stood by watching. As I came in the doctor rose, looked at the monks, and asked whether one of them would be willing to be bled as there might be some chance of saving the patient if some fresh blood could be transfused into his veins. The monks in answer to this appeal one and all cleared out, while the kavass, a lean Albanian, came forward stretching out both his bared arms saying, "Doctor, doctor, take all the blood out of me so long as you save my master's life."

The doctor then asked me to help him. I willingly assented to this request, thinking at the same time of the mysterious ways of Providence that made me be called upon to help to try to bring back to life the man who, had he had the chance, would have taken from me the life of my precious husband.

CHAPTER XIV

1882-1887

AFTER the Russo-Turkish War was ended, peace was patched up by the Berlin Conference on promises made by Sultan Hamid, promises which, by the way, he never intended to keep. This peace only succeeded in promoting discontent among the interested parties and gave Turkey a breathing time after her late exertions.

Turkey at that time possessed a great statesman and an honest man, Midhat Pasha, who endeavoured to bring about reforms on the basis of a constitutional government, and was apparently allowed a certain amount of freedom of action by Sultan Hamid. So hopeful did internal affairs look that my husband and other well-wishers of Turkey began to think that an era of better management of Turkish affairs had begun. It was at this juncture that Sir Hubert E. H. Jerningham wrote the following clever notes of my husband, which I have recently found in his private correspondence :—

> " En Bulgaie á ce qu'on dit,
> Vous avez fait merveille,
> De Salonique il m'est écrit
> Le Turc par vous s'éveille.

Recevez donc mon compliment
   Dans la vieille Angleterre,
Car on rencontre rarement
   Votre taille sur terre."

I'm said to be a polyglot,
   Le "glot" n'est pas terme "poli"
What I may be I do not wot
   Si ce n'est que je suis l'ami.

But His Majesty, Sultan Hamid, set to work
after a short time to frustrate the efforts of
Midhat Pasha and persecuted this great reformer
and his two colleagues, one of whom was Hamid's
brother-in-law, by exiling them to Asia Minor,
where, after torturing and starving the unfortunate
trio for a time, he had them assassinated, when
Midhat's head was placed in a case and sent to the
Sultan at His Imperial Palace Yildiz labelled,
"Old Antiquities," to demonstrate to His Majesty
that his commands had been carried out.   This
tragic calamity made Mr Blunt, who had been a
great friend of Midhat, feel that he must give up
all hope of the reformation of Turkey.   It was
about this time that Sultan Hamid caused seven
of his Ministers to be murdered, and after their
deaths had been accomplished he was heard to say
"Turkey needs a Hamid."

My husband's promotion to the position of
Consul-General over a vast area necessitated our
moving to a larger house on my return from
England, so that the Chancellerie could be under
the roof where we lived.

We fortunately secured a fine old two-storied
konak, from the front of which we had glorious
views over the Bay of Salonika and Mount

Olympus. There was a large garden with carriage
drive and main entrance, at what may be described
as the back of the house. A wide entrance led
into a palatial hall, which in oriental fashion had
numerous windows, while ten spacious rooms
opened on to the hall. The upper floor was
similar to the ground-floor, but in addition there
was a wide terrace, from which we enjoyed the
views and the sunsets.

I at first felt rather puzzled over the important
question of furnishing this grand old palace.
However, with the aid of carpets and oriental
stuffs, which I had collected during many years,
of old Spanish chests, beautifully carved, brought
by the exiled Jews to Salonika, of Chinese
porcelain from Bulgaria and many other treasures,
I transformed the old palace into a comfortable
home.

The next few years passed quietly. We had
our excitements certainly, one of which was one of
the recurrent great fires, which destroyed a great
part of the town but fortunately stopped short of
the powder magazine.

Several distinguished visitors came to Salonika,
one of whom was Archduke Stéphan of Austria.
The Prince one morning paid an early, unofficial
visit to my husband, and in his charming way
asked whether he could see me. My husband
sent him up to me telling Hussein to announce
that an Austrian officer desired to see me. I was
struck by the Archduke's fine personality and we
entered into an animated conversation. I had
no notion who he was and his incognito gave a
piquancy to the situation; he went for a drive

with me, and when we came back my husband told
me who my visitor was. I learned later that
encounters of this kind were amongst Archduke
Stéphan's greatest pleasures.

This visit was shortly followed by an equally
interesting one from M. Léon de Tinseau, a
French author, who was much interested in
Turkish affairs, and who was good enough on the
strength of my having written a book on *The
People of Turkey* to call me a *collègue de
profession.* I was much amused at this title
of importance, to which I hardly felt I had a
claim.

The Italian Fleet paid one or two visits to
Salonika, and every now and then one of our
British men-of-war looked in and anchored in the
Bay for a few days. It was during these years
that my boy used to come back from Wellington
to spend his holidays with us, and later on when at
Oxford he brought friends with him to enjoy the
splendid sport that the country afforded. At
times we paid flying visits to Constantinople, when
we stayed with my brother and were kept *au
courant* with the affairs of the Near East by our
friendship with the successive ambassadors, and by
our intercourse with the various Turkish officials,
most of whom we had known for years.

It was on one of these visits to Constantinople
that a ball was given at his palace by Fouad
Pasha. A party of the guests asked me whether
they might be permitted to visit the harem. I
said I thought so and spoke to Fouad Pasha who
at once assented, took a key from his pocket, and
proceeded to unlock the door leading to the ladies'

apartments. Several of the guests in their pretty ball dresses passed through the door and were being followed by some of the attachés of the various embassies, when Fouad Pasha quietly turned towards the latter, and with a smiling face said, "Messieurs, je le regrette, mais vous n'êtes accredités qu'à la Porte."

But in 1888 a new era began, for it was in that year that we learnt that the Mediterranean Squadron was about to visit Salonika, under the command of H.R.H. The Duke of Edinburgh, and accompanied by H.R.H. Prince George and Prince Louis of Battenberg. We were delighted at the news, and determined to have in readiness everything we could think of that would be agreeable for our guests whose presence in Salonika was taken as an indication of the future policy of the British Government. The Turks, who always had a liking for the English, appeared pleased on hearing the news, while the rest of the population was jubilant, each in its own sphere hoping to derive some benefit from so important an event.

When it was announced that the Squadron was sighted, Turks, Greeks, Bulgars, and Jews gathered in crowds on the shore and watched the arrival of the men-of-war with admiration, not unmixed with fear as to the direction the great power of England would take in the near future. I sat on our terrace and my heart palpitated with joy as I watched the *Queen of the Seas* glide majestically into the Bay and cast anchor facing Mount Olympus, the mountain from which the Grecian gods and immortals had darted their projectiles of thunder

and lightning, while below, by contrast, the guns
of the Squadron thundered to announce its arrival.
This contrast marked the great evolution time had
worked, transforming the poetical into real and
more effective power.

The visit of the Squadron lasted ten days and
gave fresh life and animation to the town. On
the day following the arrival, I had the honour of
entertaining at luncheon T.R.H. the Duke of
Edinburgh, Prince George, and Prince Louis of
Battenberg, and several of the captains, among
whom were Captain Boyes, Captain Alington,
Captain Cardale, Captain Rice, Captain Pringle,
and Captain Palliser.

I was much struck by the sound common sense
the Duke displayed in the knowledge of what was
necessary in the surroundings of Government
officials, for the maintenance and dignity of the
position of England. His Royal Highness complimented us on the house we had acquired for the
Consulate, and said how different it was from other
consulates he had visited, and how he wished the
Government had more consuls like my husband.
Perhaps some of my readers will find no more
interest in Consular abodes in the Near East than
did some of those in authority at home. Nevertheless, the subject happens to be an old one and
a most important one to England, as well as to
members of the Consular Service. On one occasion when the subject was before the House of
Commons a Member of the Opposition suggested,
" That consuls or Government representatives
might live in tents." It is largely due to ignorance of this kind and ignorance of the value of the

Near East to England that matters have reached the present muddle.

A few days after the arrival of the Squadron we gave a ball, when everybody in Salonika was asked to meet the Royal guests. Mr Blunt and I felt some misgivings as to the success of this ball, but thanks to the kind help of Mr Viscovitch, the Austrian Consul-General, in the arrangement of the reception, all went off very well. There was much variety in the obeisance of the ladies, some knelt on the ground, others salaamed, but many of the younger ladies, pretty and well dressed, curtsied gracefully. We arranged that there should be no introductions since all were our friends, but I was much charmed by Prince George who always came up to me and said, " Do you think, Mrs Blunt, that young lady," indicating some one, "would like to dance with me ? "

This request on his part greatly pleased me, as young as he was he must have already acquired some knowledge of human nature, and have known how the honour of dancing with him must have been appreciated. His choice invariably fell on the right person.

My husband asked one of the Duke's aides-de-camp whether we could know if the Duke was pleased with our arrangements, he replied, " If you see His Royal Highness take only one refreshing drink be sure he is not pleased, if two, leave him alone, he is quite contented."

To my joy my husband came to me when the Duke left and said, " It is all right, my dear, the Duke has had three drinks."

When I thought I had said good-night to all

our guests, to my surprise I found a fat Armenian lady covered with jewels comfortably ensconced in the corner of a sofa, smoking a cigarette, looking as if she intended to stay there. I suggested to her that the house had to be closed. "Yes, Janoum" (my heart), said she, "but it is still dark and I dare not go into the streets lest some one should attack me and rob me of my precious gems."

"Do not be afraid," said I, "I will give orders to one of the Consulate guard to take you to your home."

At a garden party given by Monsieur Charnaud a British subject, a young nephew of my husband was walking along one of the pathways down which I was conducting the Prince. This small boy, Turkish fashion, kept his hat on as a token of respect. I told him in Greek to take his hat off, when the Prince laughingly exclaimed, "I understood what you said, you told him to take his hat off." The Prince who was fond of his cousins at Athens must have picked up some modern Greek when he was there.

A big shoot was arranged at Catarina to which Prince George did not go. I asked him if he would like me to arrange a little dance for him at the Consulate free from formalities. He gladly accepted and I think enjoyed the dance. He was much amused next day to hear it said that I had invited all the cream of Salonika to meet him and had left all the sour milk behind.

The Duke's At Home on board the flagship *Alexandra* was a great success, largely owing to my husband's direction of the dances, to which he

added some novelties of his own and made it so
lively and amusing that Prince George said, "It
is worth coming to Salonika to dance a quadrille
under Mr Blunt's direction."

On certain days people of all nationalities and
of all classes were allowed to visit the men-of-war, a
privilege they greatly enjoyed, and great amazement
was felt and expressed at the order and discipline
which prevailed on board. The native people
were filled with wonder at the power, strength,
and harmonious organisation of the Navy, since
these qualities are foreign to the oriental character,
as well as at the energy and activity of the sailors
and the variety of their sports. The Governor
sat by me during a tug-of-war between the officers
and men, which he watched with the greatest admiration and said, "Now I understand the power
and greatness of the English nation which, unlike
ours, is reared from childhood in the practice of
physical and moral powers."

This dear old pasha, fat and listless, judged
and condemned his nation from his own personal
experience. In order to comfort him I said,
"Effendi, you should bear in mind the natural
wealth of the country Providence has given you,
where there is little need for energy for those who,
like your people, are content with Nature's gifts."

Owing to my husband's insistence that the
Turkish authorities must be responsible for the
safety of the officers and men of our ships who
came on shore, nothing untoward ever happened,
beyond perhaps the smashing of a few panes of
glass by some one or more men who had indulged
rather freely. Food and drink at that time were

abundant and pure, and our men spent a good
deal of their pocket-money on the good fat geese
and turkeys which were to be had so cheaply in
those days.   Occasionally a sailor had some fancy
of his own which caused much amusement, as
when one, with his pockets well furnished with
gold, could think of no better way of spending
some of it than in the purchase of a small donkey.
He deemed his pet worthy of special attention,
and took it to the chief barber in Salonika and
requested him to shave it.   The barber indignantly
refused, considering it beneath his dignity to do
so, but the persistent bluejacket put his hand in his
pocket and brought out and placed on the counter
a sovereign.   The golden piece proved so alluring
that the barber put his dignity aside and shaved,
perfumed, and powdered the little donkey, which
showed its whole-hearted disapproval of the
performance by braying and kicking all the
time, to the great amusement of the onlookers.
A small crowd collected when the proud owner,
on completion of his pet's toilette, jumped on
its back and promenaded the streets.   On finding
it was time to return to his ship he insisted on
the Jew boatmen taking both him and his donkey,
when doubtless, on arriving on board, the joke
was soon brought to an end.

We watched with regret the departure of this
fine squadron, which left a strong impression of the
power of England on the people. None of the foreign
squadrons, French, Italian, or Austrian, which now
and again visited Salonika could in any way compare with ours, nor did they gain the esteem and
confidence enjoyed by the British Squadron.

I do not intend to enter into the political reasons that had brought and continued to bring squadron after squadron to Salonika. All I can say is that we were delighted to see them, especially for a prolonged stay. Their visits coincided with troubles in Crete, Armenia, and Macedonia. Those prolonged visits gave us the opportunity of becoming acquainted with many distinguished personages whose friendship and sympathy last to the present day.

On one occasion when the Duke of Edinburgh was again at Salonika in command of the squadron an epidemic of smallpox was raging in the town, and the Duke asked me if I could recommend a reliable washerwoman to wash his and the Prince's clothes. I said my washerwoman was reliable, and that I would give her one of my visiting-cards so that when she came for the washing she might be recognised. I simply wrote "washerwoman" on one of my usual visiting-cards. A few days later to our great amusement one of the captains asked me how many Mrs Blunt's washerwomen there were in Salonika, since many cards bearing this inscription had been brought to the ship. It had not occurred to me how easily my cards could be stolen from the houses I visited at and be made use of by the washerwomen who desired work from the Squadron.

Among the foreign ships that visited Salonika those of Austria were certainly the best, and the officers were gentlemen. The captain of one of the Austrian men-of-war was an old friend of ours, and when I met him one night at dinner I cordially shook hands and asked in a bantering way when the Austrian Fleet was coming to take possession of Salonika. He looked all round and then said, *sotto voce,* "Quand nous aurons l'argent voulu, Madame." My husband came up immediately afterwards and by chance asked the same question, when the captain, reverting to his official position, said, "Jamais, monsieur le Consul, jamais."

This was at the time when Austria had begun to work seriously in Macedonia through the agency of officers disguised as engineers, pedlars, or sportsmen, who returned to the Austrian Consulate and drew maps of the places they had visited. I broached the subject with Redjeb Pasha, one of the highest and most honourable generals in the Turkish Army, who for a short time had command of the forces in Macedonia. His answer was, "I know better than anyone the work Austria is doing in the country with the object of taking possession of Salonika when a favourable opportunity occurs, but I am tied and helpless like the rest of my party under Sultan Hamid and his infamous regiment of spies whom we come across at every step."

Redjeb Pasha built himself a kiosk (country-house) close to Salonika, and thoughtlessly named it "Yildiz," after Sultan Hamid's kiosk. He gave a small party and asked us and one or two of the other consuls. On the day following the party one of the spies telegraphed to Sultan Hamid that Redjeb Pasha had turned traitor, that he intended to take possession of Macedonia, that he was conspiring with the foreign element, that he already called his house the Imperial Palace, and so on. That same evening Redjeb was dismissed from his post and ordered to leave at once for a distant part of the Empire, where he was put in charge of a body of Turkish troops without pay and without food for himself or his men. He did his best for some years when the Young Turkish Party requested his presence at Constantinople. Redjeb returned, but alas! only lived three days. At his funeral he received the honours and attentions his valour deserved, but which had been denied him in life.

CHAPTER XV

1888

IF I remember rightly it was close upon Christmas that the Mediterranean Squadron, under the command of Admiral Lord Walter Kerr, came in,.much to our delight as well as to the delight of the people of Salonika, and especially of the ladies, who appeared to have lost their hearts to the officers during the previous visits of the Squadron. The weather, though cold, was bright, and the season promised to be a gay one, except perhaps to the winged species such as the ducks and geese, disturbed from their peaceful haunts by the guns of the sportsmen. The shooting was a great attraction to the officers, and it was no uncommon sight to see the sailors taking back to the ship a fine fat goose for a roast on festive days.

We gave a ball, which everybody appeared to enjoy, and this was followed by an equally successful one given by M. Charnaud. This latter ball was a particularly lively party, enhanced by the presence of M. Charnaud's four young and pretty daughters, as well as by a number of ladies who spoke English. Free from the cares and responsibilities of a hostess, I danced until

the approach of dawn when the band struck up
"God save the Queen." Some of our gallant
young officers, full of life and energy, insisted on
unharnessing the horses of my carriage and
dragging me home in triumph themselves, a most
chivalrous attention which I had in no way
expected, and which consequently was all the
more appreciated, coming as it did from such
lovable friends.

The French Consul and Madame de Lacretelle
gave a charming ball in the refined French style
in honour of the British Squadron, where the
cotillon was specially well danced, and dainty
prizes of Parisian style were prepared and awarded
by Madame de Lacretelle. The Consul and his
wife were a most distinguished couple, with whom
we joined in efforts to introduce modern ideas
and manners into Salonika. The Jewish element
and a few Greek families left in Salonika were
among the first to adopt our suggestions. The
rest of the society consisted chiefly of Levantines
who gradually followed suit, being less under the
control of their father confessors than were the
ladies of Adrianople.

Every nation was represented at Salonika by
a Consular Agent. Some of the consuls were of
genuine nationality, others were of local origin ; the
whole posse of consuls was like a basket of fruit
picked at random in the orchard. Some few were
fine specimens, others mediocre or poor. One
gentleman was the Consular representative of four
nations, and when he received His Excellency
the Governor on State occasions he arranged four
sofas, one in each corner of his reception-room,

and took His Excellency from one corner to
another, at each of which he adopted the Consular
cap of the particular country he represented at
the moment, and gave His Excellency greetings
in the appropriate language.

The great hospitality of the officers on board
and their efforts to enliven the sleepy old town
succeeded so well, that they made that Christmas
season one of lively gaiety. Those were happy,
peaceful times; but should any old naval friends
visit Salonika at the present time of great
upheaval, they will not find it possible to enjoy
their favourite pastime of sport, nor will they
meet any of the set of old residents who formerly
welcomed them.

By way of consolation after our friends had
left, I decided to go and visit my brother at
Constantinople, and my dear mother at Brussa.
My boxes were packed, when about the eighth
day after the Squadron had steamed away, as we
were on the point of retiring to bed, we heard the
fire-alarm guns. Fires were of fairly frequent
occurrence but were always alarming, since so
many of the houses were old, and like the
Consulate, were built of wood. I went on to the
terrace to see in which direction the fire was,
and to my relief I found it had started some
miles away from the Consulate. I attached no
particular importance to the strong wind blowing
at the time. When I came down from the
terrace I found my husband ready to go out to
the region of the fire, and in accordance with his
usual habit he left things at home under my
care, merely saying as he went off that I had

better not have anything moved out of the house
before Mr Routh, the insurance agent, had been.
Mr Routh, an easy-going gentleman, remained
in his house in bed till eight o'clock the following
morning.

The fire was a terrific one and ran down the
hillside like a burning river, devouring every
obstacle in its way. The strong wind fanned the
flames and carried sparks and burning embers
right and left, so that the fire spread rapidly and
advanced in our direction. Still no one suspected
it would reach the Consulate, surrounded as it
was by its large garden. No one came in to
help or advise me. Our guards and men servants
were absent looking after their own homes and
families. Live embers fell on the house twice,
but the maids and I put them out. It made me
anxious, however, for Mr Routh had not come,
and I did not like to begin clearing the house of
furniture after what my husband had said. I
felt desperately troubled as I watched the
miserable Jewish quarter behind the Consulate
blazing, and saw the poor people stumbling along
with their furniture on their backs, some of which
burst into flames as burning bits of wood, carried
by the strong wind, fell on it, whilst others carried
little children in their arms and encouraged their
poor wives. Anxiety on our own account increased, when, on going on the roof to see the
progress of the fire, I felt a hot puff at my back
and saw a blazing bit of wood on the staircase I
had to go down. I tucked up my skirts and
beat a hasty retreat, only to find my little Greek
maid in hysterics. I shook her by the shoulders

and ordered her to stop it, and told her that if
she lay where she was she would be burned with
the house. This roused her, and her Greek
courage and intelligence restored, she was seized
with a good inspiration, and asked me to allow
her to get my boxes, all ready packed for my
visit to my brother, into the garden. She dragged
the heavy trunks down, and in this way saved
my laces and other precious possessions. In the
meantime the terrible conflagration was getting
nearer to us. On going into the garden I noticed
to my dismay a bright flame like a huge torch
on the roof. This must have given the alarm to
the people round that the Consulate was on
fire, and attracted the attention of the Turkish
authorities, who walked into the garden in a
body, headed by His Excellency the Governor
and the Commander-in-chief. Turkish fashion
they were spectators only, and all sat down and
watched the fire spread all about the Consulate
like lightning. The red tiles dropped down from
the roof like tears of blood. The Turks looked
sorry and sympathetic, and by way of comfort
said "Kismet," and that it was the will of Allah,
and that it was better that the fire should attack
property than destroy life. The only people who
displayed any energy and activity were the young
captain of the Turkish *Stationnaire* and half a
dozen of his smart sailors, who went into the
drawing - room and snatched away whatever
attracted their attention, and loaded the things
into two of the carriages, and drove them some
way up the Kalamaria road where they left them
unguarded. Fortunately a friend, Mr Alson,

noticed them as he was on his way to help us, and had them taken into his house, and then came down to see to the safety of the horses. The poor beasts were stamping and neighing with terror, but refused to move till the coachman came and led them away. The house was now nearly in ruins, but the flag was still flying on the roof. The Governor at last made a move, saying it was time to leave the burning premises, as no more could be done. I made a stand at the garden gate, determined not to leave so long as the flag was flying, and made all the women servants pass out before me to see that all were safe. They were all empty-handed except my little Greek maid, who I noticed was tightly holding something in both her hands. I asked her what it was.

"Madame," said she, with an air of great importance, "here are the keys of the house."

Everyone laughed in spite of anxiety and sorrow, as we turned and gazed on the mass of burning embers which had been the house. The flag had now gone, and as I turned to come away my husband appeared besmeared all over with black, his face smutty and half of his beard scorched away. He had spent the whole night in making efforts to protect life and property and had accomplished much. For these services he received the thanks of the Sultan and the Grand Decoration of Liakat, which I preciously guard, together with other beautiful orders and decorations he received from time to time as mementos of his long and distinguished career.

H.M.S. *Australia* came down from Athens to

help at this time, and I need hardly say how considerate the officers were towards us in our trouble and how generous they were in helping the destitute and homeless people, who were chiefly Jews of the poorest class who were reduced to living under any shelter they could find. Blankets, clothing, food were generously distributed at once, and a little later charitable contributions followed from all directions.

The fire was a great calamity for us as well, but we had to do the best we could. We regretted most of all that the gates of the fine old Consulate were for ever closed to our dear friends in the Navy, whom we had so loved to entertain there.

I paid a flying visit to my brother at Constantinople and then went on to Brussa to see my dear mother, who was now a widow, my father having died but recently. I was struck afresh with my mother's qualities of bravery and simplicity. Shortly before leaving the Consulate she had been sitting at her window overlooking the garden one morning when she saw a wild-looking man, yatagan in hand, rush in through the gate and take up a position in a corner of the garden with his back to the wall evidently ready to defend himself. He was quickly followed by half a dozen policemen, who formed a semi-circle round him, unwilling to approach within striking distance of the yatagan which he flourished at them while he said, " You know that I am Andon, the well-known brigand, whose yatagan never yet failed him. The first among you who takes a step in my direction may look upon himself as a dead man. Come on, my braves, and take your chance." My mother, hearing this and seeing the position of the police, walked down the garden and ordered the police to stay where they were. She then ordered Andon to hand his yatagan to her. Taken by surprise or perhaps lost in admiration of her courage he handed it to her, saying, "Madame, I am ready to hand over my arm of defence and my life to you, but I would not give it to those dogs," indicating the policemen, "till I had despatched a few of them to accompany me into the next world."

Having handed his yatagan to mother, he next held up both his hands for her to fasten the handcuffs round his wrists, when he quietly walked away with his guard.

Mother was well known in the country for miles round for her great kindness to the people. My sister Matilda used to tell a good story of how one day mother went into the village where everyone knew her, and where she was in the habit of getting all her servants. On sighting her arrival some of the beggarly families collected round her and poured out grievous tales of their poverty and misery, pointing to their tattered, barefooted daughters to confirm their statements. Mother, much affected by this tableau of misery, got a cart and placed as many of these tatterdemalions in it as it would hold and took them to the Consulate. My sisters went to meet mother at the door on her return home, when to their surprise and dismay they saw six or seven unkempt girls, grinning with delight, jump down from the cart. My sisters wondered what had possessed mother to bring these girls, and in answer to their looks of inquiry she said, "Dears, I found these poor creatures looking so starved and miserable that I thought I would bring them home with me, so that they could be washed and have some dinner, but if you find their presence objectionable they can go home again in the afternoon."

From her young days my dear mother showed sympathy and gave help to all the sick poor she came across. She lived in Therapia, and in those days a colony of Croatians dwelt in tents on a bit of bare ground at the back of the garden. A small gate opened on to the ground where the Croatians, who were hereditary gardeners and professional thieves when opportunity served, lived, and through which they entered to work in the garden. My mother always looked after them when they or their children were sick, and the whole colony was devoted to her, much as dogs are devoted to their master. One day when mother was walking in the garden close to the small gate, she saw it open mysteriously and one of the Croatians came in, putting the fingers of one hand on his lips to beg her to say nothing, and hurriedly placed between her hands a small but heavy bag and quickly went out closing the gate behind him. Mother took the bag into the dining-room, thinking it probably contained some fruit, and emptied the contents on to the table, when to her amazement a perfect stream of gems, emeralds, rubies, and pearls poured forth and shone with brilliance in the sunshine. Not knowing what to do with so valuable a treasure she sent for Count Pisani, a friend of the family, who was the Keeper of Archives of the Embassy, and asked his counsel.

Together they decided it would be best to send
the bag of jewels to the Mayor of Therapia as he
might possibly hear of the owner who had lost so
great a fortune. The Mayor evidently thought
"that possession was nine points of the law," since
in three days' time he had secured a post as pasha,
evidently having paid for the position with the
treasure so confidingly given to him.

I was struck on revisiting Brussa with the
method of disinfection my mother always practised
with regard to goods brought to the house. A
trough of vinegar stood outside the entrance at the
back door of the house, and into this everything
that could be washed was soused before being
brought indoors. My mother had lost her sister
Sophia in Constantinople from plague when they
were all girls together, and this had made a great
impression upon her. My Aunt Sophy was a
lovely girl, judging from a miniature of her my
mother had, which as a child I much admired.
She was a clever linguist and used to translate
documents for the Embassy in the time of Lord
Ponsonby. She was also a clever artist and
designed and worked beautiful embroideries. One
day when plague was rampant in Constantinople
and when no one left the house unless it was
imperative my aunt ran short of some silks she
needed for her work. Seeing a pedlar pass by
who sold skeins of silk, and deeming that it would
be safe to buy of him she let down a string from
her window, to which the pedlar fastened the
skeins she chose. Drawing up the string she
proceeded to use the silks. Shortly after this she
was attacked by plague and died in a few days,

having, so it was thought, received infection through her purchase.

My mother and I stayed at Kucutlu, the village a few miles from Brussa, where there were the remains of some old Roman baths, and I thoroughly enjoyed a plunge morning and evening into the deep, cool waters of the huge marble swimming-baths. But my visit had to come to an end, and I returned to Salonika to start household anew in the charming villa of " Mon Plaisir," most kindly lent us by M. Charnaud, and to prepare for a large bazaar in aid of the poor destitute people of Salonika.

The bazaar was a great success, very largely owing to the generosity of Admiral Lord Walter Kerr and the officers of the Squadron, among whom were Sir Rosslyn Wemyss, Lord Charles Beresford, and many others who in those days promised great things by their intelligence and their energy, and in these days have accomplished them.

CHAPTER XVI

1889

AFTER the burning down of the Consulate, Monsieur Charnaud most kindly offered us the loan of his house, Villa Mon Plaisir, as a temporary home. We gladly accepted this kind offer and found the villa a delightful, spacious, and well-furnished house which came as a Godsend after the disastrous fire.

Sultan Hamid had formed a Ministry of Public Works, a fraudulent body which acquired land in Salonika and elsewhere by the simple method of annexing what it required where it desired, without any reference to the wishes of the owners or compensation to them. In this way a fine part in Salonika called Boulevard Hamidia came into existence, which was set apart for the construction of fine houses suitable for consular abodes. Our Consulate was the first to be built and was promised to us by a certain date. I was fortunate enough to get Portocal Effendi, the Minister of Public Works, to allow me to make several improvements in the original plans for our house. While we were comfortably installed at Villa Mon Plaisir awaiting the building of the Consulate I asked my two nieces, Mary and Isabelle de

Bilinski, to come and stay with us for a few months. They were both sweet, pretty girls and I was glad to have them with me, especially when the Squadron under the command of Admiral Lord Walter Kerr came in. There were many old friends amongst the officers whom my husband and I were delighted to see, and we were specially pleased when we heard that there was a possibility of the Squadron making a prolonged stay. The possibility became a reality, the ships being anchored in the Bay for three months as a standing protest on the part of England during the abominable Armenian troubles. I believe. that on two or three occasions the Squadron stood in readiness to sail for Constantinople; but even in those days the policy of "wait and see" was in vogue, and stopped this most powerful and advantageous step from being taken. The brilliant opportunity was lost which would have resulted in incalculable advantages to Turkey as well as to England, by giving an entirely different turn to the train of events that ensued. The oriental character with its fatalistic belief in "kismet" is not easily moved to action or mere menace or distant danger, whilst it soon yields to determined action whether it likes it or not. In connection with this it is regrettable to have to state that the Germans by their count- less ways and devices, from treacherous actions to brutal force, which none of the sounder Ministers of the Turkish Empire were capable of opposing or resisting, gave rise to the powerful influence they acquired over the treacherous Young Turkey Party, and made this party do the ignoble work which lay beyond their reach, and which has largely con-

P

duced to bring about the present situation. God alone knows how it will end for Turkey and her people.

Exceptions of course exist among the Turks, but it is generally recognised that the love of honours, decorations, and money earned with the least possible trouble will get the better of the patriotism of the majority.

Some five years ago I had an interesting conversation on the organisation and future prospects of their constitution with a staunch member of the Young Turkey Party who was passing through Malta. The first thing that struck me in the formation of this proposed constitution was, that no mention whatever was made of any reforms, conventions, or arrangements in favour of the vast Christian element within the borders of the Turkish Empire. Passing' over several minor details the next point which specially struck me was the hungry avidity with which he broached the financial question. "Money, money, Hanoum, is all we require, and we are trying to get it on a large scale."

On my questioning him where and how they could get it, he said, "Why, from Germany, England, France, and Italy."

"But surely," I said, "these Powers are not desirous of parting with their money for nothing."

"No, Hanoum, we know that; we have already arranged to give the Powers concessions for railways and other works in close proximity to each other, relying on the objections and disputes that will arise between them; and if they come to blows we shall get the native workmen to strike or to

set the works on fire.   You are aware, Hanoum,
how clever we Turks have always been in getting
out of difficulties with European Powers."

" And what about Germany," said I.

" No fear on that side, Germany is now our
best friend, ready to help us in every way."

Poor, deluded people, they little knew how soon
that Power would become their master and hasten
on the ruin of their country.

I do not wish to include the uneducated people
in this description of the aims of the Young Turkey
Party.   The country people are still in profound
ignorance.   They are an Allah-fearing people, and
have remained content earning their daily bread
by the sweat of their brow.   Their wages allow
them to have about two pence a day pocket-money,
and in the evening after drinking a cup of coffee,
eating a small quantity of their favourite yaghourt
(soured milk), and smoking a few cigarettes, these
hard-working toilers are ready to turn in and sleep
peacefully till dawn without troubling their heads
about politics or parties.   Such at least were the
Turks of my time.

I have no pretension to a spirit of prophecy, but
when looking recently over a few notes I made in
1875, I came across this prediction.   "Turkish
affairs will never settle down until America comes
forward."   The brave American missionaries have
done wonders for the Christian population in Turkey.
The work has been able and tactful, and though
opposed to the religious interests of the Turks, yet
the Turks nevertheless highly respected these
devoted servants of humanity, and often followed
the advice they gave.

But to return to Salonika ; a Squadron, under
the command of Admiral Sir Michael Culme
Seymour was eagerly welcomed by all classes,
since its presence in the Bay of Salonika inspired
a sense of great confidence and security.   Outside
this sense of security was a genuine feeling of
admiration for the sea-power of England, and great
regard and esteem not only for the gallant admiral,
officers, and middies but also for the crews ; and the
Turks were pleased to be under the shelter of this
great fleet, which compared so favourably with the
fleets from other nations, and attracted the attention
even of the ignorant at a time when the Turks
were wont to say of their own ships, "Bizim
ghemiler bir para etmezler" (Our ships are not
worth a penny).

One late afternoon about this time I was
going to the stable to give a bit of sugar to my
favourite horse, when I was startled in the semi-
darkness by a gigantic, dishevelled individual with
a besmeared blackened face springing out of the
coal-house which adjoined the stable.   This man
fell at my feet and implored me to save his life.
Drawing him into the stable out of sight, I asked
him who he was, and what the danger was that
was menacing his life.

"I am the Hedjabachi (headman) of Cassandra,"
said he, "pursued by these dogs (meaning the
Turks) for hiding arms on my estate, which I
only have there in order to protect my family
and my farm in case of necessity."   Learning
from him that this was the extent of his crime,
and though feeling that the case was a delicate
one, I sent him back to the coal-house to remain

there till I could find out if his story was based
on fact. If it were I knew he was in danger of
losing his life or of imprisonment, which was
nearly as bad.

Fortunately there was a ball that evening,
where I knew I should meet a great friend of
ours, Redjeb Pasha, the Commander-in-chief of
the Forces in Macedonia.

I decided not to say a word to my husband,
but to make a direct appeal to the Commander-in-
chief in favour of my friend in the coal-house.

I broached the subject with all the diplomacy
in my power, and while watching his face I
noticed on it looks of annoyance at being asked
a favour beyond his official capacity to grant.
This decided me to go straight to the point and
ask him for the release of the man, and his help
to get him out of the country. He stared at me,
saying, "Great is the gravity of your request
to me as Commander-in-chief of our Forces in
charge of the protection of the country."

I answered smilingly that I knew that to be
so, and that that was the very reason I made
this request only to the kindness of his heart.

"Has Mr Blunt knowledge of this incident?"

"Certainly not," said I, "he would have been
the first to place the man in your official hands,
whilst I ignore your official position and prefer
to appeal to the kindness of your generous heart."

"Be it so," answered my gallant friend, "I
cannot refuse your appeal. Tell your protégé to
be at your garden door about three o'clock in the
morning, and when he hears three gentle taps to
open it and go out, and follow a man who will

put him on board a Greek boat which will take him out of the country."

My husband was furious when I told him the story some weeks later, but I rejoiced to think that I had been able to save the life of an oppressed man who had only made reasonable preparations in case of an attack on himself and his property.

After the Squadron left my husband and I went to England on six months' leave. This was my husband's first visit to England since he had left it on the completion of his education thirty-five years previously, and he was like a schoolboy let loose in his happiness in returning to the dear land of his birth and boyhood. His first visit in London was to his club, the Athenæum, of which he had been a member for years, but had never previously had the chance to enter. I was favoured by fortune, for I had the privilege on the Kaiser's visit to the city of London of going to the club, too, and having a place on the balcony from which to view the procession. There were many celebrities at the luncheon which followed, and it rejoiced my heart to see that my husband, in spite of his long sojourn and anxious work in the Near East, looked the youngest of them all.

CHAPTER XVII

1891-1895

HAPPY as we had been at Villa Mon Plaisir, yet I was very glad on our return from England to move into the new Consulate, a spacious modern building on the Boulevard Hamidia. The picturesque Mount Hortiach which we saw from our windows often presented one of the finest atmospheric effects I have ever witnessed. The rays of the setting sun blended in some curious way with the soft dews rising from the mountain, and appeared to form an azure curtain floating in space.

Owing to the fact that we had insured our furniture in the old Consulate, we had money to invest in furniture from England and oriental stuffs from the Stamboul bazaar. This time, thanks to the aid of Jeanne's nimble fingers, I set up house more easily and quickly than I had ever done before. We had nearly finished arranging the dining- and living-rooms, leaving the ballroom to the last, when my husband received news of the early arrival of the Squadron; good news which rejoiced everybody in Salonika.

It was, I think, during the Cretan troubles that the British Squadron paid frequent visits to

Salonika under different commanders-in-chief, among whom were Admiral Sir George Tryon, Admiral Markham, and Prince Louis of Battenberg in H.M.S. *Cambrian.* I well remember the old friends who came back on this occasion, as we gave a house-warming dinner followed by a ball, when the ballroom, not yet complete, was temporarily decorated most prettily by some of our bluejackets. Poor Admiral Sir George Tryon attracted much attention by his personality and good looks as he stood by me watching the dancers. The Italian Consul came up and paid him so many compliments on his appearance as an admiral that as he left us Sir George turned round to me and said laughingly, " Pears' soap, Pears' soap."

A regatta took place before Admiral Tryon left, and I noticed with keen interest what a great event a regatta is both for the officers and the men. Sir George asked a large party from the shore, including His Excellency the Governor of Salonika, who was so pleased at the attention that he presented as a special prize a handsome set of gold and silver coffee cups. The prize was won by one of the Admiral's favourite middies, a most charming and promising young officer, and the Admiral asked me to thank the Governor for having given so valuable a prize, and to add that he was so pleased that one of his youngest officers had gained it as he would be likely to live long, and to bear in mind all his life His Excellency's kind gift. *L'homme propose mais Dieu dispose.* A fortnight later both the Admiral and his favourite young officer passed out of this finite world in consequence of the well-remembered sinking of the Admiral's ship, H.M.S. *Victoria* (1893), during naval manœuvres. The brave young boy preferred to remain on the sinking ship to the very end by the side of his beloved chief, in spite of his chief's repeated permission to save himself. This calamitous loss of a number of brave officers and men was specially grievous to us since their recent visit was so fresh in our minds. A cloud of sorrow hung over Salonika for a time, and the deepest sympathy was felt for Lady Tryon. Much sympathy too was felt for our dear kind friend, Admiral Markham, who was well known as a very capable, brave, and distinguished officer.

Many men-of-war remained in the Bay of Salonika over a long period as a demonstration during the Armenian and Cretan troubles. Both these troubles were serious enough, God knows, but it has always been the Armenians who paid dearly. The custom of re-commissioning men-of-war every two years brought back to Salonika from time to time old friends and introduced new friends who, in due course, rose through the ranks of officers, from midshipmen to that of commander-in-chief, each standing on his own merits and steadily going up the rungs of the ladder of promotion. Jeanne asked one of the youngest of her friends what his feelings were whilst in charge of a boat full of bluejackets. "My feelings," said the bright little fellow, "are akin to those of an admiral fulfilling his duties, and," added he pleadingly, "please say something nice about me to my captain as I love him very much and I should like him to care for me." I thought this little speech a striking illustration of the harmony, respect, and good feeling that reigns on board these fine well-disciplined ships down to the bluejackets who are, as a rule, proud of and devoted to their superior officers. Even the Turks, so differently brought up, were struck by the general good behaviour of our sailors. In the few instances when a complaint was brought to my husband of some foolish conduct on the part of a sailor, and his assurance that the case would be brought to the notice of the captain, he was thanked and was asked that the case might go no further on the plea that childish pranks in brave young men, though tiresome and reported to the Consul-General, did not deserve punishment. Some of the jokes played by a few mischief-loving sailors were most absurd. Again, it was a donkey that was made to play the chief rôle. A regie gardien (civil guard) was fast asleep whilst in his sentry-box. The sailor, seeing this, brought his donkey and gently put its head through the narrow window at the side of the sentry-box, so that it was more or less on a level with the face of the peaceful sleeper. The donkey, disapproving of its head in this position, gave utterance to a bray of distress. The guard, half asleep, became conscious of the donkey's head close to his own, thought it was some strange beast come to devour him and screamed for help at the top of his voice. The sailor, after enjoying his practical joke, came to the rescue, and after a good deal of trouble got the donkey's head out of its tight prison, and at the same time mollified his victim by placing a few shillings in his hand.

Another practical joke brought to my husband's notice was serio-comic. The victim was a devout Turk who had spread his handkerchief of prayer

facing Mecca, and with his face on his knees he
bent on the ground and made his Namaz. Thus
absorbed he attracted the attention of a bluejacket
who approached from behind, seized the Turk by
the legs, and made him turn three somersaults in
succession, in spite of the Turk's protest at being
disturbed in his devotions. The Turk's turban fell
off, and his tormentor placed it on his own head
and put his cap in exchange on the Turk. The
poor Turk tried to persuade the sailor to give him
back his turban as he abhorred looking like a
ghiaour (infidel). After contemplating his handiwork the sailor put his hand in his pocket, took
out a shilling and handed it to his victim with the
turban, said, "Namaz great bosh. English shilling
bono-bono. Good-bye."

"Allah, Allah soupan Allah" (God is great),
said the Turk, but consoled by the look of the
shilling he also agreed that it was *bono-bono*.

Entertainments of one kind and another
continued to be given during the stay of the
Squadron. M. Charnaud and Mr Allatini, the
latter a well-known wealthy Jew, were both
very hospitable people, and so were one or two
of the foreign consuls. I must not forget to
note down the hospitality of M. L——, a
nouveau riche, a most avaricious Jew who, on
hearing that Captain Lord Charles Beresford
was reputed to be much the wealthiest of the
officers, said, "Je dois prendre note de cela."

M. L—— gave a dinner, when great confusion
ensued over the seating of the guests. The
Commander-in-chief was passed over by the host
in favour of Lord Charles, who was placed next

to Madame L——, a pretty young woman of
European extraction. The two officers looked
at each other. The younger in his delightful
outspoken way said, "I beg your pardon, sir,
but I had to sit where I was pressed down
unceremoniously by the waiter."

We always had a little coterie of officers with
us whenever a squadron was in the Bay, which
gave us much pleasure and was one of the delights
of the happy days in Salonika. Wit, youth, and
gaiety, as well as the stately charm of the senior
British naval officers often produced the effect
of a Parisian *Salon de Conversation*. Every
imaginable subject was discussed at one time
or another, the older members looking all the
younger, and the younger older and wiser when
talking over some of the ways of life on land
and sea. It was during one of these pleasant
gatherings that a young officer in imitation of
my nieces called me "Aunt Fanny." The
happy inspiration was enthusiastically approved,
and from that moment I was formally adopted
as "Aunt Fanny" to the Navy. These dear
"Extraordinary Nephews," as they called themselves, formed a small committee and only
admitted to this relationship such further officers
as they approved of, and this was kept up to
very recent times. Among this first set of
nephews were Admiral Sir Rosslyn Wemyss,
and many others who have carved great careers
for themselves, but who in those days were happy,
light-hearted, yet earnest young officers. One
generation of Extraordinary Nephews has followed
the other, and all, according to their age, are

occupying positions of great importance. I am now at the fourth generation, and many of the youngest set have already distinguished themselves, and show me that they are following in the footsteps of their predecessors. On a cigarette box that some of the members of the first generation gave me are the names amongst many others of Allan F. Everett, Maurice Woollcombe, Mark Kerr, all now distinguished Admirals of the Fleet.

What makes me so proud and happy in the enjoyment of this great group of Extraordinary Nephews is the wealth of friendship and affection they so generously bestow upon me, and which I retain to the present day. Few, indeed, are those of my Extraordinary Nephews in the Mediterranean Navy who, passing through Malta, fail to come and see me, now pretty well known as "Aunt Fanny of the British Fleet."

Honi soit qui mal y pense.

CHAPTER XVIII

1895-1896

NONE of the countries I have visited can compare with Egypt in stimulating the desire to see and to know more of it. What can be more impressive than the Pyramids built of huge blocks of stone bearing the marks of bygone centuries? The wonderful Catacombs, the resting cities of the Pharaohs whose spirits are thought to hover in these their mysterious domains. The Colossal Sphinx presiding above, its wonderful eyes now no longer thought to have power to harm the dead or the living. The wide desert, that land of silvery sand and sunshine dotted here and there by the comforting presence of an oasis, and the possibility of at times contemplating across it the mysterious fleeting mirage. The expeditions on the blue waters of the Nile or to the ruins of some ancient temple. Egypt is rich in interests diverse enough to gratify every taste among the crowds that used yearly to resort there from all parts of the world, and is a country where old and modern civilisations often blend incongruously, such as the ancient custom of a donkey ride combined with the irresistible fun

252

of the cosmopolitan chatter of the fellahîn who
takes charge of both the beast and its burden.

My interest in the land of the Pharaohs was
greatly stimulated by the kind hospitality of my
cousin, Sir Edward Zohrab, who had been a
General in the Egyptian Army, and was at the
time 'of my visit Under-Secretary of War. I
was greatly attached to my cousin, whose fine
qualities attracted me much, and I was much
gratified to find that Lord Wolseley, whom
I met in Malta some years back, shared my
feelings. In talking of the Soudan campaign
when he had seen much of my cousin, Lord
Wolseley said, "In all my long experience of
life I never came across any person I loved and
admired as much as I did that dear good cousin
of yours."

The season I spent at Cairo was a very lively
one, and was made especially delightful for me
as my dear son was quartered there with his
regiment, the Connaught Rangers. It was at
this time that I first met H.R.H. the Duke of
Cambridge, Lord Wolseley, General Kitchener,
Slatin Pasha, and many other distinguished men.
Balls and parties of every description were given;
the two that have remained engraved on the
tablets of my memory were the ball at the
Ghezireh Palace given by the cavalry regiment
stationed in Cairo, in honour of the Duke of
Cambridge, and the dinner given by the
Connaught Rangers. The ball was like a peep
into fairyland. The vast terrace of the palace
was hung with brilliant oriental draperies, their
bright colours held here and there by gold and

silver roses that caught the reflection of thousands
of lights.   The garden, decorated in a similar way,
its alleys perfumed by the rich scent of countless
flowers, proved a serious rival to the attractions
of the ballroom.

The Duke of Cambridge appeared to be deeply
impressed by the lovely sight, and after looking
all round asked me who had designed so beautiful
a palace.

"I believe," said I, "that it was the creation
of the Khedive Ismail in which to house his
countless houris."

"It is a pity," said the Duke, "that there
are none of them here to complete the tableau."

I demurred, and cast a look of admiration at
the groups of lovely girls flitting in and out
among the bushes.   The old courtier guessed
my thoughts, and, with a twinkle in his eye, said,
"They are well represented but they lack the
interest of novelty."

"An interest," added I, "which their rivals
must certainly have introduced into the Mohammedan paradise."

The distinguished company, the brilliant
uniforms, the excellent supper in these beautiful
surroundings made a delightful luxurious entertainment which was said to have cost about
£2000.   The habit of extravagant waste of money
introduced and practised by the Khedival family
was easily caught by other than those of the
Khedival household.

The grand dinner and ball of the Connaught
Rangers was an annual affair given to celebrate
some regimental victory.   I was much interested

in the fine display of silver, the accumulated
treasures of many years, on the dining-table.
Colonel Brook commanded the regiment at that
time. I was seated next to General Kitchener,
who was much interested in the decoration I wore,
which had been given me by Sultan Abdul Hamid
for my work amongst Turkish women. The
decoration is very beautiful and consists of a five-
pointed star of red enamel on gold. The spaces
between the points of the star are filled with gold
crowns encrusted with diamonds and green enamel.
The centre shows the Toughra or signature of the
Sultan, surrounded by a green enamel band, on
which are three words in Turkish characters in
fine letters of gold, *i.e.*, Fidelity, Friendship,
Valour.

Kitchener was at that time just beginning to
be a rising star over which slight clouds occasionally passed, owing to some difference of opinion
between him and his Commander-in-chief, which
induced the future hero of England to go on a
visit to Cyprus. Kitchener's return coincided
with difficulties the French were making in the
Soudan, causing annoyance to Lord Wolseley in
consequence of certain vexatious criticisms cast on
the English, which necessitated sending some able
person to examine into and to report on them.
The Commander-in-chief applied to my cousin to
find the right person for the mission.

"I have him ready for your service, sir," said
Edward.

"Who is it ?" asked Lord Wolseley.

"Kitchener," was the reply.

"Look for some one else," said Lord Wolseley.

Q

Next evening the same inquiry received the same reply, and it was only on the third day that my cousin's persistent recommendation of Kitchener appealed to Lord Wolseley, who, after taking a turn or two up and down the room, said curtly, "'Tell him to come and dine with me to-night."

Edward told me this story and added, "As soon as I got the order I went off like a shot and spent seven hours on horseback trying to find Kitchener. At last I came across him and told him to hold himself in readiness to start next morning on a mission to the Soudan."

"To-morrow morning, by whose orders?" said Kitchener, with a pleased surprise.

"By order of the Commander-in-chief."

"Never, the man hates me like poison, and is not likely to wish to make use of my services."

"Never mind what you think, you are to come and dine this evening and receive your instructions for to-morrow."

It did not take Kitchener long to get to the bottom of this affair and to give an able and satisfactory report.

I believe it was Kitchener's successful conduct of this mission which cleared his sky from the cloud which had temporarily veiled it.

In spite of the fact that the case had been well sifted and reported on, yet the French press continued to cast unpleasant reflections on our policy in the Soudan. Again chance decided in Kitchener's favour. It happened that my cousin and the Editor of the *Times* were in Paris together, when the latter, anxious to get correct information on the subject to enable him to put a stop to the outcry of the French papers, applied to Edward and learnt what he wanted from him. Kitchener on meeting Edward a little later spoke to him of the great change in the tone of the French press, and wondered who could have supplied such sound information to the *Times*.

"One of your friends, I expect," said Edward.

It apparently did not occur to Kitchener that it was Edward who had helped to confirm the soundness of his report, and thus further to establish the position he had won for himself.

Slatin Pasha, an officer in the Egyptian Army, was another of the interesting personages I met in Cairo. Slatin Pasha often came to my cousin's house, and his personality and conversation deeply interested me. He was an Austrian by birth, young, good-looking, and delicate in appearance. He had been Governor of the Province of Darfur when the Mahdist rebellion broke out, and was made prisoner and spent seven terrible years at Omdurman. It was a miracle how he managed to survive those long years of captivity. At one time he would be put in chains and nearly starved, and at another his position would be all that he could desire, good food, kind attention, and everything he needed when, without rhyme or reason, so far as he knew, he would again be put in chains and starved. After his escape in 1895 he told me that on his return to Austria he was amazed to find that he was the sole survivor of a small circle of friends he had left in good health, and whose lives had been lived, unlike his own, in uneventful, comfortable circumstances.

During my stay in Cairo I enjoyed the

privilege of meeting several distinguished members of the Khedival family, the descendants of Mehemet Ali, the first Khedive of Egypt.

Mehemet Ali was an Albanian born at Cavalla, where his father, a much respected citizen, had settled down, living quietly on his modest earnings. Mehemet Ali, a bright, handsome boy, was employed by Mr Chassaud, a British subject, a grain merchant, as kavass or guard. It was Mr Chassaud's son who told me the interesting details of the beginning of Mehemet Ali's wonderful career. It seems that the boy, full of life and energy, though illiterate and devoid of any means beyond his trifling salary, began to pine for some change to better his position, when fortunately he came across some Albanian adventurers on their way to visit their native land, who told him about the great country of Egypt they had just left, and of the frequent unexpected openings to make a fortune that occurred there, owing to the difficulties the Turks found in maintaining their control over the country. Mehemet Ali thought this over carefully, and made up his mind to get to Egypt by hook or by crook. Troubled by the want of means for his journey he appealed to his mother, who discouraged him as far as she could from undertaking so venturesome an enterprise, but seeing his fixed determination she at last took an old stocking from the bottom of her trunk and poured out her small savings into Mehemet Ali's hands. The amount was barely sufficient to pay for the journey to the great city of Stamboul, about which he had heard so much since childhood. Mehemet's father could not help him with money, but gave him a suit of fine Albanian clothes and a set of arms worked in silver. These treasures were Mehemet's stock-in-trade when he set sail for Stamboul.

The adventurous boy was very hungry when he reached his journey's end, as he had spent his last piastre on food the previous night. On landing at the old bridge of Stamboul, he neglected his pangs of hunger by an effort of will, cast a gratified look on the fine figure he cut in his rich Albanian clothes, inquired his way to the great bazaar of Stamboul, and swaggered along the narrow streets, his hand on his yatagan. The presence of an armed Albanian, a stranger, striding along the bazaar looking into every saraff's (money-lender's) box, alarmed the timid Armenian occupants, most of whom he passed with a look of disdain. At last at the top of a small incline he came to a solitary saraff sitting behind his portable bank. Mehemet Ali stood in front of this saraff, looked him up and down, and then said, " Saraff Effendimis, I want you to lend me £50."

"Bash-ustune" (On my head your orders), answered the money-lender, outwardly polite, but inwardly quaking with fear, "the amount is at your service if you can leave a deposit."

"I have none to leave," said Mehemet, his hand on his yatagan. The Armenian cast an anxious look on the stalwart youth and made a timid proposal that an I.O.U would be necessary. Mehemet Ali, with a bitter smile, said, "I can neither read nor write, you must therefore give me the £50, and trust to my word of honour that some day I will repay you."

The saraff pulled out his drawer and counted out £50 to the stranger whose name even he did not know. Mehemet Ali with this sum in his pocket started on the remarkable career which enabled him finally to occupy the proud position of first Khedive of Egypt. He never forgot the saraff to whom he owed his start in life, and in due course sent three of his officers to Stamboul to search him out and bring him to Cairo. The saraff, who was in reality a wealthy banker, had forgotten the incident till recalled to his memory by Mehemet Ali who said, "I wish to reward you, and appoint you, Boghos, the head of the Financial Department in Egypt, and I feel confident it will prosper under your care." Boghos Bey was overpowered by this unlooked-for good fortune, but rose to the occasion and filled well the important position given to him, and enjoyed to the last his master's confidence. Mehemet Ali, though illiterate, had a good head on his shoulders and sound foresight. He liked the English and the French, and encouraged them in the capital of his creation, and was glad when it was suggested that an hotel (afterwards Shepheard's) should be built. But when it was desired to buy the land on which the hotel was to be built he felt some anxiety, and talked the matter over with his friend Canelli, and said, "You see, Canelli, I like the English and am glad to attract them into the country, but I dislike the idea of giving them the right to purchase land, being well aware of the English method of sending first missionaries, then traders, and then the army and navy to take possession

of the country. This is sure to happen sooner
or later when Turkey goes to pieces, as she surely
will." None of Mehemet Ali's successors was
his equal in mind, power, or organisation. Each
in his way had certain qualifications of bravery
combined with marked defects, such as caprice,
favouritism, and reckless generosity, with an
excess of cruelty and oriental despotism.

The Khedive Ismail, the founder of Ismailia,
during whose reign the Suez Canal was made by
the engineering genius of M. le Baron de Lesseps,
built the three fine bridges between Cairo and
the island of Gezireh, as well as the museum.
He laid out the beautiful garden of Ezebekieh
and the zoological gardens, but came to grief,
chiefly owing to his extravagance and ignorance
of financial matters. Like most Orientals, Ismail
loved gold, but did not attach much importance
· to paper money, of which, however, he issued a
good deal, and used often to give away recklessly.
One day he desired to give a large sum to a
favourite, and ordered his treasurer to have ready
£10,000 on the following day. The treasurer,
well knowing the poverty of the Khedival purse
and the Khedive's love of gold, arranged ten
thousand bright Egyptian pounds on Ismail's
table. The Khedive, startled by the sight of so
fine a display of gold, asked what so large a sum
was doing there.

"Effendimis, it is the £10,000 my lord ordered
me to put at his disposal."

"By Allah," answered Ismail, "put it away,
put it away," and casting a glance of gratification
at the shining pieces he passed on quite forgetting,

as his wily treasurer intended he should, to give any orders concerning the gift he had promised.

Under the Turkish protectorate Egypt was going to rack and ruin, when Mehemet Ali came to the front and saved it from that curse which was fast draining the country of all its resources and carrying them off to Constantinople. But it was "out of the frying pan into the fire" under the Khedival rule. The oriental Grand Seigneur, unless he be a miser, is absolutely reckless in financial matters. He will squander all his ready cash and mortgage his property to usurers (Jews), who are careful not to press for payment of the interest until it reaches an amount beyond the power of the borrower to pay, when the property changes hands greatly to the disadvantage of the borrower.

My visit to Cairo came to an end with the outbreak of the war in the Soudan, when my son was sent up country in charge of a Maxim gun, a gun that had then only recently been introduced into warfare.

I took passage on a Khedival steamboat bound for Constantinople, and had for fellow passengers a group of pretty, bright princesses leaving Egypt on the plea that plague had broken out. These girls were under the care of a Khedival lady, and were intensely bored by the want of society on the boat. I found them pretty, talkative, and elegant. They spoke French and English fluently, as they had been brought up by European governesses. They hated their forced seclusion, and longed for the liberty and freedom that were denied them. It made my heart bleed to see intelligent young women cut off from the pleasures and duties of life. I met some of these princesses a few months later at Constantinople, where they occupied a lovely palace overlooking the Bosphorus, and found them rather happier, as they were allowed a little more liberty to go about than had been permitted in Egypt. Some of them went to Europe soon after, and the first thing they did was to cast aside their veils and wear hats!

I remember during the eighties that a charming woman with a romantic history had come to spend some months at Salonika, where I became acquainted with her. She was a Circassian girl who had been sold when a mere child in the slave market at Constantinople, and had been bought by a sister of Mehemet Ali, a princess of the Khedival House who had married, but was childless. The little Circassian, Besimé by name, was dressed as a boy by her adopted mother and carefully educated. The child grew up to be a beautiful girl, and when some fifteen or sixteen years of age was present at one of the annual gatherings of Turkish ladies, given by the Sultan as father of the Empire, when all the ladies are unveiled. Little Besimé attracted the Sultan's attention and he desired her for his seraglio. The princess objected, but after endless talk and arrangements Mehemet Ali decided that the Sultan might have her if the ceremony of nikiha or marriage was performed. This is a very rare ceremony, and I believe the case of Besimé was only the second that had occurred in the history of the Turkish Empire. After

occupying an important rôle as sultana for some
years, she became impatient of the impediment to
her free development, and tired of the jealousies
and intrigues of a household of seven hundred
women who had nothing to do but gossip, broke
away from the Court. The Sultan provided her
with a large fortune, but this she soon squandered
away, oriental fashion. Besimé was still young
and beautiful when I knew her, and she often
came and lunched with us unveiled, when my
husband· and I enjoyed her interesting conversation. After lunch she would come into my
boudoir and tell me of all the sorrows of her
adventurous life. I wrote down a good deal of
what she told me of the life and surroundings of
an oriental Sultan. The seraglio was practically
a little town with everyone in it devoted to the
interests of one man, the Sultan ; but unfortunately
all my notes were destroyed by the great fire
which burnt down the Consulate.

This story of Besimé is in marked contrast to
that of Zulfica, a real blossom of the desert who
came down to the banks of the Nile with her
water-pot on her head, her slim figure upright,
and her baby clasped in her arms. After filling
her water-pot and placing it in the shade of a
palm tree she entered the river and dipped
herself and her baby in the blue waters, then stood
for a few moments on the bank smothering the
child with her kisses. All this time she was
noticed by an unseen watcher, who followed her
home and made inquiries in her village as to who
she was. Finding she lived with her father, and
that she had but recently· lost her husband in the

war, the unseen watcher, a prince of the Royal
House, begged her in marriage and took her
home, where she became the chief wife of a
truly devoted husband. Egypt and Turkey are
full of romantic stories, but the greater number
of them develop into sadness or tragedy as the
years roll on.

CHAPTER XIX

1897

I HAD an uneventful journey to Salonika, and arrived in good time to help my husband organise some fêtes in honour of Queen Victoria's jubilee (1897). The Italian Fleet was in the Bay at that time, which gave additional animation to our festivities. We had an At Home for all the children, who were delighted by the novelty of the entertainment, and were further gratified by carrying home mementos of the great Queen of England. In the evening we had a large garden party in the public gardens which went off well, in spite of the difficulty of illuminations owing to the scanty allowance of £10 accorded by the Foreign Office for this purpose. My husband considerably supplemented this sum from his own pocket and did not, as did another consul, put the Foreign Office to the expense of spending £100 in telegrams in discussing with it his inability to do justice to his Queen and country by a meagre dole of £10 for illuminations.

It is nineteen years since I left Salonika, and I often wonder how much has been left of the old town and its well-to-do inhabitants. I hope it will remain as it now stands by its birthright,

part of the renewed, purified, and consolidated
Greece under the firm, honest control of M.
Venizelos, that patriotic genius whose short
tenure of office as Prime Minister gave such
solid proofs of his great capacity for organisation
and reforms. The speedy manner in which he
purged the whole country from the curse of
brigandage, using moral pressure far more than
the severe hand of the law, was a proof of his
knowledge of how to handle men and matters.
The success of M. Venizelos in this as in several
other reforms is little known outside Greece, but
so greatly increased his popularity there that had
circumstances been more favourable to his noble
task he would have saved his country from the
trouble she has had through the treachery of
an alien king, and of a few thousands of unpatriotic
Greeks who, brought up on German intrigues
and fed by German money, were led to become
the partisans of Germany. These Greeks pressed
the nation by every means in their power to
follow the evil example which has led Greece
to ruin, and has given her a bad reputation
amongst her oldest and best friends, France and
England. However doubtful and unpropitious
the relations of Greece may still appear to be,
there is every hope in the formation of a new
Greece reformed and ready to expiate her past
errors under the guidance of M. Venizelos, should
his life be spared to accomplish the task he has
taken upon himself. The thousands of Greeks,
too, who languish under the despicable Turkish
rule must, ere long, wake up to the necessity of
union with the mother country. Whatever the

defects of the Greeks may be they have been acquired by the force of circumstances only, whilst the virtues of a nation, like those of individuals, are inherited gifts which are passed on from one generation to another. The Greek nation has preserved a number of virtues, little known outside their own people, which are held sacred to the present day in spite of the hardships that some of them impose on individuals. Few persons have had the opportunity of seeing and studying the soundness and patriotism of the Greek home life. The father, respected and venerated, as a rule exercises full power over the whole family, and does his best for the education and prosperity of his children who are generally clever and enterprising. When the father retires from his business his sons take on their shoulders the sacred duty of working on behalf of dowerless sisters, and do not themselves marry until a dower has been provided and a husband and home secured for their sisters. I have known of Greeks even in good but not lucrative positions who have abandoned everything they possessed in favour of their sisters, and have gone abroad to earn a livelihood. No sons, on the death of their father, touch the property should any be left; it goes to the mother and her daughters. In times of trouble Greeks are helpful to one another; there is a great deal of kindness and generosity in their nature mixed up with a great amount of pride and conceit. The Greeks under the Turks, by force of circumstances, are not always as honest with strangers as they might be; but in spite of defects of this kind the Greeks

are by far the most advanced and clever of all
the races under the Turkish rule, and are the
most adaptable to modern civilisation.   These
are some of the reasons why, in my humble
opinion, I look upon modern Greece, not only
as a progressive nation which will in time acquire
influence in the Near East, but with her important
maritime positions, her excellent seaports, and
her army and navy, she should become an ally
of considerable value to both England and France.
These, no doubt, are problems reserved for the
future when Germany is forced to accept the
inevitable, and ceases to try to realise her dream
of conquering the world.

I was in Athens in 1888 on the twenty-fifth
anniversary of the coronation of the late King
George of Greece, when I found the town full
of joyful animation.   His Majesty, a kindly,
sensible king, had earned the confidence and
affection of the whole nation.   At that time
there was no German influence in the air,
Greece and her people were united and happy.
I remember that even the Turks on that occasion
seemed full of goodwill towards their Majesties,
and gave a dinner in their honour.   The funny
part of these entertainments was that my nephew,
who was Secretary to the Turkish Legation, and
Riza Pasha, the son of Raouf Pasha our great
friend, who was the Turkish Minister, asked me
to help them to arrange the Legation for the
dinner.   To my dismay I found the place as
bare as a Turk's shaved head, but fortunately
good old Mr Canelli, a Salonika friend, whose
guest I was at Athens, allowed me to borrow

a great deal of his lovely furniture, and the
Legation was soon transformed into a beautifully
furnished place, so much so that on the day
following the dinner the Athens papers were
full of praise for the Sultan of Turkey, for
sending such beautiful furniture to Athens in
honour of the occasion. T.R.H. the Duke
of Edinburgh and Prince George were present
at the dinner and ball, and the Greek and
English Royal families appeared much pleased
at the success of the entertainment. I enjoyed
it all, as well as the ball given by the Queen
of Greece. It was a great pleasure to me to
have the honour of again meeting the Duke of
Edinburgh and our charming young Prince, and
other friends in their *entourage*.

I felt much gratified to find the vast progress
Athens had made after her liberation from the
ruinous Turkish yoke. At the time of my first
visit some half century previously, the population
had appeared to consist of depressed, unkempt
people from all parts of Turkey who bore the
traces of their past serfdom. Athens was only
just beginning to show something of her old
beautiful self—many of her ancient monuments
still lay half buried in the dust, and wholesale
robberies of some of her treasures had been
committed.

At this last visit my interest in the Schliemann
collection of treasures, which had been deposited
in the museum at Athens, was heightened by my
stay at Troy some years previously.

Smyrna was one of the old cities on the shores
of the Mediterranean that I visited several times,

and which I always found interesting. Smyrna
with its fine position and its close proximity
to Ephesus with the old church of St John the
Divine, the most important centre of Byzantine
orthodoxy, had always attracted many Greeks
and foreigners since it had been granted certain
privileges by various sultans with regard to life
and property. British traders began to go to
Smyrna in the seventeenth century, and flourished
and developed into a wealthy colony, who carried
on their business in the town and had pleasant
country-houses in its vicinity. I do not remember
ever hearing that Smyrna had been subject to
any of the massacres on the part of the Turks
during the war of Greek independence, when
the Turks chopped off heads whenever they had
a chance. Smyrna, however, had her troubles
with the barbarous people farther in the interior,
some of whom, like the Albanians, lived on loot,
and occasionally came in bands to Smyrna and
its environs, carrying off property or hostages.
The situation improved after the construction
of the railway between Smyrna and Aïdin.
Dr Freshfield, if I remember rightly, had a good
deal to do with the building of the railway, as
he loved the country not only for its interesting
old Byzantine churches, but as the birthplace
of his beautiful young wife, Miss Zoé Hanson.
My husband was distantly connected with the
Hansons, and received much kindness from
them when he was a student at Smyrna College.
I became acquainted with old Mr and Mrs Hanson
when going to England as a young girl, and I
shall never forget the impression they made on

R

me, nor the charm and beauty of their only daughter. She and I met again years afterwards when we were both married, and both she and her husband were very kind to me whenever I went to England. She died when still compara- tively young, and was buried in the lovely church in Surrey dedicated to "The Wisdom of God," which Dr Freshfield built not far from his house, and to which he presented marbles from the church of St John at Ephesus and from the monastery of St John Studium at Constantinople.

Some distance from Smyrna was a district inhabited by some semi-savage tribes such as the old Turkomans, the Zeibëeks, Kurds, Lazes, and Bektashis. The Bektashis are an order of Dervishes who live under the control of a chief of their own selection. The chief, who wears a large and dis- tinctive badge of office round his neck, directs all the worldly affairs of the tribe. As a child I heard Mr Versami, the then ruling chief, relate to my mother his experiences. As a young man he came across a property belonging to the Bektashis near Smyrna which pleased him and which he rented and farmed. The tribe was kind to him and he helped them, and after a time they selected him as their chieftain. All was friendship and harmony between the chief and his subjects till one fine day, whilst all the community was at service in the Mosque, Versami's herd of pigs got loose and stampeded into the Mosque, and made noisy if not sweet sounds by their grunts and snorts. The devotees, surprised on their knees, were horrified to feel the unclean beasts lick their bare feet. Disgusted and infuriated they rushed at the chief intent on removing his badge of office, when Versami stood up, clasped the badge firmly in his hands, and in a stern voice called out, "Stop, you ignorant fools, can you not see that there must have been a visitation of Shaitans (evil spirits) on our peaceful community, which Providence in his mercy has driven into these vile beasts to punish them before the day fixed for their execution, and in the form of these unclean creatures they have rushed into this sacred building to acknowledge their acceptance of our true faith before they meet their doom."

"Is that so!" said the Bektashis.

"It is," answered Versami, with a show of handing over his badge. "Take this much-honoured badge back if you do not believe me."

His protest was drowned by a general, "Hasha, hasha, Effendim" (Never, never, Effendim); and thus ended the threatened rebellion.

Perhaps one of the most interesting things at Smyrna was the tribe of the Mamouni, a Jewish sect which originated at Smyrna but was transferred to Salonika. A Jew named Sabatay Zevy rose to great eminence owing to his learning and eloquence, but since no one can be a prophet in his own country, his brethren persecuted him and had him arrested by the Turkish authorities who sent him to Constantinople. The then reigning Sultan had heard of Sabatay as a prophet and questioned him on his power and capacity. Sabatay did his best to stand firm on his own ground; but when the Sultan informed him that the termination of his earthly existence had already been settled, and that he would be decapitated the next day, Sabatay

was nonplussed and fell at the feet of the Sultan
and declared himself a true believer of Islamism.
Thereupon he left Constantinople and worked his
way to Salonika, openly proclaimed himself as
a convert to Islamism, but privately represented
himself to his own community as a prophet and
reformer of Judaism. His success was wonderful,
especially among the Jewish women who followed
him and worshipped him, tearing their hair and
their clothes in frantic enthusiasm. Most of the
dogmas and religious ceremonies ordained by
Sabatay were based on the teaching of the Old
Testament, and were carefully carried out by the
community in secret whilst they openly frequented
the Moslem mosques. One night in the year was
set aside as a selection meeting, but small as their
community was, schisms arose and they divided
into three branches. No marriage out of their
order was ever allowed to take place. Children
were formally affianced at birth and these vows
were never broken. None of the womenkind ever
left Salonika, but the men were free to go where
they liked or their interests demanded. There
was, according to the written instructions left by
Sabatay on his death, a room always ready for his
ever-expected return, and one of the faithful
watched by the entrance gate of the town every
night to receive him. The women of the community were hysterical to the highest degree.
My doctor and some of his colleagues assured me
that when one of the women went off into a fit of
hysteria the whole street followed suit. As a race
these people were neither handsome nor sympathetic, but they were clever and open to all modern

ideas. They were charitable to each other to the extent of always supporting and setting right the economic position of any of their members who needed help. This sect had much influence with the Young Turkey Party, and it was due to one or more members of the Mamouni community who entered the Imperial Palace at Constantinople that the dethronement of Sultan Abdul Hamid was eventually brought about.

CHAPTER XX

I MADE one of my many journeys to Constantinople on board a Russian ship, and I was glad to do this since Russian vessels at that time rarely visited Salonika. The captain, a refined looking man, who spoke French perfectly, impressed me as being a good naval officer. The few first-class passengers appeared to be Orthodox devotees going to Mount Athos to expiate their sins, and to take the vow of celibacy on becoming monks in the huge Russian monastery. There was as well a considerable number of beggarly looking creatures, fine men, but unkempt and unwashed, closely grouped together on a lower deck, counting their beads, muttering prayers, and drinking tea out of a huge kettle that frequently made the round of the group when each man took a sip or two. I could not help watching these savage looking creatures at their meals. Each man carried a greasy bag which contained a coarse-looking bread and some small dried fish, and turned the contents of his bag on to the skirt of the long robe he wore, his lap serving as a plate, and ate ravenously of the simple fare which was washed down with more tea from the kettle. I must say it somewhat disgusted me to see such a fine, strong set of human beings living in such a manner, but evidently they formed a realistic picture of the Russian Moujik of that time.

We were to stop at the Holy Mountain, Mount Athos, that hill of monasteries of the Orthodox Church where no female creature of any kind, not even a hen, is ever allowed to land.

Mount Athos is the easternmost of three promontories which project from Thrace into the Ægean Sea, and it is here that Orthodox Monasticism continues to exist as in medieval times. The first monastery is believed to have been built by the Empress Helen, mother of Constantine the Great. In course of time Mount Athos became a famous resort for pilgrimages for all the nationalities professing the Orthodox creed. Of the twenty monasteries on Mount Athos seventeen belong to Greece and one each to Russia, Serbia, and Bulgaria. The moral and religious influence of the Holy Mountain continues to be very great over Greece and Russia. The wealthiest and finest monasteries belong to those two countries, especially to Greece. The Grecian monasteries made their submission to Mohammed II. before the conquest of Constantinople, and obtained from him a Firman which secured them many privileges. The Russian monastery up to a late date was richly subsidised by the Russian Government, and received as well, valuable gifts in money and in kind from distinguished Russians.

The rules followed in the monasteries were instituted by St Basil. The monks are divided into two main classes, one in which they live in community under an abbot and abstain from flesh

all the year round, the other in which asceticism is
less severe and the monks are directed by two or
more presidents.

All the monasteries possess some precious
relics. Some relate to the Nativity, others to the
death of our Saviour, others again relate to the
Virgin Mary. Some monasteries in addition have
relics of the apostles and saints, which are treasured
and venerated for the miracles they are said to
have performed. Besides these sacred treasures
many of the monasteries possess valuable gems,
gold and silver objects, as well as priceless old
manuscripts, books, and pictures, the collection
of many centuries. Nothing leaves the Holy
Mountain except the souls of the departed monks.
All their worldly goods go further to enrich the
monasteries.

The Russian monastery is said to give shelter
to many old soldiers who become monks, and who
are well furnished with arms in case of need.
Even the rocky grottos of the solitary monks
who live on the summit of the Holy Mountain are
ornamented with arms that helped to drive away
the Turks in former days. It is to be hoped that
no renewal of such attacks will be attempted by
the Turks and their associates the Huns at this
time, for, though Mount Athos could no doubt be
well defended by its soldier monks, yet the infernal
high explosives of modern warfare might greatly
damage this sacred old hill to which so many
Christians have dedicated their lives and property.

In spite of the fact that the Empress Helen
built and endowed the first retreat on Mount
Athos, yet the laws of St Basil decreed with a

quaint lack of humour that no female of any kind
be allowed on the Holy Mountain. St Basil's
ruling is, however, powerless over the ubiquitous
flea, and the monks and their attendants battle
with large family parties of these small but
determined invaders with beautifully carved long-
handled weapons (scratchers) with which they
chase or kill the greedy little pests.

As we neared the port of Mount Athos the
bells of the twenty monasteries began to ring in
honour of the new arrivals on board the ship.

The captain soon cleared out his devout
passengers, and as he turned round to say "Au
revoir" to me before he landed for a visit to the
Russian monastery, I said, "Excuse me, Captain,
but I intend to accompany you on shore."

He stared at me in amazed surprise and said,
"Impossible, Madame, impossible, cela ne peut se
faire. Ce que vous me demandez, Madame, est
contraire aux règlements de ces saints lieux qui
defendent à tout être de votre sexe humain ou
animal de pénétrer par égard au salut de l'âme des
moines."

I smiled, feeling sure that he did not believe a
word of what he told me and said, "Monsieur le
Capitaine, chaque règle peut avoir son exception.
Je suis certaine que cette exception sera faite en
votre faveur, vue l'importance que votre arrivée
vient de causer. Quant aux injures à ma personne
j'en prends la responsabilité."

He shrugged his shoulders, saying, "Soit,
Madame, je ne suis pas responsable pour la
reception que vous aurez."

I consequently followed his steps and came

face to face with a party of venerable monks who were horror-stricken on seeing a lady land. After they had saluted the captain the monks sharply turned back carrying him off. I stood for a few seconds uncertain whether to go back to the ship or to face the unpleasant ordeal of being turned into a pillar of salt, a superstition of what would happen to any woman who ventured on to Mount Athos, which was firmly believed by that ignorant community. I decided to risk the calamity, and followed the captain and his friends at a little distance up to their monastery. Before the party entered the gates one or two monks cast a scathing look at me and then disappeared. I wandered on, charmed with the beauty of the lovely site the selfish monks had appropriated to themselves. Some of the monasteries appeared to be hanging in mid-air since they were built on isolated blocks of rock, others were built on patches of fertile soil and peacefully reposed on Nature's bright green and flowery carpets, while fine old trees of every kind gracefully swayed their branches in the refreshing breeze. I felt deeply impressed by the stillness and the beauty of the surroundings as I walked upwards towards the part where the monks of solitary order lived in caves and sheltered nooks by themselves, and for themselves, in expiation of their past sins, and who from time to time peeped from under their cowls to contemplate a world they had vowed to give up with all its joys, sorrows, and vanities. A few jackdaws moped about chased by some wretched dogs equally condemned to celibacy. Absorbed by these sights which interested me much, I did not

notice that I had reached the gate of another
monastery, when I was startled by the sudden
appearance of a rather wild-looking monk who
stared at me, repeatedly crossed himself, and in
a menacing frantic voice of horror exclaimed in
Greek,—

"Ποία εἶσαι κόρη τοῦ Σατανᾶ; ἀπό ποῦ ἔρχεσαι καί τί
ζητῆς εἰς τό ἱερόν αὐτό μέρος; Καί αὐτή ἡ μήτηρ Εὔα δάν
θά ἐτόλμα νά παρουσιασῆ ἐδῶ. Φύγε ἀμέσως πειρασμέ διότι
διά τῆς παρουσίας σου ταράττεις τήν ἡσυχίαν τοῦ εἰρηνικοῦ
αὐτοῦ κοινοβίου τό ὁποίον περιεφρόνηοε τά ἀγαθά τοῦ κόσμου
ὅλα καί τάς ἁμαρτίας ποῦ τό φύλον σου παρασύρει τούς
ἀνθρώπους Φύγε ἀμέοως πρίν μέ ἀναγκάσης. νά σοῦ κατα-
ρασθῶ καί σέ μεταβάλω εἰς στήλην ἅλατος."

"Who are you, daughter of Satan, where do you
come from, and what do you want on this sacred
spot? Mother Eve herself would not have dared
to show her face here. Go away at once, you
temptress, disturbing as you do by your presence
this peaceful, holy community which has renounced
the world and all the sins your sex might lead it to
commit. Get away at once before you provoke
me to utter the curse that will surely turn you
into a pillar of salt."

"Thank you, father," said I, "for your un-
christian sentiments and your inhospitable wish
to turn me into a pillar of salt. Do not forget
in case your curse has its desired effect to taste a
bit of the salt, as salt is the savour of life."

"Φύγε ἁμαρτωλή κόρη τοῦ Σατανᾶ, φύγε."

"Go, go," said he again, "temptress, daughter
of Satan," and with this he covered his eyes with
his very dirty hands.

I hastened away really alarmed by his frantic speech. On my way down I met other monks who all crossed themselves and looked askance at me but made no ill-natured remarks. On the contrary, some of them who were returning from the ship where they had been with some small goods such as crosses, beads, and badges to sell to the passengers, stopped me and asked me to buy some of their things. I bought a few trifles, thinking to myself of the power money exercises over the world. I walked towards the port, and felt very pleased to meet my captain who was anxiously looking out for me and who said, "Ah, Dieu merci, je suis heureux de vous retrouver."

"Mais pas en bloc de sel," said I laughingly.

"Il a fallu être Anglaise pour avoir ainsi bravé le danger," answered he, adding, "Now, Madam, that your curiosity has been gratified and your presence representing the dreaded and forbidden sex has put this holy place topsy-turvy, the sooner we get on board and leave the better."

"Do you mean, Captain, that that mountain of cargo on deck has already been landed and housed in the cellars of your monastery?"

"Yes," said he, "it consists of foodstuffs for the abstemious occupants."

"Of course," added I, with a certain amount of malice, "it must have been very light if it consisted of dry fish such as I noticed some of your passengers ate."

He gave me a sharp look, and with no further interruption on the way beyond the presence of a few more monks who also wished me to buy some of their trifles, we got on board and proceeded to

Constantinople where the kind, pleasant captain dropped me and continued his journey across the Black Sea.

On the whole I considered this trip as the most interesting I had ever made. I felt gratified at having been one of the only two women who have ever landed on Mount Athos. Lady Stratford de Redcliffe with the help of her husband had visited Mount Athos in spite of protests and opposition from the monks. I had succeeded merely on the strength of my moral courage in imposing my wish on the good captain. The captain told me that this most powerful old resort of Orthodoxy in the Near East, which had played a great rôle after the conquest of the Byzantine Empire, continued to exercise up to the present time a powerful influence among all the races of the Orthodox faith. The importance of Mount Athos, though not political, has been most useful in the practical sense, as it has for ages kept open the doors of its monasteries as a harbour of refuge to great and small notabilities. Most of the Russian monks had formerly been soldiers, and the yearly cargo which reached Mount Athos and was consigned to the Russian monastery without passing the custom - house, did not consist of dried fish but of arms of all kinds.

In conversation with the captain, I heard a good deal of his country and its people before the liberation of the serfs. He described Russia as a limitless land rich in natural wealth of every kind. The people, ignorant and uncultured, were ruled by a small section of educated people who formed a highly despotic government. He thought that

when the people began to grow and develop
Russia would be split into many factions, and that
it would take a long time and need many sacrifices
before she would pull herself together and form a
nation in harmony with the other Great Powers.
I sometimes wonder if this long-sighted captain is
still alive to witness the chaotic state of his country
at the present time.

CHAPTER XXI

1897

THE Greco-Turkish War broke out in 1897 at the time that Greece was frantic over the desperate position of her Cretan brethren, and the European Powers hesitated to take any active action to prevent the massacres organised by Sultan Hamid's agents. The patriotic association in Greece, the "'Eθνική 'Eταιρεία" or National Committee, decided to send a body of troops to Crete and to declare war against Turkey, in spite of the fact that neither the King nor the nation at large approved of the step. In the meantime, the European forces which began to pour into Crete remained inactive, owing to the cunning Sultan's diplomatic double game, till the appalling massacres occurred, when many unfortunate Christian families, among whom the wife and child of Mr Kalokerinos, the British Agent, and other members of his family, were ruthlessly murdered. I do not intend to enter into the details of the Greco-Turkish War, and shall only state a few matters connected with Salonika and relate some of the rumours that reached us from the seat of war. Neither Greece nor Turkey was prepared for war, least of all the latter, whose forces were scattered all over the countries comprising the Sultan's Empire. When the town criers in Salonika called out the news that war had been declared between Turkey and Greece it took the people by surprise. The impression of unpreparedness of both countries was prevalent; but the news proved to be true, and shortly afterwards 50,000 Turkish troops landed at Salonika destined for Thessaly. It is only right, in justice to these troops, to state that there was not a single case of disorder or theft reported against them, in spite of the fact that all essentials as regards clothing, commissariat, and medical care were absent. I do not know the number of the Greek forces in Larissa under Prince Constantine that the Turks were to meet, but judging by the reports that reached Salonika the battle could not have been serious, since the Prince was reported to have left the camp at the approach of the enemy forces, a fact which made so bad an impression in Greece that the Prince found it necessary to leave the country for a considerable time.

Great dismay was caused among the Turkish authorities on hearing that the Greek Fleet was seen outside the Bay of Salonika. The Turkish Commander - in - chief, who called on us the following morning, assured us that he had not closed his eyes for three nights, since the entrance to the Bay was undefended and the Greek Fleet could have come in and taken possession of Salonika without firing a gun.

The dismay subsequent to the declaration of war was still greater among the Hellenic subjects

in Macedonia, then under the dominion of the
Turks, owing to the brutal conduct of the Turkish
authorities in driving the unfortunate people out
of their homes down to the seashore, where
they hoped, but vainly, to find ships to take them
to Greece. My husband as usual was the first
to take up the case of these destitute refugees and
went to the Governor, Riza Pasha, a kindly humane
man, who greatly helped to modify the situation
until boats could come from the Piræus to take
them away.

About half a dozen English war correspondents
turned up at Salonika with extraordinary rapidity.
They were Mr Bigham, son of Mr Justice Bigham
(now Lord Mersey), who represented the *Times*
and was a bright, clever youngster ; Mr Stevenson,
whose untimely death was, I believe, a great
loss to the literary world, owing to his many
gifts and his distinguished personality, as well as
Mr Gwynne and one or two more, who must
have made their mark, as they were all clever,
gifted men. The first to reach Salonika was Mr
Bigham at about 3 A.M. one morning. He drove
straight to the Consulate and insisted on seeing
my husband. The kavass said he did not think
his master would care to come down and see
a visitor at so unusual an hour. Mr Bigham
sent up a message to my husband, who replied,
" Ask the gentleman to come upstairs," forgetting
that I was in bed not far off. But the kavass
had already gone with the message, and I had
only time to jump out of my nice warm bed and
go behind a curtain, where I was kept for at least
twenty minutes, while Mr Bigham discussed with

S

my husband the necessity of his obtaining a permit
from the Governor in order to pass the frontier.
"Well," said my husband, amused at the persist-
ence of his visitor, "all I can do for you is to
give you a kavass to show you the way to the
Governor's house." "Thank you, sir," said
young Bigham, beaming with delight, "I think
I can manage the rest." And he did, for he got
the Governor out of his bed and obtained the
permit he wanted. The next time the Governor
met my husband he said, "What extraordinary
people the English must be, if all are as persistent
as the friend you sent me, who would not take
'No!' for an answer, but turned me out of
my bed and made me do as he wished." I got
to know Mr Bigham better when later on he
stayed with us on his return from the seat of war,
when I told him of the unpleasant twenty minutes
he had given me. He expressed his regrets, but
said that it had been worth a fortune to him as it
had enabled him to get several hours ahead of his
colleagues, so that he had had the privilege of
sending the earliest war news home. All the
English correspondents came in a body to see me
when they returned to Salonika. They were not
only unshaved but their beards were long and
they wore wonderful costumes of Greek capes, red
Turkish belts, and dust-covered clothes, so that
I hardly knew one from the other. They were
evidently well pleased with themselves, for they
jokingly asked me to go for a walk with them.
I flatly refused, saying I had no wish to exhibit
myself in the company of half a dozen outlandish
looking men, but I would gladly go if they made

themselves presentable. Most of this interesting · group of men remained about a week in Salonika, discussing the past, present, and future of Greece with surprisingly good knowledge and clear insight, especially with regard to Macedonia. They were greatly surprised that neither the Cretan troubles nor the Greco-Turkish War made the Macedonian Greeks give the slightest sign of desiring to take any part with their countrymen in fighting the Turks. Well acquainted as I was with the ideas and aspirations of the Macedonian Greeks, since I often discussed the subject with the patriotic set, I knew they had all agreed that a rising of the Macedonian Greeks would have been unwise and useless, likely to lead to great disaster, since the movement started in Greece had no serious foundation, but was the outcome of the Ἐθνική Ἑταιρεία, National Committee, which was composed of hot-headed men. At the same time rumours were afloat that Germany probably had a hand in the matter, in order to push forward her projected influence in Greece. The Greeks, far from being ready for war themselves, made no sign to their Macedonian brethren to come and help them, and these latter made no move all the time the Turkish army was present. Even the peasants in mixed villages (Turks and Greeks) went on peacefully working in the fields. The Turks, on the other hand, were pressing in from all directions to join the army on the march, though the army lacked the principal necessaries, which, however, were said to be following on from Constantinople in readiness for the great battle, which was, I believe, to be fought at Volo.

When the battle was fought there was little
damage to either side. These facts are gathered
from the Greek Archbishop at Salonika, whose
confidence I enjoyed as to what was going on
in Macedonia.

The Turks brought in about three score
prisoners with a certain display of satisfaction,
leading them through the main street of Salonika
on their way to be incarcerated in the White
Tower. I happened to be walking in that
direction when I noticed the procession of
prisoners followed by a rabble of Jews, jubilant
and noisy, and making insulting remarks regarding
the prisoners, At that very moment the coupé of
the Governor, who was a very little man, drove
up, and as he came face to face with the prisoners
and the crowd he got out of his carriage, spat
once or twice into the palms of his hands, took
a firm hold of the heavy stick he was carrying, and
suddenly appeared to be transformed into a giant
as he struck out right and left with force and
precision on the backs of the Jews. Howls and
screams ensued, and "A Dio Signor del Monde!"
was called out by one and all. The cries could
be heard at the end of the street, but did
not last long, as the crowd quickly dispersed
and disappeared.

Later on, in 1912, the taking of Salonika by
the Greeks entirely altered the situation. Prince
Constantine in the subsequent war entirely
redeemed his military reputation and became a
great favourite in Greece, until on succeeding his
worthy father, King George, he allowed himself to
fall under the damaging influence of Germany,

when he ruined his own cause as well as that of Greece.

The war came to an end through England's political pressure and her practical assistance. England lent Greece four millions at two per cent., in order that she might settle the claims of Turkey. The war was inglorious except for Koutsflena, a Greek village of a thousand inhabitants, which happened to be planted on the old Turco-Greek frontier and remained under Turkish dominion. The inhabitants of this village, all Greeks, wisely razed their village to the ground and burnt every vestige of it and rebuilt it in Greek territory.

The Near East question is so far-reaching, important, and dangerous that unless carefully revised and placed on a sound basis within a short time trouble will break out once more. May God help the people directly concerned.

Neither friends nor adversaries can put any confidence in Bulgarian promises or written conventions, for, if convenient to themselves, they will consider them worthless and of no consequence. The Bulgarians, such as I knew them, were a hard-working people, grasping and greedy for extension of territory. They understand the advantage to be derived from large homesteads, and whilst other races have to dower their young daughters when giving them in marriage, the Bulgarian father keeps his daughters at home as long as possible to cultivate the soil, and when he has to part with them it is the affianced husband who gives a dower to his future father-in-law before he can claim his bride. The Bulgarian will be found to be a tough element to deal with unless all his teeth are drawn.

Justice and generosity do not appeal to him. He neither practises them nor understands them. The Turks, who formerly lorded it over them, ordered that their heads should be shaved, except for one long tuft of hair, which must appear through a hole in the top of their sheepskin caps. This tuft of hair was used by the Turks as a handle to shake them into obedience. I much fear the indulgence of the Entente towards them will make matters very difficult to bring into line, and the sooner the Dedeagatch railway is taken out of their power the better.

The well-known inconsequent ways and dealings of the Turks, added to their late tuitions under their masters, the Huns, are sure further to complicate matters. I am sure that half measures with Turks and Bulgarians will be found in the long run to be as bad as no measures at all.

But to return to Macedonia and the problem as regards the future. I learn on good authority that the whole country is clamouring to be placed under the suzerainty of Great Britain. The English, the Macedonians declare, are the only good, generous, humane people. "The French and Italians may be good and great in their way," say they, "but they look on us as unfortunate, debased people, whilst the English respect us and show us their sympathy. Nor is there need to mention the way in which they treat our women-kind. With us our maidens are kind, pleasant, and moral in their behaviour, and therefore the saying has arisen that to be gentle and well-behaved is to be like a girl. . So strongly has the good behaviour of the English soldiers impressed

itself on us that when they are ˜seen marching
through the country it is no uncommon thing for
the peasants to leave their work in the fields while
they watch the soldiers, and to hear them call out,
since it is the highest praise they can give the
soldiers, 'The girls are passing! The girls are
passing!' When French and Italian troops are
passing no such praise is forthcoming; on the
contrary, the girls and women run away and hide
themselves."

This sentiment is so general in Macedonia that
Mr Repoulis, the Vice-President of Greece,
mentioned it in a speech in the Chamber.

Macedonia is a wealthy country, and great, I
believe, will be the future of its capital, Salonika,
if, helped by fortune, it falls under the administration of a good and wise government. The Greeks,
Turks, Jews, and Europeans of all nationalities
would then be free to develop, unhindered by
political intrigues or national upheavals.

I wish the dear old country all success and
prosperity.

CHAPTER XXII

1898

IT was after the short Greco-Turkish War and the rumours of a rising in Macedonia, and soon after the massacres in Crete in 1898, that Jeanne and I went to Kandia to spend a few weeks with my son, who was A.D.C. to Colonel Sir Herbert Chermside, the British Commissioner.

About the time of the rising the British Government, in spite of warnings, had thought fit to reduce the garrison of the Province of Kandia, the part allotted to British jurisdiction, to half a battalion under the command of Lt.-Colonel Reid of the Highland Light Infantry (71st Foot). Sir Herbert Chermside was temporarily absent when the Moslem population of Kandia massacred 700 men, women, and children of the Christian population, among whom were about 45 men of the Highland Light Infantry. A certain number of women and children in the town were saved by the bravery of Padre Antonino of the Capuchin Order, who collected them in his monastery. When the Moslems had done their worst in the town they attacked the monastery. Padre Antonino opened the gates and stood in the gateway with his arms widely stretched and called

out in a loud voice, "Come on, my friends, I am
ready for you, but before a single bullet reaches
those behind me it must first pass through my
heart." The rabble, strange to say, melted away
like magic, and the monastery was not further
attacked. When I heard of the bravery of this
heroic priest I called on him to express my esteem
and admiration of his conduct. He smiled, saying,
" It was no merit of mine, but an inspiration from
above, which helped me to save a number of
fellow creatures from death and worse."

Two young officers greatly contributed to put
a rapid stop to the carnage by giving notice, at
the risk of their lives, to our men-of-war in the
Bay. The Turkish fortress and quarter were at
once bombarded by the guns of the men-of-war
and the massacres ceased. These terrible doings
in Crete roused the whole of Europe, and troops
of all nationalities poured into the island and
men-of-war arrived, and finally this lovely old
island of Grecian fame was freed from the cursed
dominion of Turkey, and placed under Prince
George of Greece, who was nominated as High
Commissioner. St Paul states that a prophet of
the Cretans described them as "always liars, evil
beasts," and this can be readily understood. A
Christian population, under the dominion of the
Turks, has an extremely hard time, and practises
all sorts of subterfuges in order that it may be let
alone. The Turks, on the other hand, are roused
to fury against the Christians, who are hard-
working people, and murder and massacre their
Christian subjects in all parts of the Empire, as
soon as a favourable opportunity arises.

It is this cruel treatment by the Turks that
induces a certain number of Christians to take
refuge in Islamism, and it is an interesting fact
that these perverts become extremely fanatical
and are the greatest enemies of the Christians.
The best thing that could happen for the unfortunate Christian population of Crete was their
severance from the galling and degrading Turkish
yoke. The number of lives lost in the Kandia
massacre was largely, if not wholly, due to the
confidence England had placed in Sultan Hamid's
false promises of reforms to the Christian population, promises which he never intended to fulfil.
The effect of the European Gendarmerie Corps,
which was to do great things in keeping the people
in order, was accepted enthusiastically by Sultan
Hamid, since he was confident of the fiasco such a
body would prove to be, as it had no power to
arrest or condemn the Turkish officials at fault, as
they were completely protected by the secret
forces of the Sultan. The Cour Judiciare appointed
under the Presidency of Mr Alvarez, one of our
able consuls, and another European President had
no better success, and caused endless jealousies
and wranglings. The expulsion of the Turks from
the island was certainly no small success. On
this point I heard of the able and highly distinguished rôle that Captain Custance played by
shipping four thousand refugees to the island of
Milo with every comfort and security. The
expulsion of the Turkish forces is also worthy of
mention. The troops were made, much against
their wish, to embark on the ships that were to
take them to Turkey. My son, owing to his

knowledge of Turkish, was sent on board shortly
before the vessel sailed to claim the key of the
fortress, which the commander was carrying away.
My son told me that there was one moment when
he thought there was but little chance of his
getting out alive from the enraged crowd of
soldiers burning with indignation at the humiliation of their expulsion.   However, he succeeded
in obtaining the key, and on landing at once went
to the fortress and lowered the Turkish flag.   The
expulsion of the Turkish forces had been delayed
till after the arrest, condemnation and hanging
of the criminals who had murdered the British
soldiers.   In spite· of the fact that 5000 inter·
national troops were in Kandia, the chief insti-
gators of the massacre, the Sultan's representative
and the chief of the police, managed to escape.

When Jeanne and I arrived at Kandia all the
trouble was over.   The diplomatic and political
questions were settled.   Colonel Sir Herbert
Chermside, who had been High Commissioner for
some time, was a great favourite, especially among
the Cretan hanoums.   After the punishment of
the culprits the Moslem fanatical element hurried
away as fast as it could find boats to take it.

The Gendarmerie Corps, composed of a variety
of nationalities, was quartered close to the little
house I had taken.   It was an unkempt, unshaved,
poor-looking lot of men, not in any way to be
compared to our fine, trim military police, who
were imposing in appearance and correct in their
behaviour.   Many of the Christian families who
had left the island immediately after the massacre
had not yet returned, but a good many liberal-

minded Moslem families were still there, waiting to
learn the fate of their beloved island, and inspired
by the hope that it might be placed under the
suzerainty of Great Britain.   I was asked by Sir
Herbert Chermside to attend a meeting of Moslem
ladies to learn their sentiments and opinions.   I
willingly consented to do this.   On my entering
the room, crowded with ladies, they all rose and
received me most kindly and with one voice
asked me, "How is our dear friend, Sir Herbert
Chermousaki (Chermside)?   When is he going to
write to Victoria, the great Queen of England, to
ask her to take us under her protection and
appoint him our Governor?   We love the English
as they are not like any other nation.   We have
samples of all the nations in the Gendarmerie
Corps, and we cordially detest them all and their
impudent manners towards us, except the English,
who, be they officers or men, are respectful to us."

I hastened to communicate these flattering
sentiments to Sir Herbert, who was naturally
pleased to hear of them.   I felt pretty certain that
the message these ladies entrusted to his care to
be conveyed to Her Majesty Queen Victoria
would not bring about the result they desired.

The weather towards the end of February was
most delightful.   In spite of the recent ravages
and the destruction of olive groves, orange gardens,
and vineyards, the fertile country left to the free
caprice of Nature lost no time in adorning itself
with millions of anemone blossoms of every hue
and with a great variety of other plants and ferns,
which delighted Sir Herbert Chermside, who was
a true lover and student of Nature.   The country

was perfectly safe, in spite of the fact that our forces were being withdrawn. My son and his bright young fellow officers became very much at home in the little house I had secured for Jeanne and myself. We had a fat old Cretan cook, who proved to be far more eloquent in pleading the wrongs of her country than capable of the practice of her profession. At times hosts and guests had to remove her out of the way while they tried their 'prentice hands at cooking. Provisions were good and plentiful, though rather dear, but this always occurs where English gold makes its appearance. Yaghourt (soured milk), kaimac, a very rich cream, and all native products were greatly appreciated, as well as the excellent fruit. The weekly market held on the Piazza was both interesting and profitable, as the peasants, chiefly women, used to come down with their loads of edibles, as well as with home-made rugs, woven cloths, and a kind of serge of excellent quality. The people looked vigorous and healthy and had a type of their own, a sure sign that the Cretan race had remained pure in spite of its having passed through times of great national misfortunes, when it had lost its old prosperity and glory and become degraded and broken by the Ottoman conquests. No human race that in its prosperous ages has risen and distinguished itself by reason of virtues and merits ever loses entire caste, and its people, even when bottled up for centuries on an island, will be found still fresh and vigorous. This can be well said of the brave Cretans who had suffered much and suffered long in their captivity, but who have produced a M. Venizelos, a generous and gifted leader, and the able re-creator of modern Greece. In speaking of the hoped-for future prosperity of Crete, joined now to the mother country Greece, I must not forget to speak of its beautiful archæological treasures. Crete, like Troy, had for centuries had relics buried in the depths of her soft oily soil. During the Turkish domination occasional finds had been known to have been made, but unlike Troy she had had no Dr Schliemann to unearth pottery and marble and to bring them together and show examples of her past art. All I saw in the museum at Kandia was a collection of articles of no special value cast about pell-mell on the dusty ground. Doubtless there were treasures to be found among them, and it is to be hoped they were given their proper place by Sir Arthur Evans, a great student of Grecian antiquities, who was an old friend of mine, and who reached Kandia just as I had gone on board ship to return to Salonika. I left Crete rather hurriedly as I had received a telegram from my husband telling me he had been appointed Consul-General at Boston. I learned later that Sir Arthur Evans' explorations in Crete had been most successful.

Before leaving Crete I paid a visit to Canea. It appeared to have preserved a good deal of its ancient remains about the port and old bastions. I stopped a few days under the hospitable roof of the Consul-General and his wife, Sir Alfred and Lady Biliotti. Sir Alfred's intelligent and useful services during the rebellion were much appreciated by our Government. In spite of being as deaf as a post it was astonishing how he managed to carry out successfully his arduous diplomatic relations with his numerous colleagues, who were in anything but cordial relations with one another. I had a pleasant time here, and even assisted at the marriage of one of Lady Biliotti's granddaughters, a thin, delicate looking child of sixteen, to a gigantic Montenegrin, who was a Captain in the Gendarmerie Corps. I felt sorry for the child when I thought of the hard work that awaited her in her new home, where the kneading of bread and the drawing of water from the public fountains would fall to her share. Years ago I remember a Slav doctor with the Turkish army told me that he had heard on the best authority that the valiant King of Montenegro washed his own socks at night in order to have them dry and ready to put on in the morning. Stories of much the same practical kind are told of the sweet Queen of Italy, and her knowledge of home industries is said at times to astonish the Italian *haut monde*. I consider it a great privilege to understand household work and to practise it occasionally, for one never knows what destiny has in store for one. Luckily the modern girl, owing to the many and varied works she has been called upon to do in consequence of this long and trying war will have something to thank it for in making her familiar with many phases of household and other work.

CHAPTER XXIII

1898

On arrival at Salonika on my return from Crete I found my husband buried beneath a mound of letters and newspaper cuttings he had collected during nearly fifty years' official life, and which fortunately he had been able to save at the time the Consulate was burned down. As he was a great newspaper reader and a most orderly person in the management of his private and official correspondence, he had dated and numbered each letter or cutting, had noted his own reflections on the latter and arranged them in indexed volumes, so that when writing on any subject concerning Turkey he could at once refer to his notes. The volumes of these cuttings filled many boxes, and before my husband left for Boston he entrusted them to my care to have them sent to whatever place we should choose for our permanent home. I had them all brought to Malta, thanks to some of our kind friends in the Navy. I sometimes peep at this accumulation of interesting papers, and regret that up to the present time I have not been able to make use of them.

My husband's appointment to Boston as British Consul, while retaining his title of Consul-General, had been a surprise to me and to many others interested in his work in the Near East. One or two papers criticised his transference to the New World as an error since it took away one of the oldest and best informed British Agents in Turkey. Be this as it may, my husband was a *persona grata* with the Americans, and was well known in their Government Department as having rendered good service to American subjects, many of whom were missionaries in Upper Macedonia and Bulgaria and in places where America had no representative. My husband had received the thanks of the President of the United States on three occasions, and after the lamentable murder of Mr Merion, one of the missionaries at Philippopolis, he was offered the post of American Consul in Macedonia. This position, however, he was unable to accept in addition to his work as British Consul.

Sir John's appointment to Boston was to fill up his final term of three or four years in the Service. Its object was a gracious attention on the part of Lord Salisbury to modify as far as he could the small salary my husband had had as Consul-General at Salonika, since an additional two hundred pounds per annum was given in the pension to the holder of the Boston post. Unfortunately my husband only enjoyed this addition to his pension long enough to pay off the debts he had incurred at Salonika in consequence of his determination to represent Her Majesty Queen Victoria's Government adequately.

Some of our men-of-war were still at Salonika, but busy as we both were pulling down, packing

T

up, and setting apart for sale such of our furniture as we could not take away, we neither of us missed any opportunity of seeing our naval friends, among whom were Admiral Troubridge and his officers. We had a farewell lunch with them, and drank the last bottles of champagne from the cellar to wish God-speed to my dear husband, who, alas! left next morning for Boston.

After lunch we went on to the verandah and were photographed in a group.

It was on his departure that I realised how popular my husband had made himself in Salonika. Half the town was at the station to bid him farewell, and he felt much .affected on leaving the country in which he had spent a life-time, and in which he had made so many good friends. But such is life. Who can control the turns of the wheel of fortune?

After my husband had gone, Jeanne and I had hard work to settle everything and to hand over the dear old Consulate to an ungracious Austrian Consul, and his still more ungracious Slav wife, who insisted on taking possession of the house within two days of my husband's departure, and who refused my request that I might leave one or two of my boxes in the basement till I could find some other place to house them in. The fatigue and worry of those two days were so great that for the first time I felt really exhausted, and realised that the years which had slipped by so quickly in the enjoyment of peace and comfort in my home had left their mark upon me.

I went to stay for a few days' rest with some friends before I started for Constantinople on a

visit to my dear brothér, Sir Alfred Sandison.   I
was very glad in after years that I had made this
journey to Constantinople, as it was the last time
I saw my brother, my sister, Mrs Longworth, and
my good kind cousin Edward, the three dearest
relatives I had, who all passed away in the course
of the next few years. These losses weighed
heavily on me in after life. Some people are
happy enough to be able to live on their remem-
brances of the past. I never could bring myself
to do so, as, when these are pleasant, I cannot but
regret them, and when the reverse they cause me
sorrow.

During this visit to Constantinople I found the
place changed for the worse. It was after the
massacre of the poor Armenian community, and
wherever I went I found that sad, cruel affair the
chief topic of conversation. The doors of innocent,
harmless families had been marked during the
night, so that their houses might be recognised in
order to separate them from other European and
Christian communities. The horror of the scenes
baffle description. Men, women, and children
were cut up, wherever they could be found, or
drowned or caused to disappear, never to be seen
or heard of again. The worst of it was that these
people do not seem to have given the least
provocation, nor had they the least knowledge
of what was awaiting them.

I heard much talk, during this visit, of the
Germans and the influence they had begun to
exercise over Turkish affairs. The Turkish Army
was under German control and largely officered by
Germans, and the Germans and their wives were

busy in their efforts to ingratiate themselves with
Turkish families, in order to create an easy
entrance into the commercial world. A number
of German shops had sprung into existence filled
with German goods at such low prices that everybody rushed to secure what they could. I
remember buying for a shilling a good knife,
which I still possess. I am sure a similar pocket-
knife could not have been bought for less than
six or seven shillings in London. Beer-shops
increased vastly in number both in Pera and
Stamboul. I was passing one of these beer-shops
one day when a German, accompanied by a native,
came to a standstill. The native indicated the
beer-shop ; the German stamped his foot and said,
"Die kirche, die kirche, ich würde an die kirche
gehen." The man turned to me and asked me
if I could tell him what the German wanted.
When I told him he said, "How could I guess he
wanted a church, when all the Germans I see ask
me the way to the beer-house."

I do not think that the Germans were ever
popular at Constantinople, nor was the Kaiser's
visit with the Empress and his staff much appreciated, owing to the large amount of money it
cost the Treasury. The Sultan, Abdul Hamid,
had made it a point that all the expenses of the
Kaiser's journey to Jerusalem were to be defrayed
by the Turkish Government. I happened to be
at Constantinople at the time, and felt amused
after the Kaiser's departure to hear the reflections
made in Turkish circles on the meagre return His
Majesty made to the Sultan for the very valuable
and beautiful gems and other precious things

he and the Kaiserin had received. The Kaiser presented to his Imperial host a stick which had belonged to his great-grandfather. Was this to show that he intended the Turks to obey him? On his return to Berlin the Kaiser was more generous in his gift to the Governor of Jerusalem and sent a life-size portrait of himself in rich robes and decorations, to be hung in Government House. No sooner did the picture reach Jerusalem than the German Consul came to announce officially the arrival of his master's promised gift, and to desire that it should be hung in accordance with the Kaiser's order next to that of his beloved friend, the Sultan. The poor Governor could not but draw a comparison between the magnificent portrait of the Kaiser and the twopenny halfpenny oleograph of the Sultan which hung on the wall, and whilst profusely thanking the Consul for the gift, he said he felt it was beyond his power to place the Kaiser's portrait next to that of the Sultan.

"Well," said the Consul, "I want to see it placed according to the instructions I have received, next to that of H.M. the Sultan."

The Governor, who felt he must temporise, said, "Of course, Effendin, of course, but before hanging the portrait I must have some repairs done to the room." The Consul, feeling it would not be tactful to show any opposition to this suggestion, withdrew, but begged that the Governor would lose no time in getting the repairs done.

As soon as the Consul had taken his departure the poor Governor rubbed his hands in despair,

called his Council to his aid and explained the
situation to them.

"If this grand portrait of the Kaiser is hung
beside the miserable portrait of the Sultan, everyone in the country will consider that the Kaiser
and not the Sultan is the master of Jerusalem."
The Council, embarrassed, decided to telegraph to
the Porte for instructions. The answer came
back "Temporise," not reckoning on the German
Consul's insistence to see the portrait hung at once.
After a warning or two the Consul threatened that
if the portrait was not put in the place indicated
within twenty-four hours he would report the
Governor, when he would have to suffer the
consequences. A fresh despatch of telegrams to
the Porte ensued, when the Sultan, though
annoyed, had to submit and gave the necessary
order.

I wonder if our glorious Army found the
portrait still there when they entered Jerusalem,
and if so if they turned its face to the wall in the
same way that Abd-el-Kader at Brussa turned the
portrait of Napoleon III. to the wall after the
French escort left him. Anyhow, the best use
that our brave soldiers could make of the portrait
would be to use it for a target to practise upon.

I did not enjoy this visit to Constantinople at
all. There was a dulness about the place and a
disquieting agitation among the diplomatic corps
of no good omen. Even at my dear brother's
place there were comings and goings of worried
looking people who came to talk over matters
with him. I felt I should be more comfortable
and more at my ease in Salonika and returned

there to spend a few weeks at Sedes, a charming watering-place a few miles from Salonika, where my husband and I had frequently stayed, as we greatly enjoyed the walks in the country towards the Hortiach mountain, from the summit of which we had frequently watched the beautiful effects of the setting sun. I do not know whether the waters at the Sedes baths had ever been correctly analysed, but they contained sulphur, iron, and alkalis, and were most efficacious in some cases. I had seen people doubled up with rheumatism arrive at the baths, and after a few days become so much better that they were able to walk easily. My own experience was that a few weeks' stay at Sedes now and again kept me free from the horrid articular rheumatism to which I have now become a victim, and which only allows me to take a few steps outside without support. How I wish I could return to Sedes for a course of baths! In my time there was no proper accommodation, only a wretched han and three or four miserable cottages. The baths were of Roman construction, patched up here and there with wood where they had given way. Sedes itself is placed on a fertile plateau and is a healthy, breezy place, close to the foot of the Hortiach mountain, and not far from the marshes, much appréciated by sportsmen for the snipe and wild fowl of all kinds to be found there. I hope the waters at Sedes are being made use of by the wounded as well as by the rheumatic patients of our Army.

During the year I spent in Salonika after my husband had left for Boston, I felt much *en l'air* and spent six months with my good friends, Mr and

Mrs Charles Allatini, who had a beautiful house in the country, which was always hospitably open to the many friends they had in the Navy. Later on, when the Allatinis made their home in England their house was bought by the Young Turkey Party, who used it as a prison for Sultan Abdul Hamid and part of his harem. Sultan Hamid remained there until a few years later, when he was removed to one of the small islands near Constantinople, from whence I hear he has just passed into the next world to enter, I suppose, the Gates of Gehennem, as the Turks say, to expiate all the crimes he committed here. It is due to the evil genius of Sultan Hamid that Turkey has been brought to the verge of ruin, yet, in spite of all his double dealings, he managed, as he justly boasted, to keep the country together, leaving to the Young Turkey Party the work of its dismemberment and the delusion of rebuilding Turkey as a purely Osmanli power and of making it the conqueror of the world.

Salonika I hear is much changed since I left it nineteen years ago, and it is thought that in time it may become a prosperous important town. I also hear that it is the hope and ambition of the Greek population to see Salonika, and in fact the whole of Macedonia, pass under British protection. This hope and ambition appear to take root wherever our glorious Navy and Army set foot, but this is in no way surprising, for the people say : "Wherever the English go, instead of taking from us, as the other nations do whatever they can, they mend, build, and help in every possible way." I believe there is much wealth to be found in minerals of every kind around Salonika. An English engineer, who inspected the country in search of coal some years ago, stated in his report that a huge bed of lignite extended from the town of Salonika to some distance into the country. Agriculture could yield much better returns than it does if there were better irrigation. I had a maid from a Greek village not far from Salonika whose father, a very respectable peasant, came one day and asked to see me.

"Kyria" (Madame), said he, "I come to ask you to purchase a very fine chrome mine for thirty liras." This reminded me of my silkworm experience at Adrianople in my younger days, but as I knew my husband would object to my embarking on any speculation of the kind I refused with thanks. Later on, I was told that Sultan Hamid's Comptroller of the Civil List had bought the chrome mine and within a short time realised £10,000 out of it. Such unbelievable cases occurred frequently in Turkey owing to the incapacity of the Turks to form companies, and also because there was much difficulty in getting the necessary concessions from the Sultan. In those days Yildiz, the Imperial Palace, was a nest of shameless corruption, where one favourite tried to nullify the promises made to another to obtain the Sultan's signature. It cost the applicant a fortune to settle the claims of the various people who promised to obtain the Sultan's wished-for signature, the Sultan himself, it was more than suspected, having a share in the spoils.

CHAPTER XXIV

1899

THE prospect of travelling to Boston alone was not cheering. I had been constantly surrounded by many friends for twenty-five years in the interesting old country of Macedonia, the home of the Grecian gods and goddesses, who, in spirit, had reigned supreme over its fertile valleys beneath the shelter of the snow-covered Mount Olympus and its sister Mount Pindus, where mortals, when Greece was at the zenith of her art, had built temples and had adorned them with exquisite taste for the benefit of devout worshippers. The Roman and Byzantine Powers had also left treasures of art, some of which fortunately had not been entirely devastated by the Ottoman conquest. In course of time other forces had aided in making the history of Macedonia and in Salonika, its old capital, changes had been made and continue to be made, which I trust are of good omen. Foreseeing more or less of what was coming I felt very sorry to leave Salonika after the good times I had enjoyed there with the coming and going of our Squadrons, and the never-to-be-forgotten six months during which our ships had remained in the Bay. The amount of

British gold spent in the markets during that six months was said to be about £1000 a day. Sultan Hamid, who never had enough money, on hearing of this, ordered the Governor of Salonika to send £10,000 a month to Yildiz, the Imperial Palace. On receipt of this order the Defterdar, or treasurer of the Vilayet, resigned, since at the same time the Sultan told him to send all the quarterly revenue. The poor Governor tore his hair in despair as to how he could squeeze out the amount for the salaries of the officials of the Vilayet and the other local expenses.

We all had such good times in those dear old days, full of harmless fun and amusing, practical jokes, engineered by the sporting young officers, " my extraordinary nephews." I remember a grand picnic organised by Lieutenant S. at the Horticultural Gardens at Sedes. Everyone was happy and in high spirits. After luncheon S., delighted with the success of the party, came up to me and whispered, " Aunt Fanny, I intend to take the prettiest ladies for a walk one by one and to kiss them all." " Nonsense," I said, " you risk a box on the ears from some and a cartel from a jealous husband or two asking you to fight a duel."

" Wait and see," answered he, and disappeared into the garden with the prettiest girl. He came back after a time looking well pleased with himself, and went on with this amusing game to the end, and then came to report " That it was all right, as he had not received any blows, nor did he expect to be called out."

It was my duty to punish him for his

impudence, but I never could put on a serious face with him, he was so full of fun and good nature.

Most of the youngsters on the ships were daily in and out of the Consulate, playing pranks whenever they got a chance. If at tea-time one or two of their superior officers were to be seen reflected in a mirror coming through the drawing-room door whilst they had their backs to it, they made dreadful grimaces and tried to upset the dignified look they assured me I assumed. On one occasion half a dozen of these boys came in to be dressed up for a charade. It happened that we were expecting Lord Charles Beresford to stay a night or two with us on his return from home. My husband, who greatly loved a joke, noticed in the group a young middy, dressed up as a housemaid.

" Come along, future admiral," said he, according to his usual habit in addressing a middy, " I shall need your services presently to take Lord Charles up to his room and to unpack for him."

Before the boy had time to answer Lord Charles was announced, and my husband turned to meet him, and after talking for a little while pointed out to him, on his way to his room, the soi-disant maid, who was to attend to his needs. Lord Charles was much too hot and tired to pay any attention to the maid, who unpacked deftly for him and laid his clothes out in approved fashion. At supper, when he came in after the charade was over, he noticed, much to his amusement, the pretty housemaid, apparently quite at her ease, chatting to those around her. He quickly realised the joke that had been played on him, and burst out laughing as he shook his finger at my husband as the instigator of the joke. Lord Charles was renowned for having been a regular pickle in his young days, and most good-naturedly did not mind the tables being turned upon him.

Another time I asked Lieutenant S. to take the place of the missing fourteenth at a dinner I was giving to some admirals and captains. He demurred at first, but yielded to my request. My maid, Elvira, a nervous creature, helped to wait that night. After she had served "my extraordinary nephew" I noticed that she stood as far away as possible from the other guests and held the dish she was offering at arm's length. This attracted my attention, and when she served me I taxed her with her awkward waiting. Forgetting herself, she justified her action in a voice loud enough to be heard by my guests, "Madame, Monsieur S. m'a pincé les jambes."

When after dinner I asked S. what he meant by his atrocious behaviour, he said, "Aunt Fanny they *are* such sticks."

Of course the story went the round of the Squadron and amused everybody.

But I must not forget the good Turkish saying, "Vakit yoldjouya yol" (Do not linger on the road), and must bring my recollections of Salonika to an end and bid farewell to the dear old place.

I began my journey for the New World via Uskub on the Dedeagatch railway line, which

passes through Bulgaria. On reaching Uskub
I was reminded of my youthful days in that God-
forsaken country, and I wondered how I had
stood it. Uskub, still under the Turkish
dominion, looked even worse than formerly in
spite of the railway from Constantinople to
Vienna, via Belgrade, the capital of Serbia.
There was only one wretched hotel in Uskub,
kept by a beggarly blonde German, who, a couple
of years previously, had married the blacker of my
two blackies. A year later the poor thing returned
to her old home to die.

My reflections were anything but joyful as
I wandered in the parts where the best years of
my youth had been spent, and to which the
evolution of time had not brought any improvement. Even the railway carriage, dirty, dusty,
and uncomfortable, seemed in harmony with the
country. On crossing the frontier into Bulgaria
I rejoiced to notice the changes and improvements
that had taken place, and the air of prosperity that
prevailed. In Sofia, the capital, fine houses,
good shops, and public gardens had sprung into
being like magic.

"Decidedly," I said to myself, "old Bulgaria
has awoke."

A great step had been made in creating a
House of Parliament in a population essentially
agrarian, of few words and less eloquence. I
thought I might still find the members of
Parliament in their sheep-skin caps and coats,
but instead, I found that Vienna had furnished
the honourable members with plenty of black
cloth and many pairs of white kid gloves, the use

of which was taught by the few Bulgarians who had travelled in foreign countries, or by the civilised young men from Robert College. The proper use of gloves and handkerchiefs was, however, still a matter of some difficulty to a few, who did not quite know whether they had to put on their gloves before they blew their noses, or whether the pocket-handkerchief was a cover in which to wrap up the gloves. Indulgence must, of course, be shown to all beginners. No doubt the admirers of the Bulgarians in England see these external signs of civilisation, and do not give sufficient attention to the inherent characteristics of the Bulgarian nation. These characteristics call for the greatest care of the Entente in the settlement of the Balkan States. On arrival at Sofia M. Stambouloff honoured me with a visit. M. Stambouloff was the Venizelos of his country, whose ambition, so he told me, was that the Bulgarian Army should reach Constantinople. On noticing my questioning looks he banged his fist on the table, saying, "Et quand même Madame nous le ferons."

The untimely death, or rather murder, of this great patriot and, I believe, honest man, deprived Bulgaria of a great leader at a critical time in her history.

I must give a bit of unwritten Bulgarian history, which strangely enough passed through my hands. During one of my visits to Constantinople, when Bulgaria had begun seriously and justly to clamour for reforms, a deputation of Bulgarians walked in to solicit my help in asking the English Ambassador to receive into the

Embassy one of the clever students from Robert College. M. Tchomakoff, the spokesman of the deputation, which by the way was chiefly composed of old Philippopolis friends, said, "We want one of our students to have free entrée into the Embassy, so that he may have the opportunity of giving proof of the miserable condition the Bulgarians find themselves placed in at the present time. We do not mind how humble a position our representative has, he might even be a shoe-black, so long as he is there to give a truthful account of Bulgaria's needs and aspirations."

I could not refuse to render to my old friends what I considered a simple service. They cordially thanked me, and said they would return in twenty-four hours for the reply.

I passed on the request to my brother, who was Oriental Secretary and First Dragoman, asking him to report it to His Excellency the Ambassador. My brother did not look at all encouraging, but said, "Come and see me later on."

His answer, however, was, "Impossible, it cannot be done." .

"Nonsense," said I impulsively, "What harm can there be in the Government being informed of the condition of Bulgaria."

My brother smiled, saying, "Who tells you, silly little advocate of the Bulgarian cause, that the British Government wants to know at this moment what is going on in Bulgaria?"

Next morning the deputation returned for the reply. I softened it down as much as I could by expressing the regrets of the Ambassador on the inability of his Government to take up the

Bulgarian question, since it was busy with other important State affairs.

"Is that so," said my disappointed friends. "We neither like nor trust Russia, but *faute de mieux*, we go from here to the Russian Embassy to settle matters with Russia."

Shortly afterwards Russia declared war against Turkey. The Bulgarian troubles were just the excuse Russia wanted. The Bulgarian patriots neither loved nor trusted Russia, and were very much in dread of her influence over the country. The patriots were a set of honest men, justly anxious to clear the nation from the degrading power of Turkey, whose sole aim was to depress the unfortunate people in every way, and to hinder their advance towards progress and civilisation.

I was especially interested in Serbia and her pretty picturesque capital, Belgrade, situated on the banks of the Danube, which alone separates Serbia from Austro-Hungary. Belgrade struck me as being greatly improved. The town, bright and peaceful, gave no sign of the coming storm and tragic end, in after years, of its young King and Queen, murdered to gratify party vengeance. By the extinction of the Obrenovitch family dangers of this kind were thought to have been removed for good, but alas! luckless Serbia never expected to have in the twentieth century the deplorable set-back she has had at the hands of her cruel enemies, who are determined, if possible, to totally destroy her. There is hope that this will not be realised, since England and her Allies are deeply interested in Serbia's destiny. A short

U

sketch of Serbia's history may not, I hope, be
found out of place in these memoirs.

The origin of the Serbs, like that of the other
Balkan peoples, is rather hazy, beyond the fact
that they sprang from the regions of the Car-
pathian Mountains. They were a tribal race,
under the control of a chieftain. They appeared
in the Balkan Peninsula and crossed the Danube,
encouraged by the Byzantine Empire, since they
formed a bulwark against the invasions of other
barbarous tribes. The Serbians flourished, and in
the seventh century spread over a considerable
portion of the Balkan Peninsula, extending their
conquests into Macedonia and making Ragusa
their capital. Growing strong and self-confident,
in spite of their endless wars against their deadly
enemies, the Bulgarians and other tribes, they
prospered and formed their republic into a king-
dom. Becoming more amenable to the influence
of civilisation they adopted Christianity. In 1336
the nation had reached its zenith, and the country
was raised to the rank of Empire during the reign
of Stéphan Dushan, the great Slavonic genius.
The short-lived empire began quickly to decline
under the rising star of Turkey, which overpowered the Serbian forces at the famous Battle of
Kossowa. The result of that battle sealed the
downfall of Serbia. Serbia's civilisation at that
time was in advance of some of the other states,
and she might have become a fine European
Power had she been fortunate enough to escape
the degrading influence of the Osmanli domination.
Of late years Serbia was taken up by Austro-
Hungary, whose treatment of her has been even

more cruel and unjustifiable than that of the Turks.

I left Belgrade with my heart full of sweet memories of the time I spent there with my dear sister, Mrs Longworth, and her clever, delightful husband, who was one of the finest men I ever knew. After Belgrade my journey to London via Vienna was comparatively commonplace.

CHAPTER XXV

1899-1900

I LEFT for Boston on one of those large liners, which appeared to me to be a floating town in miniature, where people lived, loved, married, and died, with no other marked difference than that in the latter case the wide ocean and not mother earth received their mortal remains.

On reaching Boston our huge boat appeared dwarfed by the vast quays, where wonderful machinery such as I had never dreamed of in the Near East took up, carried from ship to shore, and gently set down quantities of luggage or letter-bags. My husband who had come to welcome me looked so small down below under immense cranes that I hardly recognised him. Once landed he put me into a carriage. The custom-house officials graciously passed my boxes at once, and we drove away, while many of the lady passengers were still wondering how best to hide some of their precious Parisian purchases.

My husband took me to an hotel which occupied the whole of one side of a street, and with his latchkey opened a door and ushered me into a sweet, pretty apartment in the annexe of the vast building. He had to go off to his office so left me with his blessing. I sat there by my solitary self a little uncomfortably dazed in mind and body after the sea journey, as we had been caught in the end of an Atlantic storm during the last day or two of our voyage. I noticed a bell and rang it. A fat, jolly looking Irish girl presented herself with a look of petulant surprise upon her face. "Madame," said she, "did you ring?"

"Yes," I said, but before I could add another word she said, "Madame, let me at once tell you that it is not customary to ring up servants at undue times. The service, once done in the morning, suffices for the rest of the day, and any little extra thing the lady wants she has to do herself."

"But suppose," I began.

"There is no 'but,' Madame, unless you pay down half a dollar each time."

I thanked her for her timely information and began to look about me. Everything seemed beautifully clean, elegant, and orderly, but of bedroom furniture such as I knew it there was none, and I began to speculate whether my husband slept on one or two chairs, whether he went to the pump for a wash, and whether he did his shaving on one of the elegant little tables that appeared to me to be more ornamental than useful. Puzzled in my mind as to how I should accommodate myself to this new style, and where my clothes were to be put, I tried to open a big glass cupboard, misplaced as I thought in a sitting-room. It refused to open to all the efforts I made. I next tried a smaller article of furniture,

which looked like a chest of drawers, with no
better result. On examining what appeared to
be a table I unknowingly pressed a spring, when a
lid suddenly sprang up and hit me on the nose.
I looked round for some water to bathe my nose,
but there was none to be seen. Finding myself
thus nonplussed in every way I sat down on a
rocking-chair and nursed my poor nose with my
pocket-handkerchief, and wondered whether all
American ladies were in the habit of rocking
themselves to sleep at night, and whether I should
ever be able to do so, when my husband suddenly
and silently walked up to me on the soft carpet.
Seeing my distressed face and my red nose he
anxiously asked me whether I was ill.

"Of course not," I said, "at least I hope not,
but how on earth do you expect me to live in
a room that is all show without a single object of
practical use."

"Is that all," said he, with a smile, "shut your
eyes for a minute till I tell you to open them."

My husband was greatly amused at my
surprised look when he bade me open my eyes,
and I saw the rapid transformation of what I had
taken for a pretty sitting-room into a perfectly
furnished bedroom. The glass cupboard I had
tried to open turned out to be a bed, the deep-
bottomed table, the lid of which had hit my nose,
was an elegant wash-stand, and the rest of the
furniture through the agency of springs or elec-
tricity was transformed into something adapted for
a bedroom.

"There," said my husband in a triumphant
voice, "this is not Turkey but America, a new

world which has made a rapid advance over the
old one. You, a child of the sunny East, have
much to see and to learn. Everything here is
done on a large scale as well as on practical lines,
but hurry up, as we have to go down to luncheon
in a few minutes." My visit to America proved
to be a long series of surprises of the labour-saving
methods employed.

The day following my arrival a meeting of
Christian Scientists was held by order of Mrs
Eddy, the great prophetess.

I thought to myself that that would be another
novelty worth seeing. I found that most of the
Christian Scientists were sober, solemn-looking
people of both sexes and all ages. Some of them
looked not too healthy, and I was told that on
principle they neglected their physical ailments,
speaking of them as not existing, and leaving them
to the care of the "healers," who prayed for them
and over them at so much an hour, in addition to
other formalities which interested me much owing
to the similarity of this newest form of faith with
that of the old Islamic one. The Turks do not
give any serious attention to diseases, and even the
most enlightened among them first have recourse
in cases of illness to one of the learned hodjas or
priests for prayers, amulets, and texts from the
Koran, which they put on their heads or hang
round their necks and arms. There is no show
about these matters, they form part of the Islamic
faith and are reverently and sincerely followed.
On both sides no doubt wonderful cures are
claimed in cases of neurotic complaints or of
slight derangements,

I had the good fortune to come across Mr and
Mrs Kerr, dear old friends from Constantinople.
Mr Kerr was a nephew of Admiral Lord Walter
Kerr. We had delightful times together, and
shared the comforts of my pretty apartment
whenever they came to Boston, and amused
ourselves by making dainty little Turkish dishes.
We wandered about the town by day and often
played bridge in the evening. I did not visit
much, as I was not well, but occasionally I joined
progressive bridge parties and played for prizes,
though I did not care very much for these parties ;
but bridge was the great rage in Boston at that
time.

There are two or three great forces in America,
such as the Trusts, the Press, and the Police,
which can make or mar the success of individuals
as well as of great enterprises, and which are not
always in harmony with public interests. In spite
of all these things the New World is one of steady
progress, in a way outdoing the Old World. The
American descendants of the old country are
a fine and gallant race who are developing in our
times many of the old virtues which have brought
the old and new countries close together in a
lasting Entente Cordiale, much to the advantage
of both. There is much to say in praise of
America's share in the present troublous war,
but I think it is best to let events speak for
themselves.

Unfortunately I could not go about much
owing to my increasing rheumatism. I was
very sorry that this prevented my visiting Canada
with my husband, when he went at the head of

the Veteran British Subjects to welcome Their
Royal Highnesses the Prince and Princess of
Wales. I saw the deputation, full of pride and
joy at the prospect of doing homage to the future
King of England, start from Boston. Needless to
say Their Royal Highnesses received the deputation with great kindness and courtesy. The Prince
recognised my husband and talked to him of
the old days at Salonika, and expressed his regrets
that he could no longer enjoy the excellent
cigarettes I used to offer him. The deputation
was deeply impressed by the gracious attention bestowed on my husband, and heartily cheered him.

My husband was delighted with his visit to
Canada, and felt that that vast land was one of
our finest colonies, which only needs the presence
of some enlightened capitalists to develop more
fully its wonderful natural resources.

The ladies of Canada presented to my husband
a beautiful piece of needlework as a souvenir of
the pleasant time he had spent there. It is always
with the deepest interest that I give myself the
pleasure of becoming aquainted with Canadian
and other colonial ladies in Malta. I find them,
with hardly an exception, simple, charming person-
alities, strong, healthy, and practical.

My stay in Boston came to a sudden end
owing to my dear son's return to England from
West Africa, where he had contracted blackwater
fever. I travelled home on one of the big liners,
and felt more at ease than I had done on my
outward voyage, as I had become familiarised
with the large scale on which everything connected
with the New World seemed to be done.

My son and I went to Germany for treatment for him, and were given by a German doctor the address of a rest-house. No sooner had we entered the house than the door was locked behind us and two or three powerful men came and inspected us. We were ushered into the presence of the head of the establishment, who wanted me to sign a contract for the term of our stay; but since his personality did not appeal to either of us, I declined to do so. As there was no room in the rest-house for me I found a lodging close by. Directly I left my son was put to bed, and his clothes were taken away. The medical attendant, perfectly drunk, went to his room, and finding he was an English officer, began to insult the English and the army in so violent a manner that my son, weak as he was, felt he must leave the place immediately. It was only then that he realised that he was in a lunatic asylum, locked up in a room with barred windows. Next morning I got access to his room with great difficulty, when I found him crazy with his experiences of the previous evening and intent on leaving the place at once. It cost me two hundred francs to get away, but we left that morning. This is a strange world where the unexpected often happens. Neither my son nor I had reckoned to get out of the frying-pan into the fire, but within twenty-four hours we found ourselves in a very similar sort of place; but this time the director was honest enough to tell us that his place was for the mentally diseased. We tried no more rest homes after this, and after a short visit came away determined never to visit Germany again.

CHAPTER XXVI

1901

THE climate of England gave me no pleasant welcome on my return from Germany, and I had to go to Woodhall Spa for my rheumatism, and was advised to live in the south of Europe. I decided to make Malta our permanent home, and, since my son was quartered there, I determined to start at once. I travelled on the *British Queen*, a cargo boat as uncomfortable and small as its name was good and great. I transhipped at Leghorn, where I had much trouble with the custom-house authorities. My luggage was taken into three different offices for the sake of the few pence each set of officials claimed after overhauling my things. A couple of agents of the famous Mafia Association followed my carriage and then got into the boat which took me to my steamer, in order to make sure of the tax which they imposed on both driver and boatman. I thought regretfully of the facilities of travel in Turkey, where once on arriving at Constantinople my maid went to the custom-house with my boxes and handed to the official in charge an advertisement from a biscuit box, which he gravely looked at upside down, nodded

299

his head in approval, and on the receipt of a
shilling passed all my belongings.

I had visited Malta in my girlhood, but on my
arrival there this time I was considerably impressed
by the quaint-looking old town, or rather fortress,
planted in a vast expanse of the Mediterranean,
with azure waves beating against its time-worn
walls and ramparts. The historical remains in
Malta add a great charm to the island, which
is said to be in the form of a huge mushroom, *i.e.*,
a large domed surface on a narrow stalk of rock.
In winter and spring Malta's rocky surface is
covered with a velvety green carpet, interspersed
with anemones, narcissus, blue iris, and other
lovely flowers, while in the gardens a perfect
wealth of roses is to be seen practically all the
year round. In autumn and winter the blossoms
are pale and sweet, like a timid maiden receiving
the first kiss of love, whilst in spring and early
summer the buds develop into blossoms of deeper
colour and sweeter perfume. The orange and
lemon trees take their share in adorning the island,
with their gold and yellow fruits reflecting the
bright soft shades of the stars above. All these
beauties justify the Maltese in calling their island
"Il fior del mondo." Many people come each
year to seek the winter warmth and sun in spite
of the drawbacks, such as the absence of good
hotels, and of lifts to the many flats up long
flights of stairs, and other minor discomforts felt
by those who come from highly civilised countries.

Newcomers usually seek a home in Valetta,
where the chief officials are quartered in fine old
palaces and mansions built by the knights of St

John. Most of these lovely old auberges are full of paintings and decorations, relics of the knights. Some of these fine houses are said to be haunted by the spirits of knights and others of bygone centuries, who occasionally visit their old dwellings. Some spirits are said to inflict marks of their displeasure on one or more of the present inhabitants they do not approve of. Others silently walk in and out of their old homes and give no sign beyond their passing apparition. The Maltese are naturally the most numerous inhabitants of the island, and it is mostly they who receive these mysterious visitors.

Malta has great value and importance as a naval station with its numerous fine harbours and busy dockyard, and offers an ideal resort to our ships for rest and repairs, and a base from which they can guard the Mediterranean and the Near East. For these purposes Malta's value is priceless. It is England's care and money which have transformed the little island into a prosperous place, and she enjoys a peaceful security, in spite of the grumblings and murmurs of a few discontented inhabitants who sigh over the loss of cheap German-made goods, prompted probably by German spies and agents, who stuff the minds of ignorant people with wonderful promises of all that Germany would do for them should the island pass under the power of the Huns. These things would not be worth mentioning in themselves, but they show the efforts Germany is making here to diminish England's prestige.

But to return to my arrival in Malta. My son came on board to fetch me. We looked about

for a flat and took one in Strada Mezzodi. Jeanne
joined us from Salonika, and, as my son was sent
shortly on a mission to Italy, we two set to work
to make our new home presentable before my
husband should arrive from Boston. I must say
that at the beginning I felt being cooped up in
a little flat with only a few of my pretty belongings
about me, and with but one servant, an ignorant
Maltese maid of all work, as my domestic staff.
Neither Jeanne nor I had much knowledge of
housekeeping. I had forgotten all I knew, and
Jeanne had had no experience. One day the maid
was told to bring a fowl from the market. Jeanne
inspected the bird and told Carmella that she had
bought an old cock instead of a tender fowl.
Carmella protested that it was a fowl, and when,
on cleaning the bird, she found some eggs in
various stages of development, she put them on
a plate and triumphantly marched into the room,
exclaiming, "Miss, miss, come and look! This
cock must be from your country as Maltese cocks
do not make eggs."

The scene was too funny for words, but I had
to look serious in order not to hurt Jeanne's
feelings.

My husband joined us soon after this. He
liked Malta at once, and enjoyed meeting many
friends who were resident here, and quickly won
the hearts of the Maltese by taking a deep interest
in their concerns. He made friends, too, with the
old ladies, and much to the delight of the children
used to throw chocolates to them in the street.
My husband liked the club, and helped by an
old friend, Admiral Hammet, he organised bridge

parties, which were then coming into fashion in Malta. With other friends he arranged some entertainments, combined with good lectures on many subjects, which satisfied all tastes and delighted the young people.

One of my husband's chief interests was the creation of a body of Boy Scouts, and he was the first Honorary President of the movement in Malta. I wish he had lived long enough to see the success of this highly civilising movement, and the happy results it is having in a place where compulsory education, with its elevating influence, is non-existent. The fact that the Boy Scout movement has been accepted without controversy and is very popular, shows that the Maltese have accepted the fact that discipline is good for their children.

Lord Grenfell, the Governor, was a delightful personality and enjoyed great popularity, and was aided by his charming niece, Mrs St Aubyn. The fine Squadron was under the command of Admiral, Lord Fisher, with Lord Charles Beresford second in command. The ships were all under the control of distinguished men, most of whom we had known at Salonika. It was a great joy to us to meet our old friends again and to become acquainted with their families. Everyone was most kind to us.

Lady Dingli was amongst my earliest friends, and her permanent home being in Valetta was a great comfort to me. I very much regret that of late years, owing to the war, her visit to England has been very prolonged, and I have seen nothing of her; but her letters are a great pleasure to me.

Among the great number of friends I made

at this time I would specially mention Lady Barry, Lady Adelaide Colville, Lady Domvile, Lady Drury, Lady Curzon-Howe, Lady Phillimore, Lady Poè, and Lady Wemyss, who not only added much to the enjoyment of our life in the early days at Malta, but who showed me such extraordinary love and sympathy when the dark days of sorrow overtook me.

Those were, indeed, good times for Malta, undisturbed by political agitation or coming trouble. The officials, in peaceful enjoyment of their positions for a certain term of years, had no cares and responsibilities beyond the welfare of the inhabitants and the improvement of the island, and displayed hospitality with true British lavishness. Valetta teemed with life and animation, everyone ready to enjoy the bright sunshine, the delightful bathing, and the many other outdoor amusements.

It was during our first season in Malta that my husband, while absorbed in a game of bridge at the club, received a telegram telling him that he had received à knighthood. He read the telegram and passed it to Admiral Hammet, making a sign to him to say nothing. As soon as the game was finished the Admiral disappeared. He came straight to our flat, rushed into the drawing-room, took me in his arms and embraced me, and so scandalised the astonished Carmella that she rushed into Jeanne's room, crying out, " Miss, there is an officer in the drawing-room who must be mad. Come and see."

It was certainly a happy bit of news, which caused me much pleasure, as I felt my dear

husband had well earned a recognition of his long
and loyal services to his country during half a
century. I cannot remember how long after this
it was that H.M. King Edward paid a visit
to Malta. The visit was a great event and new
roads were made in anticipation of the Royal
visit, old roads were restored, ugly buildings were
pulled down, and the neglected bit of land between
Valetta and Floriana was laid out in pretty
gardens. Most of this work was well and
quickly done under the supervision of Sir Edward
Merewether, one of the most distinguished and
clever lieutenant-governors that Malta has ever
had. His Majesty received a most hearty
welcome, and gave great pleasure to all classes
by walking freely about the town and chatting
with people he recognised. There is no doubt
that kindness and thoughtfulness for others are
special gifts of our Royal Family. The Duke of
Edinburgh was a great favourite in the Navy and
at Malta, and so were all the other royal
personages who honoured the island with a visit.
I believe it was Queen Alexandra who won the
hearts of the Maltese boatmen by going out alone
in a dghasai, and who gave a sovereign to the
delighted men on her return to shore. In a few
hours this story was told all over Valetta.

The Duke of Connaught came as High
Commissioner, and was accompanied by the
Duchess and Princess Patricia. Malta was proud
and delighted to have members of the Royal
Family resident in her midst, while the Duke
and Duchess appeared to like the little island with
its sunny skies and the freedom from court

x

restraint. Both Sir John and I had most happy memories of the two years the Duke and Duchess were here, and I was very grateful for the special kindness they showed to my husband, who was beginning to feel his advancing years after the fatigue of incessant work for over half a century in the Service.

It was on the day of his arrival that King Edward asked for my husband and knighted him, saying, " Rise, Sir John, I am very glad to knight you with my own hands." I shall never forget how proud I felt that evening at a ball at the Palace to find my self in the midst of a large circle of old and new friends, who congratulated us on the happy event.

King Edward paid a second visit to Malta some time later, when I had the privilege of talking to him of the bygone Constantinople days.

The last Royal visit that Malta received was that of Their Majesties, King George and Queen Mary. The King is well known in Malta and everyone rejoiced to see him again. The Queen being with him gave double pleasure to all the inhabitants. Both Sir John and I have received so many kind attentions from the many members of the Royal Family it has been our privilege to meet, that I have an irresistible desire to put down in these my memoirs my humble thanks and my grateful feelings towards them.

It was on some of the State entertainments given at night that our glorious Squadrons looked their best. In peaceful repose in the Grand Harbour they showed thousands of electric lamps, which shed their bright lights all around and seemed to reflect the stars above. Fireworks were sent up to return in showers of golden sparks, crossed and re-crossed by the wonderful beams of the searchlights, which revealed in the darkness the outlines of the great vessels of might and power. On guest nights these great giants were transformed intó hospitable homes. Dancing-rooms, ornamented with beautiful flowers and flags, offered welcome and pleasure to the fortunate guests who entered this temporary fairyland. Those were happy, peaceful times, when a squadron of England's fine battleships, with its contingent followers, were all anchored in the Grand Harbour to enjoy rest, but ready at a moment's notice to put to sea for action if necessary.

Unfortunately the years that succeeded these happy times have brought cares and anxieties to the nation incidental to the evil times that have fallen on us, but the King and his people have bravely determined at all costs to uphold the freedom of the seas and the independence of small nations. The Kaiser must surely realise the error he has committed in overlooking the sea power of England and the loyalty of her splendid colonies and dependencies. One of the great blessings this savage war has produced has been the bringing together in closer and more intimate relations all parts of the Empire, as well as demonstrating the true friendship of America.

Everyone is of the opinion that up to the present time this sunny island is the safest and pleasantest residence in the world. Everything

appears to run smoothly and comfortably except
the cold, which has been unusually severe and long
this winter, and which has been felt a good deal
owing to the dearness of coal and scarcity of
paraffin. Of course many things formerly thought
to be indispensable are lacking, but the untiring
solicitude of His Excellency, Lord Methuen, and
his Staff, and Lady Methuen's thoughtful care for
distressed families, tend to make things work
smoothly. Under the heavy pressure of this
terrific war everyone is full of anxiety for the
heroes fighting and many have the sorrow of
recent partings. My pen refuses to dwell either
on the no distant past or the present.

I am rejoiced to say that at times my sorrows
are greatly lightened by the kindness and affection
bestowed on me by many dear good friends,
especially those in the Navy who from far and
near do not forget me. I receive many delightful
letters from some and enjoyable visits from others
when they are in Malta.

I heartily wish every good luck and happiness
to all my "extraordinary nephews" and others to
whom I will not wish a final good-bye, as I have
every hope, should I live a while longer, to see the
harbour of Malta free from all signs of war and
become again the peaceful resting-abode of our
splendid ships.

INDEX

PRINTED BY OLIVER AND BOYD, EDINBURGH, SCOTLAND.

Lightning Source UK Ltd.
Milton Keynes UK
UKHW010352130119
335431UK00007B/504/P